追逐流逝的光芒

美国报刊中的赛珍珠

匡霖 ●————● 编著

江苏大学出版社
JIANGSU UNIVERSITY PRESS
镇 江

图书在版编目（CIP）数据

追逐流逝的光芒：美国报刊中的赛珍珠／匡霖编著
. -- 镇江：江苏大学出版社，2023.11
ISBN 978-7-5684-2091-4

Ⅰ.①追… Ⅱ.①匡… Ⅲ.①赛珍珠（Buck，Pearl
1892-1973）—人物研究 Ⅳ.①K837.125.6

中国国家版本馆 CIP 数据核字（2023）第 227787 号

追逐流逝的光芒：美国报刊中的赛珍珠
Zhuizhu Liushi de Guangmang：Meiguo Baokan zhong de Sai Zhenzhu

编　　著/匡　霖
责任编辑/汪再非
出版发行/江苏大学出版社
地　　址/江苏省镇江市京口区学府路 301 号（邮编：212013）
电　　话/0511-84446464（传真）
网　　址/http：//press. ujs. edu. cn
排　　版/镇江文苑制版印刷有限责任公司
印　　刷/扬州皓宇图文印刷有限公司
开　　本/700 mm×1 000 mm　1/16
印　　张/18. 5
字　　数/405 千字
版　　次/2023 年 11 月第 1 版
印　　次/2023 年 11 月第 1 次印刷
书　　号/ISBN 978-7-5684-2091-4
定　　价/78. 00 元

如有印装质量问题请与本社营销部联系（电话:0511-84440882）

前言

　　2022 年是赛珍珠诞辰 130 周年，我很荣幸地获得了镇江市赛珍珠研究会和位于美国宾夕法尼亚州佩尔卡西镇的赛珍珠国际的热忱支持与帮助，使这本汇集了关于赛珍珠在美国的主要活动报道资料的书能够与广大读者见面。

　　1892 年，当赛珍珠还只是一个三个月大的婴儿时，她就被身为传教士的父母带到了中国的镇江。从那时起，她就长期生活在中国，并以汉语为第一语言开始了启蒙教育。实际上直到 1910 年进入了弗吉尼亚州的伦道夫-梅肯女子学院之后，赛珍珠才开始真正了解美国这个国家。1914 年从伦道夫-梅肯女子学院毕业后，赛珍珠急不可待地回到了中国。她在学校里讲授英文，那时她也是一位传教士。她的文章和有关她的故事经常在《大西洋月刊》（*The Atlantic*）和《国家与亚洲》（*The Nation and Asia*）等刊物上出现。1932 年，赛珍珠获得了普利策奖。1938 年，她获得了诺贝尔文学奖。作为美国作家，赛珍珠是镇江的女儿，是中国的女儿，是"中国土壤培育了赛珍珠"，"但是，这位写出了划时代作品《大地》的了不起的女性，发现她最伟大的时刻并不是在其作品被承认时，而是在《大地》的孕育中"①。

---

　　① 原文：But the wonderful woman who has written one of the greatest books of this generation found her greatest moment not in the signal recognition accorded her work, but in the actual work itself. 引自 *Iowa City Press Citizen*，1932-06-03.

赛珍珠不仅仅是一位著名的作家，她还是一位哲人，更是一位社会活动家。赛珍珠具有卓越政治家的思想和洞察力，即使在中美关系极其困难的时期和极其复杂的环境中，她也不曾放弃为中国故乡和中国人民摆脱战争、贫困和帝国主义的压迫而作出努力。

一天，我读到了赛珍珠写给美国女画家利奥尼贝尔·雅各布斯（Leonebel Jacobs）的一封信①。其中的一段写道："每当想到我们都不再有机会去探望那个美丽的国家和那里优秀的人民，真的是令人痛心。"我深深地被她这句饱含对中国人民的炙热、深厚、真诚情感的话吸引着，于是开始了对赛珍珠的穷根溯源——追逐那一道流逝的光芒。

我发现，赛珍珠和雅各布斯这两位伟大的美国女性都有着强烈的中国情怀，都曾为增进中美两国人民之间的了解与友谊而不懈努力。即使是在中国人民最为艰难的抗日战争时期，他们对东方的这片故土和这里的人民的深厚感情始终不渝。她们各自成立了援助中国的募捐基金会，而且基金会都是由罗斯福总统的夫人担任名誉主席。随着研究的深入，我发现赛珍珠对于中国人民的感情和为中国人民所付出的精力是其他任何一个西方人都无法比拟的。

赛珍珠的一个个闪光的身影，在几万条美国报刊的报道中被深深地镌刻下来。她每每焦虑和发出呼吁，大多是为了中国故乡的人民，为了在美国的华人，为了被遗弃在亚洲的孤儿，为了世界和平与人类平等，这是慈善关爱的声援行动，亦是她对于事实、真理和正义的追求。这些报道时时在我脑海中回放，并引起我内心的共鸣。

以下是关于赛珍珠的一些历史点滴。

---

① 2013年，我开始研究一幅北宋赵令穰的青绿山水画。画框背面有一张纸条，写明它原属于女画家雅各布斯。为了查清这幅画的传承历史，我开始研究雅各布斯的生平。雅各布斯曾在北京、天津等地生活了三年多。1927年由于战争逼近，她回到了美国。她的家里一直保持着中国式的环境陈设。在日本侵华战争期间，雅各布斯曾为支援中国人民抗日募捐。为了纪念八十岁生日，雅各布斯出版了传记《我的中国》。通过好友菲利斯·芬纳，雅各布斯将一本《我的中国》送给了赛珍珠。雅各布斯居住的曼彻斯特镇与赛珍珠居住的丹比镇的车程距离只有25公里。赛珍珠收到书后，写了这封信。

1923 年

赛珍珠的故事和文章开始不断地出现在《大西洋月刊》和《国家与亚洲》杂志。

1932 年

赛珍珠以传教士的身份而不是作家的身份和丈夫一起回到美国纽约。

"中国土壤培育了赛珍珠"，但是，"这位写出了划时代作品《大地》的了不起的女性，发现她最伟大的时刻并不是在其作品被承认时，而是在《大地》的孕育中"。

1938 年

在诺贝尔奖晚宴上，赛珍珠说："目睹中华空前之众志成城，卫自由，御凶顽，令吾犹敬。此深刻之意，乃中华天然本性之所善兮。故知，中华不可征服。"

1939 年

赛珍珠在文兰高中礼堂讲演。她说，中国哲学认为"战争的胜利，属于战争结束后还活着的人"。赛珍珠宣传中国的持久战方针。

1940 年

赛珍珠在美国发起了筹集一百万美元的活动，以赈济受战争灾害的中国人民。罗斯福总统的夫人埃莉诺·罗斯福是基金会名誉主席。

1941 年

赛珍珠担任"联合中国救济会"的董事，目标是筹集五百万美元。
"美国再不对日本行动，任何一天都可能为时已晚。"
同年，日本偷袭珍珠港，太平洋战争爆发。

1942 年

赛珍珠断言：如果日本征服了中国，它可能会在一夜之间成为我们（美国）最危险的敌人。"但我们仍然没有从睡梦中醒来。我们对中国的帮助远远低于应有的水平。从政府贷款到红十字会救济，我们提供的帮助太慢，而且也太少。"

赛珍珠宣称："中国永远不会屈服，但她越来越绝望，她非常了解她正在进行的战争。"

赛珍珠以南京大屠杀为背景，写出了长篇小说《龙子》。

1943 年

赛珍珠向美国众议院移民委员会提出废除排华法案的请求。她说："虽然中国人是我们的盟友，但我们仍然在排斥他们。日本人正在用同样的方式对中国人进行宣传。"

赛珍珠说："中国人忍受着饥饿，但士气旺盛。""中国不会倒下。"

"日本人永远无法安抚中国人。日本从恐吓到'和解'政策转变的伎俩，在中国永远不会成功。"

"美国必须将所有敌人视为敌人，将所有盟友视为盟友，并且不歧视任何一方。"

赛珍珠在《生活》（Life）杂志上发表"关于中国的警告"，指出"重庆没有自由，没有民主，……各级官员在腐败。"

1949 年

赛珍珠认为中国人民接受共产党，"是因为他们已经对蒋介石总统失望。"

1950 年

赛珍珠对 3,000 名教友派教徒听众说："我认为我们在朝鲜所做的事情是必要的。但是作为一个美国人，我感到深深的羞耻，而不是民族自豪。……如果你使用武力，你就承认了你的失败，如果这是我们所能做的全部，那我们就失败了。……与中国开战会输掉一切。"

1951 年

赛珍珠在致《波士顿环球报》编辑的信中写道："亚洲人和欧洲人为美国感到难过，因为美国缺乏智慧。"她在信中引用了中国哲学家孔子的话"君子求诸己，小人求诸人"。

1952 年

赛珍珠说："大多数人想要一个更美好的世界，而不是一个糟糕的世界。有少数变态和可怜的灵魂，享受灾难和毁灭。还有一些人不介意冷漠和病态，也许是人类灵魂和身体的某些隐性的侏儒造成的。但我发现，大多数人都在诚实地寻找金色的未来。"

1955 年

赛珍珠驳斥"东西方不能交往"。

赛珍珠在自传《我的多重世界》①中写道：

"然而，当令人厌恶的浪漫主义逐渐净化了自己，最坚强的思想开始回归自己的人民。周树人，或自称鲁迅，也许第一个察觉到，虽然他的灵感可能来自西方文学，但只有将他的新发现灵感应用到自己的人民身上，他才能摆脱模仿。因此他开始写小品和故事，最后是关于普通人的小说。郭沫若成了我自己的最爱，尽管有时只会带来破坏性的玩世不恭。……丁玲和冰心……这两位曾经让我如此骄傲的勇敢无畏的女作家……我记得的是，他们为我提供了我们当时共享的世界最清晰的镜子，通过他们和读他们的书，我明白了否则可能无法解释的事情。"

1961 年

关于台湾，"中国人民从历史上就认为台湾理所当然地属于大陆"。

赛珍珠强调："红色中国是美国必须面对的现实。"

她认为美国对中国采取的政策是一种过时的外交模式。美方与中国人民加强沟通势在必行。她还提到首先启动两国之间的贸易和旅游，"两国领导人将找到共同利益与合作之道"。

赛珍珠呼吁肯尼迪总统取消禁止向中国出售价值四亿美元谷物的决定。

赛珍珠和一些妇女领袖呼吁裁军、禁止核试验，"联合国接纳中华人民共和国"。

---

① 《我的多重世界》（*My Several Worlds*）书名在国内被译为《我的中国世界》或《我的几个世界》。

1964 年

"随着红色中国作为核武器大国进入世界舞台，美国人必须更多地了解中国人民。"

"我不相信中国人会炸毁世界，这样做不符合他们的利益。……拥有核弹会给中国人带来新的面貌，这对世界和平来说是个好兆头。"

赛珍珠呼吁："救救被抛弃在韩国的孩子们！（混血）私生子们在他们的家乡被遗弃。美国父亲们冷漠地对待他们成千上万的亚洲孩子。"

1965 年

赛珍珠入选全球十位最受敬佩的女性名单。

旨在资助生活在亚洲国家（主要是韩国）的美亚混血儿童的赛珍珠基金会成立。

1967 年

赛珍珠在即将迎来她的七十五岁生日之际，将她的财产和大部分收入，共计超过七百万美元，捐给她自己设立的赛珍珠基金会。该项目为生活在亚洲国家（主要在越南南部）的美亚混血儿童而设立。在她去世后，她的所有稿费也将捐献给赛珍珠基金会。

1971 年

赛珍珠、钱学森的名字被收录在一份 23 年来联邦调查局秘密搜集的涉嫌颠覆国家政权的个人和组织的名单上。该名单于 1971 年 9 月 7 日被封存。

1972 年

已经八十岁高龄的赛珍珠，前往纽约霍尔马克画廊参观表现现代中国成就的摄影展览。

5 月 17 日，赛珍珠的私人访华签证申请被拒。

1973 年

巨星陨落。她的墓碑上只镌刻着三个篆书汉字"赛珍珠"。

美国总统尼克松高度评价称："赛珍珠是沟通东西方文明的一座人桥。"

作为一个传教士，作为一个几辈传教士家庭的后代，赛珍珠不信仰共产主义，但是她赞同八路军和游击队抗日，也赞赏红色中国的成就。虽然受到西方环境对于红色中国的不实舆论的影响，但是赛珍珠对于中国故土的眷恋和对这片土地上的人民的情感依旧十分强烈。她不愿意以尼克松总统的随行团员身份回到中国，而是申请私人访华签证。在前往纽约参观现代中国成就摄影展览后不久，她获知申请被拒签了。即使是向多方求助也于事无补，她感到无比的痛苦、失望与无助。十个月后，巨星陨落，回归了大地。

对于哲人赛珍珠，大地虽分东西，但是天下为一。

本书所整理的报刊片段，可以编织成一篇波澜史诗。我深深地被赛珍珠的每一个故事所吸引和感动。每一个故事片段，都记述着一段艰苦卓绝的过程，这不是一个个短暂的瞬间，而是历史的天空中一道道闪烁着的长长的光芒。这一道道光芒，冲击着我们的灵魂。

赛珍珠不是中美人民交往长河中的一朵浪花，而是一块磐石，甚至可称为民间交流的中流砥柱，无人能够替代。现实世界需要让更多的人了解这些历史，更好地研究和认识赛珍珠，通过东西文化交流传承博爱精神，继续"人桥"使命，相知互鉴向未来。这样的愿望驱使着我持续研究赛珍珠并编写本书，衷心希望更多的读者成为东西方文化交流和中美两国关系发展长河中的一朵朵浪花。

需要说明的是，本书整理收录和编译的部分报道为节选、节译，书中的脚注均为本书作者的注释。因能力和水平所限，书中关于赛珍珠的报道和旨意难免有疏漏，敬请读者批评指正。

目录

前言

壹　巨星陨落 —— 〇〇一

贰　赛珍珠的成长 —— 〇一五

叁　东风、西风与大地 —— 〇二九

肆　中国不会亡 —— 〇六三

伍　中国最好的朋友 —— 〇九九

陆　博爱 —— 一一七

柒　不灭的期待 —— 一三五

附壹　雅各布斯 —— 一六五

附贰　报刊报道原文 —— 一八七

后记 —— 二八一

壹

巨星陨落

1973 年 3 月 6 日，赛珍珠去世，享年 80 岁。

赛珍珠出生时的姓名是珀尔·康福特·西登斯特里克（Pearl Comfort Sydenstricker）。赛珍珠的父亲有个自己取的中文名字"赛兆祥"，这是由于其姓氏 Sydenstricker 的第一个音节不是读［si］，而是发音［sai］（赛）。珀尔是 Pearl（珍珠）英语发音的汉语标注。1917 年赛珍珠结婚后，她随丈夫姓氏改称为珀尔·巴克（Pearl S. Buck），巴克是她丈夫的姓氏。1935 年赛珍珠再婚，她仍然沿用了珀尔·巴克作为自己的笔名。如无其他说明，本书所用到的报刊资料中出现的姓名称呼珀尔、巴克、巴克夫人、巴克小姐、珀尔·巴克夫人、珀尔·沃尔什夫人均指赛珍珠。

我们从记者琳达·威·理查森最后一次采访赛珍珠的报道和赛珍珠 80 岁时的手迹开始对赛珍珠的追忆。①

赛珍珠：最后一次采访①

《曼西晚报》（*Muncie Evening Press*），1973 年 3 月 10 日

《曼西晚报》报影（1973-03-10）

［编者按］　以下是对赛珍珠的最后一次采访。采访配合了她最后一部非小说作品《中国：过去与现在》的出版而进行。赛珍珠于 3 月 6 日去世，在她去世前六天，约翰·戴公

---

①　1973 年 3 月 10 日《曼西晚报》的这篇《最后一次采访》和《林肯杂志之星》1972 年 11 月 13 日的报道《赛珍珠：一位亚洲头脑的美国人》出自同一位记者琳达·威·理查森的采访。

出版了她的最后一部小说《天下》。

[佛蒙特州丹比，记者琳达·威·理查森报道]　当我还是个小姑娘的时候，我相信赛珍珠是一位敢于接受挑战的人，她以特殊的角色左右了我认知世界的方方面面。我没有完全意识到她是个男人还是女人，我只知道赛珍珠是如此伟大，没有人可以质疑她的力量或她的能力。

我最近访问了赛珍珠。除了能证实她的确是一位非常美丽、和蔼可亲的女性之外，我意识到我童年的想象是完全正确的。

赛珍珠是美国文学史上作品被翻译数量最多的作家，出版的图书数量与她80岁的年龄相同。她是诺贝尔文学奖和普利策奖以及无数其他荣誉的获得者。这位世界上最权威的中国问题专家在关爱和收养美亚混血儿童方面也取得了前所未有的进展——这些孩子是我们所了解的在遥远的战争地区和贫困背景下由美国父亲和亚洲母亲所生的。

赛珍珠现在住在新英格兰①的一个叫作丹比的小镇上，该小镇已有两百年历史。丹比位于佛蒙特州7号州际公路旁边，拉特兰以南约10英里。

赛珍珠在客厅接待了我。她穿着一件中国传统式样的宝石蓝色锦缎长袍，光彩照人。她的出现瞬间让我感到轻松，同时，我觉得只要能和她一起共度时光，自己便是一个朋友、一个知己、一个重要的人。

她很有风范地坐在舒适的椅子上喃喃地说，这个佛蒙特州的村庄坐落的地方让人联想到一个中国山地区域，她就在那一带长大并且生活了40年。②

她说话时身体几乎不动，即使是在做手势时亦如此，她并非主要透过她的讲述向我传递热情活力——尽管在当时和过后回想起来，她的幽默、敏捷和措辞得体的回答让我感到惊叹——而是通过她对生活全部意义的明确认知。

1926年的中国革命期间③，巴克小姐和家人被暂时逐出中国后在日本生活了一年。我刚结束在东京生活和工作的三年而回国。我确信我对亚洲人思想的有限认识促进了我与巴克小姐的交流，因为赛珍珠具有并将永远有亚洲头脑。

以这种方式谈论一位父母是美国人、出生在美国并且在中国这个国家度过了40年的女性，这不可能吗？

————————————

① 新英格兰是由美国东北部的六个州，即康涅狄格州、缅因州、马萨诸塞州、新罕布什尔州、罗德岛州和佛蒙特州组成的地区。
② 美国著名肖像画家雅各布斯带到美国的北宋赵令穰的青绿山水画《春山待客图》，描绘的正是这样的一个地区。
③ 指1926年开始的国民革命军北伐。

不，并非不可能。因为巴克小姐自己也承认，她仍然先用中文思考，然后用英语表达。她说的话是经过仔细权衡的，在她的谈话里没有废话，没有多余的话。她天性中有如此精致的亚洲式的细腻，以至于我感觉自己坐在一位儒家学者、一位菩萨、一个西方人永远无法完全理解的神秘东方的稀世珍宝的旁边。

当我送给巴克小姐我的象征性礼物时——这是访问亚洲家庭时遵守的一种礼节，她非常欣赏包装，认为装饰纸是我带来的书签。当她发现里面有东西时，并没有为自己的误解表达歉意。她查看了来自日本札幌山区的素雅的编织布条，更加赞不绝口，立即夹进了她正在看的书里。

赛珍珠家的一楼杂乱无章地摆满了她过去在亚洲的宝贝。但二楼的客厅和接待区却装修成了轻快的色调，这种风格被称为"永不过时的舒适"风格，另外还有些许中国特色的装饰摆放其间。然而，在西边的房间，赛珍珠的出现使它变成了当代的皇宫。

离开时，我克制了自己以亚洲人的方式鞠躬致礼的强烈想法，我们轻轻地碰了碰手。我感到一种人们所期望的敬畏之意，不是因为她是不朽的赛珍珠，而是因为我觉得她是我所认识的最完美的人。从本质上来说，赛珍珠具有贵族精神所孕育的谦逊和高雅。

（英文原文见附贰：1. Pearl Buck：A Last Interview）

赛珍珠：一位亚洲头脑的美国人——《林肯杂志之星》（*Lincoln Journal Star*，1972-11-13）

《圣路易斯邮政速递》（*St Louis Post Dispatch*），1973 年 3 月 6 日

Pearl S. Buck Dies; Author, China Expert

Pearl S. Buck
Author dies

《圣路易斯邮政速递》报影（1973-03-06）

[佛蒙特州丹比，美联社报道] 赛珍珠出生于传教士家庭，因写作有关中国的作品而获得诺贝尔文学奖和普利策奖，今于家中去世，享年 80 岁。

赛珍珠的私人秘书贝弗利·德雷克说，这位作家安详地离世了。去年秋天，她接受了胆囊手术。

1892 年 6 月 26 日，赛珍珠在西弗吉尼亚州出生，她在中国长大，并且在学习英语之前就学会了说汉语。她说，正是这种背景不仅影响了她的写作主题，也影响了她的写作风格。

她在中国度过了人生的前 17 年，之后返回美国一段时间，而后从 1914 年到 1935 年在中国担任长老会的传教士。去年 10 月，中国政府拒绝了她重访中国的请求。

1932 年，赛珍珠凭借《大地》获得普利策奖，这本书详细描述了一个中国农民的发家兴旺。1938 年，她成为第一位获得诺贝尔文学奖的美国女性。该奖项特别提到了她 1936 年的两部

传记作品——《异邦客》和《战斗的天使》①。

去年，赛珍珠的身体已经每况愈下。

去年7月，她在胸膜炎发作后住进了医院，并在那里度过了将近一个月的时间。10月，她再次住院两个月，进行胆囊手术治疗后的恢复休养。

今天，在西弗吉尼亚州希尔斯伯勒（Hillsboro），赛珍珠出生地基金会（Pearl S. Buck Birthplace Foundation，Inc.）发言人表示，私人葬礼将在宾夕法尼亚州巴克斯（Bucks）县举行，"以便靠近她的孩子们"。

在赛珍珠的几十部作品中，最受欢迎的是《大地》。它被翻译成30多种语言，还被改编成了一部戏剧和一部电影，这部电影为路易斯·雷纳（Luise Rainer）赢得了1937年的奥斯卡奖，该片由保罗·穆尼（Paul Muni）主演。

终其一生，赛珍珠都在写作，每年出版三部作品。她还以John Sedges的笔名出版了五部小说。

赛珍珠说，她发现大多数当代作家都"无聊地沉迷于（描写）性爱"②。她说："我根本不是道德家，这并没有让我感到震惊。它比什么都更让我开心。"

去年6月，赛珍珠期待着庆祝自己的80岁生日。她回忆生活，其中包括1927年在中国革命者手中与死亡的擦肩而过③。她评论道："我不会错过任何一个机遇。有些虽然是触手可及的，但每一件事似乎都有意义。"

赛珍珠的写作给她带来了财富，其中的大部分都捐给了赛珍珠基金会，这是一个致力于帮助美国军人所生的亚裔儿童的组织。该基金会成立于1964年，已经帮助了五个国家的两千多名儿童。

这位作家有过两次婚姻。她的第一任丈夫约翰·洛辛·巴克（John Lossing Buck）是就职于金陵大学的传教士。他们于1935年离婚，这场婚姻持续了18年。后来，她嫁给了她的出版商理查德·沃尔什（Richard John Walsh）。沃尔什于1960年去世。

赛珍珠与她的第一任丈夫生了一个女儿卡罗尔④。这个孩子患有代谢紊乱疾病，大部分时间都在新泽西州的家中度过。赛珍珠收养了九个孩子，并在她位于宾夕法尼亚州巴克斯县的农场里抚养他们长大。

（英文原文见附贰：2. Pearl S. Buck Dies；Author，China Expert）

---

① 这两部传记分别记述赛珍珠的母亲和父亲。

② 赛珍珠反对过多地描写性爱。

③ 应该是1926年。

④ 赛珍珠的女儿卡罗尔·巴克（Carol Grace Buck）患有智力障碍征。他们在中国时，赛珍珠便为了日后有人能够照顾卡罗尔，领养了一位美国女孩珍妮丝（Janice Buck）。为了照顾姐姐，珍妮丝终身未嫁。赛珍珠去世后，珍妮丝成了卡罗尔的监护人。

赛珍珠去世，魂归大地①

《朗维尤日报》（*Longview Daily News*），1973 年 3 月 6 日

Pearl Buck dies, goes home to 'The Good Earth'

《朗维尤日报》报影（1973-03-06）

「佛蒙特州丹比，美联社报道」 赛珍珠出生于传教士家庭，因写作有关中国的作品而获得诺贝尔文学奖和普利策奖，今于家中去世，享年 80 岁。

巴克小姐的私人秘书贝弗利·德雷克说，这位作家今天早上大约 7 点 25 分悄然离世。去年秋天，她接受了胆囊手术。

巴克小姐 1892 年 6 月 26 日出生于西弗吉尼亚州，她在中国长大，在学习英语之前就已学会中文。她说，正是这种成长经历不仅影响了她的写作主题，也影响了她的写作风格。她在中国度过了人生的前 17 年，然后返回美国居住一段时间②，接着从 1914 年到 1935 年在中国担任长老会传教士。去年 10 月，中国政府拒绝了她重新访问中国的请求。

1932 年，她的《大地》获得普利策奖。这本书以"史诗般的磅礴、独特而感人的人物形象、充满趣味的故事情节、简明而色彩丰富的风格"详细地描述了一个中国农民的发家史。

1938 年，她成为第一位获得诺贝尔文学奖的美国女性。该奖项特别提到了她 1936 年的两部传记——《异邦客》和《战斗的天使》。

过去一年，巴克小姐的健康状况一直不佳，两次长期住院。

去年 7 月，她胸膜炎发作后在医院住了近一个月；10 月

---

① 此篇报道与前一篇报道《作家、中国专家赛珍珠逝世》内容基本相同。显然，美联社的记者深深地认同赛珍珠是大地的女儿。此回归大地是西方的大地，她在此为了促进与东方大地的交流和理解，顽强地、艰辛地、满怀希望地耕耘了四十年。赛珍珠的教育背景和成长经历使其坚信，东方和西方大地的人民终将友好地交往互助。正所谓大地分东西，天下为一。

② 赛珍珠 1910 年至 1914 年回美国读大学。

份，因为胆囊手术后要恢复，再次住院两个月。

她的秘书德雷克夫人拒绝就巴克小姐的去世发表任何评论，只说她安详地离世。她补充说，按照巴克小姐的意愿，其葬礼将不会公开，也不会在佛蒙特州举行。

她说赛珍珠的家人不打算透露告别仪式将在哪里举行，但确实表示赛珍珠家人正在考虑在西弗吉尼亚州举行葬礼。

位于西弗吉尼亚州希尔斯伯勒的赛珍珠出生地基金会的发言人今天表示，赛珍珠的私人葬礼将在宾夕法尼亚州巴克斯县举行，"以便靠近她的孩子们"。

在她的几十部作品中，最受欢迎的是《大地》。它被翻译成30多种语言，并被改编为戏剧，拍了一部电影，该片为路易斯·雷纳赢得了1937年奥斯卡最佳女主角奖，保罗·穆尼也主演了这部影片。

巴克小姐终其一生都在写作，一年写出三篇小说。她以笔名John Sedges出版了五部小说。多年来，她一直是美国最畅销的作家之一，但她说她最大的读者群体在欧洲。

巴克夫人在1969年的一次采访中说，美国评论家倾向于将她视为"女性作家"。她说："美国评论家习惯于与美国作家打交道，他们应该面对事实——我不是一个纯粹的美国作家。我的小说观念基于中国小说，具有简单、直接的风格。在我来美国上大学之前，我几乎只看中国小说。"

巴克小姐说她发现大多数当代作家都"无聊地沉迷于描写性爱"。她说："我压根就不是道德家，这并没有让我感到震惊。它比什么都更让我开心。"

近年来，她一直忙于建立基金会，她的基金会旨在帮助那些美国大兵与亚洲妇女所生但却被遗弃在亚洲的儿童。基金会在七个亚洲国家开展工作，并于去年9月在越南西贡①开设了办事处。

她自己向基金会捐款一百万美元②。

最近，她在佛蒙特州丹比镇购买了房子。多年来她一直试图通过鼓励旅游业、开设新商店和进口亚洲礼品在当地销售来振兴该镇。

她说，具有商业价值的丹比项目基于这样一个信念——"一个国家的生命之血来自其村庄"。

出生于西弗吉尼亚州希尔斯伯勒的珀尔·西登斯特里克（Pearl Sydenstricker，即赛珍珠）在还是婴儿时就被其身为长老会传教士的父母带到了中国。

---

① 即今越南胡志明市。
② 作者注：应该是七百万美元的收入和财产。

1917 年，她嫁给了农业传教士约翰·洛辛·巴克博士。他们于 1935 年离婚。同年，她与约翰·戴公司总裁理查德·J. 沃尔什结婚。沃尔什于 1960 年去世，享年 73 岁。

巴克小姐在她的第一次婚姻中生了一个女儿，是一个有智力障碍的孩子。1950 年，她在一篇期刊文章和一本书《从未长大的孩子》中讲述了这个女孩的故事，并将收益捐赠给了一所培训学校和智力障碍的研究工作。

（英文原文见附贰：3. Pearl Buck Dies, Goes Home to "the Good Earth"）

赛珍珠：连接东西方之间的人桥

《新闻民主党人报》（*The Press Democrat*），1973 年 3 月 7 日

PEARL BUCK
'Human Bridge Between East, West'

《新闻民主党人报》报影（1973-03-07）

[佛蒙特州丹比，合众国际社报道]　赛珍珠是第一位获得诺贝尔文学奖的美国女性，尼克松总统说她是"连接东西方文明的人桥"。

巴克夫人星期二在她位于佛蒙特州中部社区的家中去世，享年 80 岁。

本周晚些时候，将为她在宾州的白金汉举行私人葬礼，时间未定。

巴克夫人是《大地》的作者，该作品描绘了一对中国夫妇在困难面前对土地的热爱。

在华盛顿，尼克松总统称她是"连接东西方文明的人桥"。"通过她的眼睛，数以百万计的读者能够在无法直接接触的情况下，看到中国及其人民的美。很幸运，赛珍珠在有生之年看到了她如此深爱的两个民族在她最后的岁月里靠得更近。"

去年 6 月 26 日她生日后不久，巴克夫人患上了一系列疾病，多次住院。9 月①，她接受了胆囊切除手术。巴克夫人是西弗吉尼亚州希尔斯伯勒人，在中国长大，父母都是长老会传教士。她在学习英语之前先学会了说汉语。

1931 年，她凭借《大地》获得普利策奖，此书后来被翻译成 30 多种语言。这本书是一部戏剧和电影的基础，路易斯·雷纳出演该影片并获得奥斯卡年度最佳女演员。在获得普利策奖的七年后，赛珍珠成为第一位获得诺贝尔文学奖的美国女性。授奖辞写道："中国农民生活的丰富而真实的史诗般的写照……"

中国最近拒绝了巴克夫人重新进入中国的申请，理由是她的作品被认为是持"对中国人民及其领导人的歪曲、抹黑和诽谤的态度"。

她总共写了 84 本书，其中许多反映了她对爱的力量的坚定信念，她认为爱能改变人类的生活。

（英文原文见附贰：5. Pearl Buck——"Human Bridge Between East，West"）

1973 年 3 月 6 日，美国总统理查德·尼克松为赛珍珠逝世发表声明：

穷其毕生，赛珍珠是连接东西方文明的人桥。她用简练朴素的修辞，将她对中国人民和文化的个人热爱转化为丰富的文学遗产，为亚洲和西方人民所珍视。

作为专长语言者、妻子、母亲和慈善家，她过着漫长而充实的生活。通过她的眼睛，数以百万计的读者能够在无法直接接触的情况下，看到中国及其人民的美。很幸运，赛珍珠在有生之年看到了她如此深爱的两个民族在她最后的岁月里靠得更近。尼克松夫人和我与所有美国人一起，向她的家人表示同情，并为一位伟大的语言艺术家和一位敏感、富有同情心的人的逝世而哀悼。

RICHARD NIXON

37th President of the United States: 1969 - 1974

Statement on the Death of Pearl S. Buck.

March 06, 1973

第 37 任美国总统理查德·尼克松关于赛珍珠逝世的声明

---

① 此篇报道中关于赛珍珠患病住院治疗的时间与前一篇报道的记录不一致。另外，此篇报道中赛珍珠获得普利策奖的时间存在笔误。

（原文见附贰：5. Statement on the Death of Pearl S. Buck，引自美国总统项目网站：https：//www. presidency. ucsb. edu/documents/statement-the-death-pearl-s-buck）

　　尼克松总统的评价巧妙地回应了美国学术界一些学者长期以来对赛珍珠获奖的批评，他赋予了赛珍珠沟通东西方文明的"人桥"这一庄重、崇高、精辟、准确和富有深意的评价。桥梁用于沟通，承担着使命。她必须承载负荷，必须面向风暴激流，必须抗御地震和战火的冲击而屹立千年。赛珍珠更是"护桥人"，尼克松正是这一切的见证者之一，才能因此得出如此精辟的总结。

　　赛珍珠一生在出版物和信件上可能留下了数万枚签名。1972年6月，为祝贺赛珍珠80岁寿辰，纽约约翰·戴出版公司（John Day）精选发行了赛珍珠小说的限量版，上有赛珍珠的亲笔签名 Pearl S. Buck。我们俯观老人家80岁寿辰时的笔迹，时光似乎停留在昨天。

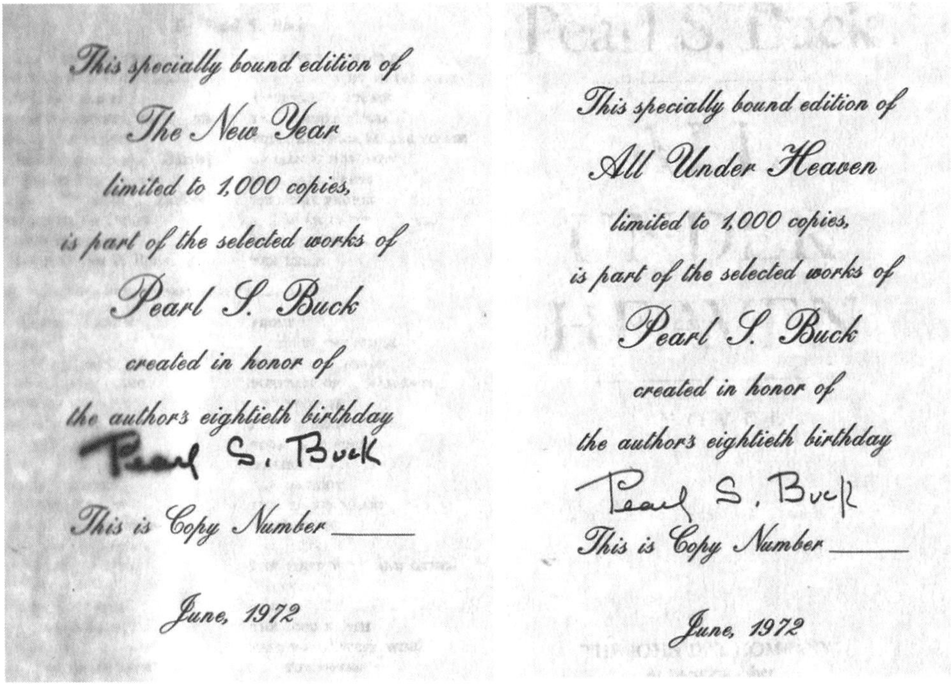

This specially bound edition of
The New Year
limited to 1,000 copies,
is part of the selected works of
Pearl S. Buck
created in honor of
the author's eightieth birthday
Pearl S. Buck
This is Copy Number _____

June, 1972

This specially bound edition of
All Under Heaven
limited to 1,000 copies,
is part of the selected works of
Pearl S. Buck
created in honor of
the author's eightieth birthday
Pearl S. Buck
This is Copy Number _____

June, 1972

约翰·戴出版公司（John Day）发行的限量版赛珍珠小说中的赛珍珠亲笔签名，左图为《新年》（*The New Year*），右图为《天下》（*All Under Heaven*）（火星云美术馆藏品）

当记者理查森还是一个小姑娘时，她对于赛珍珠的遐想意味着赛珍珠对一大批青少年，特别是对女孩的影响，直至后来影响到成年人和政治家对于中国的认知及对赛珍珠的尊重与敬仰。许多与赛珍珠同龄或者年龄更大的记者和作家，介绍中国时或多或少地以夸大甚至故意扭曲的手法描写中国人民的行为、习俗和信念。而赛珍珠却是用朴实的语言和真实的表达，突出中国人民对美好未来的向往和勤劳质朴的优良品质，描述根植于传统礼教和文化的个性与整体社会的相融，向西方介绍她所熟知并深深热爱的中国大地及其人民。赛珍珠回到美国近40年，可是她的中国文化之根丝毫没有动摇。她不仅穿着中国传统的宝石蓝长袍，她的气质、她的言行举止、她的眼睛传递的情感和思想，也展现了她的中国智慧和品格。因此，记者理查森觉得赛珍珠是她"所认识的最完美的人。从本质上来说，赛珍珠具有贵族精神所孕育的谦逊和高雅"。

从尼克松总统就赛珍珠逝世发表的声明中可以清晰地看到这位政治家和战略家对于赛珍珠的深刻洞悉。赛珍珠是中美两国交流史上的瑰宝，无人能够替代。早在1961年（当时尼克松是美国副总统，总统是德怀特·艾森豪威尔），即中国敞开大门欢迎尼克松或者说尼克松叩响中国门环的十年前，赛珍珠便提出"红色中国是美国必须面对的现实。可以首先启动两国之间的贸易和旅游……两国领导人将找到共同利益与合作之道"。

赛珍珠不愿以美国访华代表团成员的身份看望她魂牵梦萦的故土和人民，于是她申请了私人访华签证。那时正是中国的"文革"时期，她的申请被拒绝了。在焦急地等待签证批复期间，赛珍珠参观了在纽约举办的展现新中国成就的摄影展。收到签证申请的拒签信后，赛珍珠十分沮丧。但她没有想到，那里的人民已经远离了战争、远离了贫穷和饥饿，他们在那片充满阳光的土地上，独立自主，幸福地学习、工作和生活。

巨星陨落了。在生命的最后几年，赛珍珠始终在推动慈善事业，而且给丹比这个大约只有900名居民且经济上主要依靠伐木和皮革生产的贫穷闭塞的小山村①打开了通向富裕的大门。赛珍珠在 1968 年和 1969 年购买了 4 座楼房，建筑外部采用红白配色，并被命名为佛蒙特村广场（The Vermont Village Square）。她成立了一家叫作"创造力"（Creativity, Inc.）的公司，拥有这些楼房的所有权。来自得克萨斯州利文斯顿的艾伦·康克林夫妇（Alan & Wendy Conklin）的一张明信片记录了佛蒙特村广场的概貌，他们在这里经营着一家名为"埃兰尼斯小姐之家"的陶瓷店。

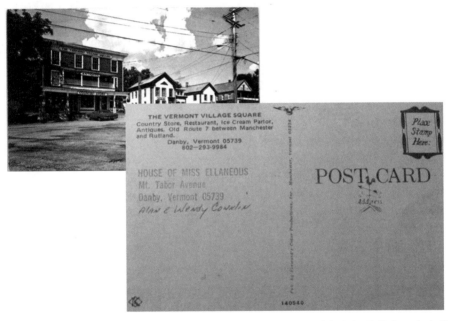

佛蒙特村广场明信片——明信片的主人是来自得克萨斯州利文斯顿的艾伦·康克林夫妇，他们在这里经营着一家名为"埃兰尼斯小姐之家"的陶瓷店（火星云美术馆藏品）

---

① 丹比的山水风貌极似赛珍珠的中国故乡——镇江。

丹比即将再次兴旺

《拉特兰每日先驱报》（*Rutland Daily Herald*），1969年10月9日

RUTLAND DAILY HERALD, THURSDAY MORNING, OCTOBER 9, 1969.

Danby to Be On Beaten Path Again Soon

Author Pearl Buck Behind Tourists' Cultural Center Development.

By ALDO MERUSI

DANBY — (Special) — Danby, isolated when U.S. Route 7 was rerouted, will soon be on the beaten path again.

Several dilapidated buildings huddled together just north of Griffith Library on the west side of the narrow twisting Main Street are being rapidly restored by the Vermont Village Square Inc., whose principal stockholders are Miss Pearl Buck, noted author, and her biographer, Theodore Harris.

Harris, who has just completed his second volume on the life of Miss Buck, said Wednesday, a country store will be opened in the long vacant Rosen General Store, and an arts and crafts center, antiques shop and restaurant in the adjacent homes sold to the corporation by Mr. and Mrs. Alvin Reed and Mrs. Mabel Stevens who are in the process of moving out.

The original tannery building, owned by Mr. and Mrs. Philip Barnes of Greenville, Pa., which was once the town office, will

Four Danby Main Street buildings now being converted into a cultural center by a corporation headed by Miss Pearl Buck, the well-known author. At left is the Rosen Business Block, to be a Country Store. Houses were owned by Mr. and Mrs. Alvin Reed and Mrs. Mabel Stevens. At right is old tannery building, later used for town offices. (Herald photos— Merusi)

《拉特兰每日先驱报》报影（1969-10-09）

丹比大街的四栋建筑现在正被一家公司改造成一个文化中心，该公司由著名作家赛珍珠小姐领导。左边是罗森商业街区，将成为乡村商店。房子过去归阿尔文·里德夫妇和梅布尔·史蒂文森夫人所有。罗森商店由丹比的木材大亨西拉斯·格里菲斯于1865年建造，曾一度被认为是佛蒙特州南部最高的商业街区。右边是旧制革厂大楼，后来用于镇政府办公室。

一位吸着老烟斗、吐着烟雾的农民说："我们丹比镇将再次被标注在地图上了。"①

（英文原文见附贰：6. Danby to Be on Beaten Path Again Soon）

---

① 丹比以前由于7号州公路改道而闭塞。创造力公司的子公司位于佛蒙特村广场，该公司一直经营到最近出售了位于赛珍珠避暑别墅的斯特拉顿的老磨坊企业。

追逐流逝的光芒

贰

赛珍珠的成长

赛珍珠大学毕业后回到中国，她励志当作家，将她熟悉和热爱的国度及其人民介绍给世界。她潜心阅读中国的文化经典，特别是中国小说。赛珍珠经常在美国的报刊上发表文章，她发表的第一篇文章是《也发生在中国》，第一篇小说是《东风·西风》，成名作是《大地》。赛珍珠写作的步伐直至80岁也没有停下来，她用笔在不同的民族和文明之间搭建了一座文化的桥梁。

小珍珠的一家，有爸爸、妈妈、哥哥、珍珠和妹妹：

爸爸阿沙龙·安德鲁·西登斯特里克（Absalom Andrew Sydenstricker，中文名赛兆祥，1852—1931），妈妈卡罗琳·斯图廷·西登斯特里克（Caroline Stulting Sydenstricker，1857—1921），哥哥埃德加·西登斯特里克（Edgar Sydenstricker，1881—1936），妹妹格蕾丝·西登斯特里克·尤基（Grace Sydenstricker Yaukey，1899—1994）。

赛珍珠的全家福——爸爸、哥哥、妈妈、珍珠和妹妹

赛珍珠和妹妹（右图为局部放大）

妈妈、珍珠（右一）和妹妹

（以上图片引自西弗吉尼亚州坡卡昂塔斯县数字档案馆 Pocahontas County W. Va. Digital Archive）

在另一幅全家合影中，小珍珠（左一）搂着爸爸的脖子，妈妈抱着妹妹，退休护士王阿妈站在后面。王阿妈有讲不完的故事，她知道许许多多习俗和说法。王阿妈十分宠爱珍珠，常常偷偷地帮珍珠完成妈妈布置的任务。可以说，王阿妈是小珍珠中国传统文化最早的启蒙老师。当珍珠学会了汉语之后，妈妈才开始教她英文。她少年的正规教育主要由妈妈和曾是前清秀才的私塾孔先生承担。1900年，珍珠8岁那年，由于义和团驱赶洋人，珍珠的邻居小姐妹们不再同她玩耍，她很委屈，很伤心，她不懂其中的原委。这是小珍珠第一次感到伤心委屈，是孔先生给她讲清了是非由来，安慰了她幼小的心灵。孔先生是1902年到赛家的，这一年秋赛家返回镇江。1905年9月，孔先生死于霍乱。

Pearl Buck as a child, with her arm around her father, Absalom Sydenstricker; her sister, Grace; and her mother, Caroline. In back is her nurse, Wang Amah, who taught her about Chinese culture.

小珍珠的全家福：小珍珠（左一）搂着爸爸的脖子，妈妈抱着妹妹，王阿妈站在后排
——《费城询问者报》（ *The Philadelphia Inquirer*，1999-06-28）

　　后来（1909年）赛珍珠去了上海的教会学校上学。1910年赛珍珠一家返回美国休假，她在当地的伦道夫-梅肯女子学院（Randolph-Macon Woman College，简称R-MWC）注册入学，并于1914年获得伦道夫-梅肯女子学院哲学专业艺术学士学位（22岁）；1926年赛珍珠

获得康奈尔大学文学硕士学位（34 岁）；1933 年获得耶鲁大学荣誉文学硕士学位（41 岁）；1942 年 6 月 8 日获得圣劳伦斯大学荣誉法学博士学位（50 岁）。

伦道夫学院，即原伦道夫-梅肯女子学院，其主楼与同在一排的其他楼房横跨将近 300 米，几乎所有建筑都由颜色相同的红砖砌成，被树木和草坪包围。通向各个楼房的狭窄路径亦由红砖铺设，别具幽静情趣，使校园魅力无限。现在的伦道夫学院，共有 30 个专业，550 名本硕学生，仅是 1891 年注册学生人数的 4.4 倍。在 2021 年《普林斯顿评论》的大学指南"最容易获得教授指导的学院"一项中，伦道夫学院排名第 16 位。如此优越和特殊的学习环境，令莘莘学子心驰神往。从 1893 年威廉·沃·史密斯（William Waugh Smith）任校长起，伦道夫-梅肯女子学院因其学术严谨而在全国声名鹊起，并开始吸引来自全美各地的女性。1893 年，R-MWC 为年轻女士们提供与亚什兰学院男生同等优势的教育。全新建筑物和设备耗资 7 万美元，学院还获得了 10 万美元的捐赠，是弗吉尼亚州唯一的一所接受资助的女子大学。R-MWC 是在美国南方第一个建立了心理学实验室的学校。1902 年，R-MWC 成为第一所被南方各州大学和预科学校协会接纳的女子学院。1916 年，R-MWC 也是波托马克以南第一所获得 Phi Beta Kappa（PBK）[①] 认证的女子学院。赛珍珠是 1914 届哲学专业的

赛珍珠于 1910 年进入弗吉尼亚州伦道夫-梅肯女子学院（现伦道夫学院）学习

　　[①] PBK 协会是美国历史最悠久的学术荣誉协会，也是最负盛名的协会，部分原因在于其悠久的历史和严谨的治学态度。

学生，是学院最知名的毕业生。作为《大地》的作者，她获得了普利策奖和诺贝尔文学奖，为母校赢得了特殊的荣誉。

今日伦道夫学院的主楼局部，该学院 2007 年开始招收男生

赛珍珠 1910 年来到美国求学时，中国还处于清朝时期。赛珍珠对校园的第一印象便是那些红砖建筑，很有中式园林的感觉。而她再回到中国时，中国已经进入了民国时代。

伦道夫-梅肯女子学院 1914 届毕业生资料是如此记载的：

Pearl Sydenstricker Buck

Randolph-Macon Woman's College
Class of 1914

Pearl Sydenstricker Buck was born in Hillsboro, West Virginia, on June 26, 1892, to Presbyterian missionary parents. Her family returned to China when she was an infant, and she spent her early years in the city of Zhenjiang. Buck received her early education from her mother and a Chinese Confucian scholar, later attending missionary schools and a high school in Shanghai. She entered Randolph-Macon Woman's College in 1910. A philosophy major, she was active in student government and the YWCA and wrote for the college's literary magazine and yearbook.

Soon after her graduation in 1914, she left again for China, which she considered her true homeland. In 1917, she married John Lossing Buck, an agricultural specialist who was also doing missionary work in China. They lived for several years in North China, then moved in 1921 to Nanjing, where she was one of the first American teachers at Nanjing University and where her daughter Carol was born. In 1927 her family escaped a brutal anti-western attack through the kindness of a Chinese woman whom Buck had befriended.

Buck was deeply touched by the simplicity and purity of Chinese peasant life and wrote extensively on this subject. In 1931, she published *The Good Earth*, a novel about the fluctuating fortunes of the peasant family of Wang Lung. For this work, generally considered her masterpiece, she received the Pulitzer Prize in 1932. *The Good Earth* was followed by two sequels: *Sons* (1932) and *A House Divided* (1935). *The Exile* and *Fighting Angel*, biographies of her mother and father, followed in 1936 and were singled out for praise by the committee that awarded her the Nobel Prize in Literature in 1938.

伦道夫学院网站上有关赛珍珠的资料

珀尔·西登斯特里克·巴克①于 1892 年 6 月 26 日在西弗吉尼亚州的希尔斯伯勒出生，父母是长老会传教士。她的家人怀抱着还是婴儿的赛珍珠回到了中国②，她的早年在镇江度过。巴克从她的母亲和一位中国儒家学者那里得到了启蒙教育，后来在上海的教会学校和一所高中就读。她于 1910 年进入伦道夫－梅肯女子学院，主修哲学，并活跃于学生会和基督教女青年会（YWCA）③，为学院的文学杂志和年鉴撰稿。

　　1914 年毕业后不久，她再次前往中国，她认为中国是她真正的祖国④。1917 年，她嫁给了同样在中国传教的农业专家约翰·洛辛·巴克⑤。他们在华北生活了几年，然后于 1921 年搬到南京。她是金陵大学的第一批美国教师之一，南京也是她的女儿卡罗尔出生的地方。1927 年，在巴克结识的一位中国妇

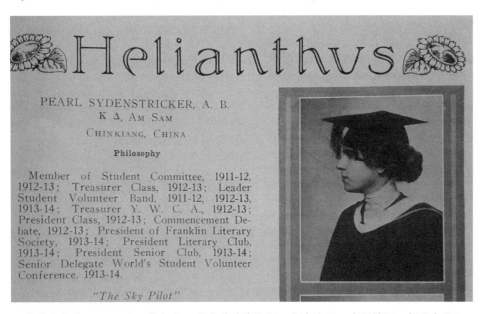

伦道夫学院"1914 向日葵年鉴"的赛珍珠毕业照，旁边注明"中国镇江，哲学专业"

---

　　① 即赛珍珠。
　　② 赛珍珠母亲有不幸夭折的孩子，她怀了赛珍珠后回到美国其母亲的家中待产。
　　③ YWCA 即基督教女青年协会。成立 160 多年来，该组织站在最紧迫的社会运动的最前沿，其成员为超过 200 万名妇女、女孩及其家庭提供服务。她们号召立即行动起来，捐款，消除种族主义，赋予女性权利。
　　④ 虽然赛珍珠和与她相同肤色的同学们一起上学，并且积极参加和组织校园活动，但她总是隐隐约约地感觉这里不是她的家，她的同学们反而好像是外来人。
　　⑤ 赛珍珠的丈夫约翰·巴克虽然是传教士，但是他对传教并不热心，而是致力于研究和改造中国的传统农耕方式，为金陵大学农学系的建立奠定了坚实的基础，培养出了金陵大学的第一代农业专家，他当时的一些工作成果直到现在仍然具有指导意义。也正是他带着赛珍珠长期在中国农村考察和工作，给赛珍珠提供了"源泉和土壤"，助力赛珍珠最后写就《大地》。

女的善意帮助下，她的家庭逃脱了一次针对西方人的粗暴攻击。

巴克深深地被中国农民生活的朴素和纯洁所感动，并就此主题进行了大量的写作。1931年，她出版了小说《大地》，讲述了农民王龙的家庭的命运起伏。这部作品被普遍认为是赛珍珠的代表之作，她因此获得了1932年的普利策奖。在《大地》之后是两部续集：《儿子们》（1932年）和《分家》（1935年）。随后的1936年描写她父母的传记《异邦客》和《战斗的天使》，得到了授予她1938年诺贝尔文学奖的委员会特殊赞誉①。

1934年，她永久移居美国。第二年，她与约翰·洛辛·巴克离婚，并嫁给了她的出版商理查德·沃尔什。在以后的生活中，她大量写作，总共创作了一百多部小说和其他作品。她的个人生活也很充实，因为她和沃尔什收养了8个孩子。

她成为许多人道主义事业工作的杰出倡导者。她是东西方协会的创始人，致力于增进亚洲和美国之间的了解。身为智障孩子母亲的体验促使她为智障群体开展了广泛的工作，并出版了感人而颇有影响的著作《从未长大的孩子》。被两个世界拒绝的美亚儿童②的困境也引起了她的同情，她于1964年成立了赛珍珠基金会以改善这些儿童的生活。

她于1973年3月6日去世，留下了众多的著作与一个致力于促进宽容和相互尊重的生命的记忆。

本传记梗概为1992年3月26日至28日在伦道夫–梅肯女子学院举行的赛珍珠百年诞辰研讨会的活动而作③。

（译自伦道夫学院网站 https://library.randolphcollege.edu/archives/Buck，英文原文见附贰：7. Pearl Sydenstricker Buck, Randolph-Macon Women's College, Class of 1914）

---

① 赛珍珠认为纪念父亲的《战斗的天使》写得更好，但是瑞典读者更青睐记述母亲的《异邦客》。

② 指美国军人在日本、韩国和越南遗留的孤儿。"两个世界"指美国和孩子们的出生国。美国父亲不要他们，韩国和越南也都歧视和不接受他们。

③ 很显然，伦道夫学院的传记梗概完全没有意识到尼克松总统所概括的赛珍珠的"人桥"作用，更没有提及赛珍珠捍卫"人桥"的精神和事迹。文明的交流、传播、沟通、融合需要桥梁，捍卫文明需要斗争和勇气，这两者都需要智慧、策略和意志。是中国土壤孕育和培养了哲人赛珍珠，正所谓："假舆马者，非利足也，而致千里；假舟楫者，非能水也，而绝江河。"

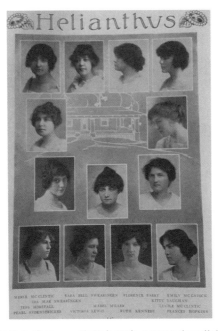

基督教女青年协会成员——伦道夫学院"1914向日葵年鉴"的记录

《盐湖城论坛报》（*The Salt Lake Tribune*），1932年4月17日

左图是《盐湖城论坛报》报影（1932-04-17），
右图是"1914向日葵年鉴"的局部

亚历山大·伍尔科特（Alexander Woollcott）似乎激起了一点争议。他撰写了赛珍珠的概况，作为赛珍珠4月份发表在《大都会》（*Cosmopolitan*）上的新小说《儿子们》的介绍。他描述了赛珍珠在美国的大学生活，说她被认为是"那个有着古怪名字，从远东而来，独自四处游荡的思乡女孩"。

格蕾丝·亚当斯（Grace Adams）是伦道夫–梅肯女子学院一位教授的女儿，在她的整个大学生涯中都认识巴克夫人，那时称珀尔·西登斯特里克，她给这个现在因《大地》的写作而驰名的女孩描绘了一幅截然不同的形象。亚当斯说："因为在各种活动中展现出能力与自信的领导气质，她在同学中出类拔萃——不仅包括基督教女青年协会（YWCA）和学生管理委员会的正式工作，还有社团女生联谊会中更细碎的事务和最高级秘密社团的神秘仪式。"所有这些意味着她不是一个"思乡"的女孩，毕业时她是学生团体中最受欢迎和最杰出的成员之一。

格蕾丝的一个社团女生联谊会的姐妹讲述了她欠巴克夫人一个人情的故事①。当时学院的传教士回来招募新人，"我被怀特博士关于她在中国工作的激动人心的故事所吸引，立刻报名加入三年或五年的传教士队伍，我忘记了具体是几年——也许是我的一生"。

"嗯，我刚上床，觉得自己很了不起。这时房间里的灯亮起，我看到珀尔·西登斯特里克站在我旁边，手里拿着我的宣誓卡。我起身，期待她的热烈的祝贺。但珀尔漫不经心地说：'杰斯，我刚刚发现了这个。我很高兴在它传给基督教女青年协会的其他人之前自己就看到了它，因为我知道，即使你不这样做，今晚之后你也会再也不想成为传教士了，所以我只是过来让你看着我撕掉它。'"②

（英文原文见附贰：8. Pearl Buck in Her College Days）

---

① 《盐湖城论坛报》上登载的故事的主人公杰斯·霍斯法尔（Jess Horsfall）的照片在学校的"向日葵年鉴"上找到了，报纸将杰斯（Jess）的名字误拼成Tess（泰斯）。此时的赛珍珠看起来稳重，不苟言笑。

② 杰斯违规了。这个故事说明了赛珍珠的善良和处理问题的灵活性。

中国的人民和土壤培育出的赛珍珠

《爱荷华市新闻公民》（*Iowa City Press Citizen*），1932 年 6 月 3 日

Great Moments -:- In the Lives of Great People -:- By ALICE ALDEN

Pearl S. Buck—Student of China and Its People.

TO undertake a task for the sheer joy of accomplishing something, without thought of gain or fame, and later find that it wins the approbation of the whole world, means the attainment of one of life's great moments. But the wonderful woman who has written one of the greatest books of this generation found her greatest moment not in the signal recognition accorded her work, but in the actual work itself. To Pearl Buck the award of the Pulitzer Prize for her novel, "The Good Earth," does not mean half as much as the knowledge that her book has helped the world to understand the Chinese, the people she knows and loves and with whom she has spent the major part of her interesting life.

Her Style of Simplicity

Millions of people are forever seeking rules that will enable them to become great writers. It is to be hoped that they will study Pearl Buck's style and learn that simplicity—the art of putting down clearly what one observes—is the secret of all great writing. When Pearl Buck painted in words and phrases a true picture of the people and the life about her, it was not with the desire to write a "best seller," but to show the world that there is intense drama in the lives of simple peasants, whether Caucasians or Mongols. Well may Mrs. Buck be happy that her great talent has been recognized in the signal honor of the award, but how much greater is

Pearl S. Buck

satisfaction in knowing that the world's intense interest in her undistorted epic of peasant life in China has contributed to a better understanding among the races.

Pearl Buck was born in Hillsboro, West Virginia. Her parents, whose name was Sydenstricker, were missionaries and took Pearl to China when she was still a little girl.

Pearl Sydenstricker returned to the land of her birth to attend college in the South, and her school companions recall that the shy girl from China became voluble only when she talked about the women of China and the unhappy conditions. After two years she eagerly returned to China, where a few years later she married John Lossing Buck.

Soon after Mrs. Buck's marriage they went to work in a city in which, for a part of the time, they were the only white people. And so her brilliant mind had ample time and uninterrupted opportunity to study the Chinese. Before she ever wrote a line she spent ten years in reading all the novels of China, which means that her knowledge of Chinese and the thousands of characters that make up the language is unsurpassed. She knows the Chinese classics, too, but feels that the real China, the pulsating heart of the people, is in their primitive naturalness, in the simple annals of a simple country family, not in stories of the scholars and sages.

The Pulitzer Award

So Pearl Buck set down a story of the life about her and sent it to America with the hope that perhaps some publisher would print it, so that the world could learn about China as it really is. To her amazement the book became a "best seller" overnight. And now has come the further recognition of the Pulitzer award.

《爱荷华市新闻公民》报影（1932-06-03）

[作者：爱丽丝·奥尔登] 　纯粹为了愉悦而承担一项工作，不计名利，而后来发现这赢得了整个世界的认可，这意味着获得了一次人生中的辉煌时刻。但是，这位撰写了这一代最伟大著作之一的出色女性发现，她最荣耀的时刻不是在她的作品获得认可和褒奖之时，而是她实际写作的过程本身。对珀尔·巴克来说，她的小说《大地》获得普利策奖本身的意义远不及她的书帮助世界了解了中国人，了解她所认识和热爱并与之度过了她大部分有趣时光的人。

她的朴素风格

数百万的人一直在寻找能够使他们成为伟大作家的秘诀。他们希望能够研究赛珍珠的风格，并学习朴素——清晰记录一

个人的所见所闻的艺术，那是所有伟大写作的秘诀。当赛珍珠用词语描绘真实的人民和她自己的生活时，并不是为了写一本"畅销书"，而是为向世界展示朴素农民生活中的强烈戏剧性，无论他们是高加索人还是蒙古人。巴克夫人可以十分欣慰，她的伟大天赋由于这一奖项的标志性荣誉而得到认可，但是她知道更强烈的满足感在于她对中国农民生活真实、史诗般的描述引起了世界的高度关注，促进了各国之间更好的理解。

赛珍珠出生于西弗吉尼亚州的希尔斯伯勒。她的父母姓氏是西登斯特里克，他们是传教士。在珀尔还是个小婴儿的时候，父母就把她带到了中国。

珀尔·西登斯特里克回到她的出生地，在南方上大学①。她的学校同伴回忆说，这个来自中国的害羞女孩只有在谈到中国的女性和不幸的情况时才会变得健谈。四年后②，她热切地回到了中国。几年后，她在那里嫁给了约翰·洛辛·巴克。结婚后不久，巴克夫妇去了一个城市工作，有一段时间他们是那里仅有的白人。因此她聪明的头脑就有了充足的时间和不受干扰的机会了解中国人③。在她正式开始写作之前，她花了十年时间阅读了各种中国小说，这意味着她对汉语及构成中文的数千个汉字的了解是卓越绝伦的。她也了解中国的传统经典，但她感觉真正的中国——人民的心脉所系在其原始的自然本性中，在其农村朴素家庭的淳朴历史中，而不是在读书人和圣人的故事中。

普利策奖

于是赛珍珠写下了她的生活故事并寄到美国，希望也许有出版商能付印，以让世界了解真实的中国。令她惊讶的是，这本书一夜之间成为"畅销书"。而现在，得到进一步认可的普利策奖已经来了④。

（英文原文见附贰：9. Pearl S. Buck—Student of China and Its People）

---

① 伦道夫-梅肯女子学院在弗吉尼亚州的南部。历史上的美国南北战争时期，弗吉尼亚州属于美国南方。

② 原文误写成两年。

③ 应该是专研中国文学，体验农民的生活。

④ 此文的最后一段写得太跳跃了。赛珍珠好多次向美国投稿，都没有被录用。第一部被出版商录用的书稿是《东风·西风》，出版正是纽约的约翰·戴公司。公司的沃尔什夫妇被赛珍珠的经历所震撼，也被她的语言才能深深吸引和折服，决定出版该书稿。《东风·西风》出版后受到广泛好评，沃尔什决定只要是赛珍珠投的稿件，一概录用。赛珍珠给约翰·戴公司的第二部书稿是《大地》，《大地》的出版顿时激起狂澜，原本负债累累的约翰·戴公司瞬间成为当时赫赫有名的出版商。

现代基督教传教士

《晨报》（*Morning Tribune*），1924 年 10 月 26 日

The young pagan is not only very likely to be studying world history, geography and institutions, but he may also be studying modern science and thinking a lot for himself. Miss Pearl S. Buck, a missionary in Nanking, China, writing in the New York Christian Advocate of her experiences as a missionary, says: "Today one has to stand before a crowd of hypercritical young students who know more about Darwin and Huxley and Dewey and Russell and all the ancients and moderns than an old missionary can ever hope to know. Stand before some of these, and remembering the great war and the morphine traffic and indemnities and extraterritorial demands and other things that exist alongside Christianity in one's own country, and try to preach with the cocksureness of the old days, and here is what happens:

《晨报》报影（1924-10-26）

[加利福尼亚州，圣路易斯奥比斯波] 年轻的异教徒不仅很可能在研学世界历史、地理和制度，而且他也可能在研学现代科学，并且自己做了很多思考。在中国南京的传教士赛珍珠小姐在《纽约基督教倡导者》上撰文讲述她的传教经历，她说：

"今天，人们必须面对一群苛刻的年轻学生，关于达尔文、赫胥黎和罗素，关于古代的和现代的，他们了解的比一个老传教士曾经希望知道得更多。面对他们当中的一些人，记住第一次世界大战、吗啡贩运、赔偿、治外法权①要求，还有其他与基督教共存于自己国家的事情，并尝试以过去的自信来布道，下面就是要发生的事情。

成百的问题会直冲你回击，'你如何解释这些现象？''你相信耶稣的神性是来自内部还是外部？''解释耶稣的神性意识。''一个人的死如何才能真正将其他人从罪恶中拯救出来？''天堂和地狱是实体的还是抽象的，你怎么知道？你怎么能证明它？''鉴于西方目前的情况，你如何证明基督教在推动道德文明与精神文明上的有效性？'

'你怎么证明——你如何证明'——这些不安的、年轻的东方人从各个角度提出了质疑。我认为与那些年老的、易说服的、温和的街头小教堂的会众交谈起来很容易，这毫无疑问。

①　即长臂管辖。

THOMASTON'S NEW CHURCH

(From the Methodist Record)

On March 11th, 1906, Rev. S. W. Roberts, preacher-in-charge of the Dayton Circuit, Selma District, Alabama Conference, M. E. Church, South, called a conference of resident Methodists of Thomaston at the Presbyterian Church, for the purpose of organizing the First Methodist Church, Thomaston, Alabama. The following members enrolled as members of the new organization: in Thomaston, the same determination and zeal has accomplished their original though long delayed desire for their own building of worship.

With slow though steady growth, the congregation continued their work using the Presbyterian Church so freely tendered for their use. The year 1910 shows no less than eighteen new members added to the roll. During the three years pastorate of Brother McGlaun (1910-1912) a total

held there by the Methodists. A few additions to the number of members are recorded during the few months following the organization, among them appears the name of Mrs. Pearl S. Buck who still remains a member, she being second only to Brother Cuningham on the chronological roll of members.

赛珍珠所在的阿拉巴马州托马斯顿小镇教堂——《民主党记者报》（ *The Democrat Reporter*，1923-06-07）。赛珍珠在教会中的排名仅在库宁安弟兄（Brother Cuningham）之后（图右）。

这些年轻人既不轻易相信也不盲从迷信，当然他们并不安逸。"

　　根据以上以及其他最近报道的传教士消息来看，很明显，现代基督教传教士的任务与该国现代基督教牧师所面临的任务大致相同。对刚刚放下显微镜或刚离开生物实验室，或刚放下对地质学、天文学或对选集研究的年轻人，让他们相信自己所看到和研究的事物是妄想和错误的，这种试图说服的努力是徒劳的。没有什么传承自遥远而虚无缥缈的过去的圣经真理的阐释，能使他放弃自己的第一手知识和基于知识的结论，而去接受一个从未拥有过他所具备的知识或经验的人为自己制定的教义。想帮助这样的人成为基督徒，必须帮助他将基督教教义与所有已论证的、实际的知识相融合协调，正如正确理解的那样。①

（英文原文见附贰：10. Modern Christian Missionaries）

---

　　① 此文需要说明的是，当时美国的传教士认为他们要努力向东方有知识的人传播基督教信仰。他们认为聪明的异教徒对他在世界另一端的基督徒兄弟，对他的政府、机构，对人民的性格和习惯有了更多了解。这与当时的社会背景有关，比如日本的教育越来越普及，比如孙中山这样的中国的新领袖坚持认为连"苦力"（Coolies）都应该得到知识的眷顾。赛珍珠出身于传教士家庭，不但她的父母是传教士，她父母的前几辈家族——西登斯特里克和斯图廷家族都是从德国移民到美国，后来迁居到了西弗吉尼亚州的希尔斯伯勒（赛珍珠的出生地）的德国传教士家族。赛珍珠反对宗教殖民，更厌恶对东方国家的掠夺。《匹兹堡新闻》1933 年 4 月 13 日转载了美联社的报道，赛珍珠利用她在中国做长老会传教士的经历写了两篇"畅销"小说，因近期写了两篇与教会的传统教义观点不同的文章而面临被开除的后果。消息是在一次新布伦瑞克省长老会会议上被披露的。在《哈珀杂志》（ *Harper's Magazine* ）1933 年 1 月刊的一篇关于传教的文章中，赛珍珠不赞同除非异教徒种族接受基督教福音，否则就要被诅咒的学说观点。

叁

东风、西风与大地

1930 年《东风·西风》出版后畅销美国，受到持续关注，书评不断，吸引越来越多的读者将目光投向古老而神奇的中国。《东风·西风》为 1931 年赛珍珠小说《大地》的横空出世营造了天时、地利、人和。在最后一本书《天下》出版六天后，赛珍珠去世，回归了大地。

《檀香山星报》（*Honolulu Star Bulletin*），1930 年 2 月 5 日

《檀香山星报》报影（1930-02-05）

首先是《小说中的中国》，作者是一位女性——赛珍珠。她多年来一直对中国小说和民间文学的起源进行专门研究。

巴克夫人在中国长大，她接受过中文书写和口语教育。正如她解释的那样，关于自己的祖国和人民，她的反应更多是指中国，而不是西方。巴克夫人为美国读者所熟悉，是因为她为许多美国期刊撰稿，并且她的第一部描写中国人生活的长篇小说《东风·西风》即将在纽约出版。

（英文原文见附贰：11. *Pacific Affairs* Out in New Form）

《奥克兰论坛报》（*Oakland Tribune*），1930 年 4 月 13 日

"East Wind, West Wind" Romance of the Orient

The poetry of the East is in the writing of Pearl S. Buck's "East Wind, West Wind" and with it a gentle romance of a Chinese woman who marries a westernized modern husband.

Kwi-Lan, schooled in the old traditions, comes into conflict with

《奥克兰论坛报》报影（1930-04-13）

　　东方的诗情存在于赛珍珠的小说《东风·西风》中，书中描写的是一个温柔的浪漫爱情故事，一位中国女性嫁给了一个受西方现代教育影响的丈夫。于是桂兰所接受的旧传统与新观念开始发生冲突。

　　在缓慢的调整开始之前，她发现了自己的悲伤和苦难，她的故事以适合主题的风格来叙述而变得具有文学和人文的吸引力。

　　魅力常见于陌生的世界。这位作家曾生活在东方，读者可以接受她的诠释是因为她如此地了解中国人。

　　要不是丈夫的爱和奉献，桂兰不会在旅途的尽头看到彩虹，她无法理解的事情太多了。作者让读者透过这位中国妻子疑问和困惑的眼睛，让他们分享这个发现。

　　（英文原文见附贰：12. *East Wind*，*West Wind*—Romance of the Orient）

Missionary From China to U.S.'

"WOMEN ARE
JUST AS ANXIOUS
TO PLEASE MEN
AS EVER"

MRS. PEARL S. BUCK, winner of the Pulitzer prize for her book, "The Good Earth" has been called a "renegade missionary" for her criticisms of the conduct of American missions in China. She is a missionary herself, home from Nanking on furlough. Her sister, Grace Sydenstricker, once attended Maryville College. Mrs. Buck attended Randolph-Macon.

Mrs. Buck has her ideas about American women. Having spent most of her life in China, she finds the women of her native land are just as dependent on what men think of them as ever.

因《大地》而获得普利策奖的赛珍珠，因其对美国在华传教活动的描述而被称为"叛徒传教士"（英文原文见附贰：13. Missionary "From China to U.S."）——《诺克斯维尔新闻哨兵报》（*The Knoxville News Sentinel*，1933 − 01−11）

Notes of

A novel, beautifully written and far-reaching in its implications is "East Wind: West Wind," by Pearl S. Buck. It shows the inevitable clash in modern China between two cultures, two traditions that are a world apart. Yet its author reaffirms the essential sisterhood of women, if not the brotherhood of men, and shows that East and West do meet and mingle.

The story, written in a poetic vein, is cast in the form of a first person recital made by the gentle and aristocratic Kwei-Lan to her American sister-in-law.

Miss Buck, the author, has lived all her life in the Orient with the exception of a few years spent at an American university. Her writings have appeared in leading periodicals in this country. The present book is published by John Day.

❧ ❧ ❧

《东风·西风》文笔优美，影响深远，展现了在现代中国的两种文化、两种传统的不可避免的冲突——《旧金山考官报》（*The San Francisco Examiner*，1930 − 04−27）

《新闻先驱报》（*News Herald*），1993 年 6 月 2 日

《新闻先驱报》报影（1993-06-02）

　　6 月 13 日，星期日，辛迪加脱口秀节目主持人、1991 年赛珍珠女性奖的获得者莎莉·杰西·拉斐尔（Sally Jessy Raphael）将在希尔敦（Hilltown）村赛珍珠基金会国际总部文化中心举办"《东风·西风》——拥抱世界的女性赛珍珠"预展。

　　《东风·西风》是一部 90 分钟的纪录片，记录了赛珍珠丰富而充满活力的一生。这部电影由西弗吉尼亚州贝克利的公共电视台 WSWP-TV 以及康涅狄格州韦斯特波特的瑞福克斯影业公司（Refocus Films）制作，由女演员伊娃·玛丽·圣（Eva Marie Saint）解说。

　　1938 年度的诺贝尔文学奖授予了珀尔·西登斯特里克·巴克（赛珍珠）。直到今天，她仍然是唯一获此殊荣的美国女性。赛珍珠是有史以来作品被翻译得最多的美国作家之一。而且，她最终因为促进亚洲与西方之间的理解以及倡导美亚混血儿童事业而被铭记。

　　这部纪录片以对许多最了解巴克的家人和朋友进行的采访

为主要内容，重点突出了赛珍珠的个人家庭以及她在中国南京的邻居的影像，其中有她的妹妹格蕾丝·尤基，南京传教士伙伴、103 岁的科妮莉亚·米尔斯（Cornelia Mills）和作家詹姆斯·米切纳（James Michener），他们毫无保留地分享自己的回忆。历史学观察的内容由世界上研究中国的一些著名学者提供，包括已故的哈佛大学的约翰·费尔班克，波士顿大学的詹姆斯·托马斯和（中国）南京大学外语系主任刘海平。

影片《东风·西风》追踪了一个传教士孩子的非凡道路。这个孩子在世纪之交出生在西弗吉尼亚州，并在中国农村长大，后来成为 20 世纪最受欢迎的作家之一。口述历史和史料影像的融合，勾画出这位女性的多面肖像。

这部电影将于 6 月 10 日在华盛顿特区的史密森学院举行全国首映。宾夕法尼亚州的首映式将在作为国家历史地标建筑所在地的青山农场举行。赛珍珠在那里生活了 38 年直到 1973 年去世。①

赛珍珠在其漫长的职业生涯中写了 100 多部作品，但最著名的小说无疑是《大地》。她在 1930 年代、1940 年代和 1950 年代有一系列畅销书，但她远不止是一位受欢迎的小说家。实际上，早在小说家的名衔为人们熟悉之前，她就已经是一名活动家。在 1930 年代和 1940 年代，她倡导了许多事业活动，包括争取妇女权利和民权、废除《排华法案》、领养混血儿童、包容和理解智障者。这部影片的最后一部分聚焦于她最大的遗产——赛珍珠基金会（Pearl S. Buck Foundation），该基金会努力为美亚混血儿和其他流离失所的孩子提供终身机会，以使他们摆脱贫困，免遭歧视和其他困境，使他们成为自给自足、自食其力的社会成员。

左图：《东风·西风》1930 年版，封面是《大地》获普利策奖之后的版本

右图：《东风·西风》：引人注目的中国背景的小说（英文原文见附贰：14. *East Wind, West Wind, A Striking Novel, Set in China*）——《萨克拉门托蜜蜂报》（*The Sacramento Bee*，1930-04-26）

---

① 此报道有误。赛珍珠 1970 年定居在佛蒙特州的丹比镇。1973 年在丹比去世。

影片《东风·西风》是独立电影制片人克雷格·戴维森（Craig Davidson）和联合制片人唐·罗戈辛（Donn Rogosin）历时五年艰辛的努力和研究的成果。（英文原文见附贰：15. Sally Jessy Raphael to Host Buck Documentary）

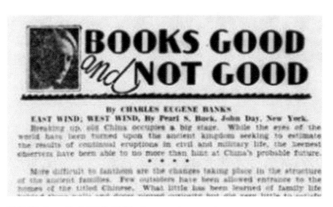

书分优劣（英文原文见附贰：16. Books Good and Not Good）
——《檀香山广告商报》（*The Honolulu Advertiser*，1930-04-13）

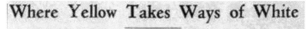

黄种人接受白种人的方式（英文原文见附贰：17. Where Yellow Takes Ways of White）
——《帕萨迪纳邮报》（*The Pasadena Post*，1930-04-12）

火星云美术馆收藏的赛珍珠签名的图书
左起：《巨浪》《赛珍珠的美国》《怀着爱写给女儿们》

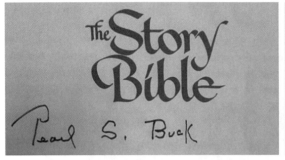

火星云美术馆收藏的赛珍珠签名的图书
（左起）：《故事圣经》《中国之我见》

　　赛珍珠的《大地》于 1931 年 2 月由纽约的约翰·戴公司出版。从 1931 年 2 月 20 日的《缅因州列维斯顿》（*Lewiston Maine*）的报影可以看到，该书列在"月度图书精选俱乐部"3 月书单，当时定价 2.5 美元。

BOOK CLUB SELECTIONS

Book League, February—"Festival," by Struthers Burt (Scrib.). $2.50.

Book League, March—"Mrs. Fischer's War," by Henrietta Leslie (H.M.). $2.50.

Book of the Month Club, February—"Grand Hotel," by Vicki Baum (D.D.). $2.50.

Book of the Month Club, March —"The Good Earth," by Pearl S. Buck (Day). $2.50.

Business Book League, February —"J. C. Penny: The Man With a

《大地》横空出世——《缅因州列维斯顿》（*Lewiston Maine*，1931-02-20）

《布鲁克林时代联盟报》（*Brooklyn Times Union*），1931 年 3 月 15 日

"The Good Earth" Story of Chinese By Pearl S. Buck

THE GOOD EARTH, By Pearl S. Buck. New York: The John-Day Co. Book of the Month Club selection for March.

MANY stories and novels have been written about China, for the most part by authors remaining only for short periods in the big seacoast centres. These deal with life in the big cities and hardly scratch the surface.

Mrs. Buck, on the other hand, was born in China, the daughter of American missionaries; China has been her home except for the few years during which she was being educated in the United States; Chinese is as much her language as is English; her home is in Nanking, where her husband is in the faculty of the College of Agricul

《布鲁克林时代联盟报》报影（1931-03-15）

　　关于中国的故事和小说已经有了许多，其中大部分的作者在沿海城市仅是短暂驻留，即使是触及大城市生活的作品，也只是浅尝辄止。

　　另一方面，巴克夫人出生在中国①，是美国传教士的女儿。除了在美国接受教育的那几年，中国一直是她的家，汉语和英语一样都作为她的语言。她的家在南京，她的丈夫在农学院任教。她懂得这块土地上的中国人。

　　赛珍珠写在《大地》中的这些民众人物——这是她出版的

---

① 此处原文有误。赛珍珠出生在美国西弗吉尼亚州的希尔斯伯勒。

第二部小说，一部真实的关于中国人的小说——如同她的第一部小说《东风·西风》，这是一部关于大众的小说，书中的民众生活在他们自己的世界，几乎不知道世界上有与他们完全不同的人。

也许是真的——也许不是——富不过三代，许多小说可能只是潜意识地建立在这个主题之上的。这是《大地》的主题。

但是，巴克夫人对这些朴素群众的生活赋予了极大的同情。她笔下的人物只是中国千千万万的中坚力量中的一小部分，他们住在破烂的泥土屋里，墙上留有小洞通风，在寒冷天气里小洞要用纸糊起来。极度贫困的他们生活在小河旁边，如果想要生存，小河是必不可少的，因为必须找到水来防止庄稼枯死。然而，在洪水泛滥时，小河又成了他们的巨大威胁。

他们的家园和庄稼都被冲走了，生活就又变成了一场抗争。

《大地》在王龙的婚礼那一天开场。王龙的父亲身患疾病，母亲已去世多年。你看到，那天早上他起床并决定（如读者看到的）将所有可用的水用来给自己洗澡。那天故事随着王龙所做的事展开，他的脑海里一直在想，家里来了一个女人而他不用再被召唤着做家务、做饭、照顾生病的父亲等等。自从母亲去世后，这些都是他必须做的事情。

王龙穷，阿兰也是如此。他所娶的这个女孩，除了贫穷、奴性和能生育之外，既没有美貌，也没有任何活着的期盼。她曾在全省最大的豪门黄家当过丫鬟，实际上是一个奴隶，有时被殴打，永远吃不饱，也看不到任何希望，嫁到这里已是一种摆脱。

黄家的儿子们无所事事。王龙则不同，他是一名长工，他的妻子是他们家中的奴隶。靠着不断勤劳和节俭，王龙凑到了足够的钱，从黄家买了一小块地——一块稻田，继续劳作。

这是他登上财富阶梯的第一步，而卖掉一块地则是黄家走向贫穷的第一步。然后饥荒来了，王龙、阿兰和他们的大儿子与其他人一起，被迫到其他地方寻找食物，来到了城墙下。

革命来了。王龙不知道这到底是怎么一回事，他也不太在意。城市被占领，他与其他人一起参与了抢掠。有了足够的黄金再投入他的土地，王龙、阿兰和孩子开始回来了。他们从黄家买新的土地，最终，黄家的土地都为王龙所有了。他富有了。

正是在这里，巴克夫人展现了她对中国人的了解。中国人不曾改变，王龙改变了他的生活方式，但阿兰仍然是他的财产。他买了一个茶楼女孩，而阿兰一直待在厨房里直到她因劳动和生育而累死。

那里依旧在周而复始。王龙现在很懒，因为他不需要劳动。他的儿子们从来不用劳动，什么活都不会干。王龙的孙子们会重回我们看到的王龙大婚的那天吗？

《大地》是一个动人的故事，讲述得很好，充满了人性和生活之事。

（英文原文见附贰：18. *The Good Earth*，Story of Chinese by Pearl S. Buck）

关于《大地》的作者

《檀香山星报》（*Honolulu Star Bulletin*），1931 年 7 月 4 日

约翰·戴公司推出了一本宣传册，内容包含赛珍珠的自传和她的小说《大地》梗概。3 月 21 日《星报》（*The Star-Bulletin*）评价的《大地》仍然在个人年度最佳小说榜单上排名第一。

Pearl S. Buck, author of "The Good Earth."

About the Author Of 'The Good Earth'

《檀香山星报》报影（1931-07-04）

巴克夫人是美国传教士的女儿，她的童年是在中国内地度过的。她在那里的教育由母亲负责，后来在上海上学，但赛珍珠也从她的中国护士①那里学到了很多，她告诉赛珍珠自己童年的故事，还有太平军造反的事；同时，赛珍珠也了解了父亲在传教过程中四处云游的许多冒险经历。

　　17岁时，她被带到欧洲和美国，在弗吉尼亚完成学业，然后返回中国。两年后，她嫁给了美国人约翰·巴克，他们在中国北方的一个城镇②生活了5年，有段时间他们是附近仅有的白人。

　　"从表面上看，我们的生活已经足够令人兴奋了。"她写道，"我们经历了一场饥荒，面临着袭扰城市的匪徒间的战斗，子弹如鸟群般密密麻麻地飞过我们那紧贴在城墙内侧的小房子。我们时不时去乡下，有时走路去，有时路途较远，我就坐在轿子里，丈夫骑自行车。我们去了白人女性从未去过的地方，我确信我备足了好几周的话题。"

　　过去10年，巴克先生一直担任金陵大学农村经济与社会学系主任，他关于中国农业的著作即将面世。

　　巴克夫人对她自己生活的描述清楚地表明，她是如何能够如此自然而令人信服地呈现中国生活并使她的人物如此人性化和真实的。

　　"我的兴趣和关注的重点一直都是人，因为我生活在百姓中间，中国的百姓中间。"她写道，"当我被问到他们是什么样的人时，我不知道。他们不是这个，也不是那个，而是人。我无法更多地描述他们，就像我无法描述我自己的血亲一样。我与他们太密切并且太近距离地分享了他们的生活。"

　　"正因如此，我不喜欢那些把中国人写得离奇古怪的文章，我最大的愿望是让我书中的人物如同我感到的那样真实。"

　　巴克夫人在中国的大学里教过英国文学，但她说她觉得这份工作有乐趣主要是因为通过她的学生得到了新知识。

　　巴克夫妇有两个女儿，一个在学校读书，另一个孩子5岁，每天在家接受中国家庭老师的指导学习中文的阅读和书写，这位老师也是巴克夫人多年的中国文学老师。

（英文原文见附贰：19. About the Author of *The Good Earth*）

---

① 应该是指退休护士、保姆王阿妈。
② 今安徽省的宿州。

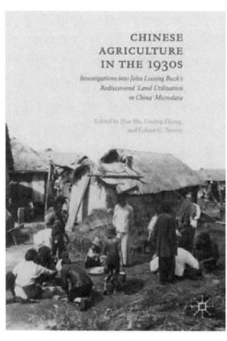

左图：农村经济学家约翰·巴克的《1930 年代中国农业调查》（1937 年）

右图：关于《大地》的书评（英文原文见附贰：20. Book Review: *The Good Earth*）——《伊萨卡杂志》（*The Ithaca Journal*，1931-03-26）

捕获中国魅力

《帕萨迪纳邮报》（*The Pasadena Post*），1931 年 4 月 11 日

《帕萨迪纳邮报》报影（1931-04-11）

《东风·西风》，赛珍珠著。约翰·戴公司，1930 年

《大地》，赛珍珠著。约翰·戴公司，1931 年

[海伦·史蒂文森] 去年出版的一本与同题材作品截然不同的名为《东风·西风》的书，可能没有引起读者的注意。实际上作者几乎一直都在中国生活，这部小说以一种尖锐的方式揭示了西方对现代中国的影响。一个迷人的中国小女孩，她在中国传统习俗中长大，嫁给了一个在国外受过教育的中国人。她保留了中国的观念，而她丈夫接受了西方的思想。她试图自我调整以适应令人惊奇和革命性的方式，塑造了令人感动和迷人的故事画面。她的兄长，也是家主地位的继承者，去美国学习并带回了他的新娘——一个美国女孩。发生在中国的现代转变和影响被如此般描绘成两个戏剧性的情景并赋予了这本书的书名。作者对中国真切的认知以及她对新老习俗的深切同情，赋予这个故事一种真实和不寻常的趣味性基调。这里没有出现在大多数关于中国生活的小说中的虚假伤感。《东风·西风》以简洁、精致和魅力写作，美不胜收。

之所以在这里提到它，不仅因为它本身的优点，也不仅因为它可能没有引起你的注意，还因为巴克夫人今年出版的新书《大地》也描写了中国。

这一次书写的是一个中国农民和他对土地的情感。两本书都因为对中国风土人情的巧妙交织和对人物淋漓尽致的刻画而备受关注。

（英文原文见附贰：21. China's Charm Captured）

出生地为她骄傲①

《号角纪事报》（*Clarion Ledger*），1932 年 3 月 18 日

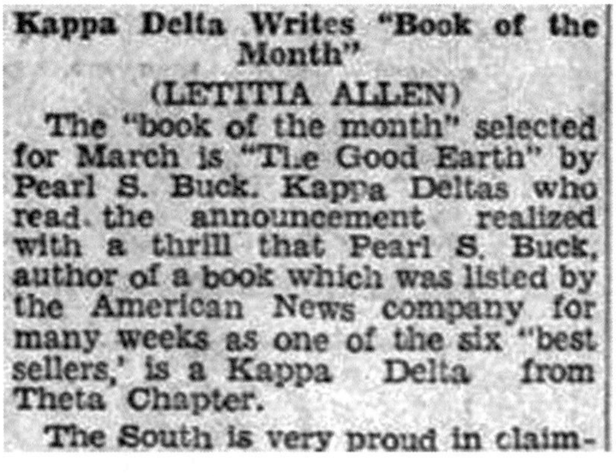

Kappa Delta Writes "Book of the Month"

(LETITIA ALLEN)

The "book of the month" selected for March is "The Good Earth" by Pearl S. Buck. Kappa Deltas who read the announcement realized with a thrill that Pearl S. Buck, author of a book which was listed by the American News company for many weeks as one of the six "best sellers," is a Kappa Delta from Theta Chapter.

The South is very proud in claim-

《号角纪事报》报影（1932-03-18）

———————————

① 此篇文章的标题是本书编著者所加。文中的卡帕·得尔塔（Kappa Delta）是由美国人埃默里·博加杜斯（Emory Bogardus）于 1920 年创立的社会学荣誉协会。该组织的最初目的是"激发学术研究，促进社会科学研究"。

[塔蒂亚·艾伦]　　赛珍珠的《大地》被选为三月的"月度之书"。卡帕·得尔塔人读到这则公告后，激动地意识到赛珍珠——其作品连续数周被美国新闻公司列为六大"畅销书"之一，竟然是一名来自茜塔查普特的卡帕·得尔塔成员。

南方人因拥有赛珍珠而感到非常自豪，因为她出生在西弗吉尼亚州的希尔斯伯勒。巴克夫人由身为传教士的父母养育成人，她本人是一名传教士，她是一个女儿，也是一名妻子。巴克夫人一直在中国生活，她只是从她在弗吉尼亚州林奇堡上学的经历中了解到这个国家①。人们可能会想知道，在伦道夫-梅肯女子学院1914届的学生中有多少人能将她与那个古怪的珀尔·西登斯特里克对上号。在伦道夫-梅肯女子学院和康奈尔大学学习后②，巴克夫人前往中国在一所中国的大学里任教。

她的故事和文章不时地出现在《大西洋月刊》和《国家与亚洲》。她的第一部长篇小说《东风·西风》也是关于中国的。

《纽约时报》书评评论如下：赛珍珠写了一部关于中国的小说《东风·西风》，广受赞誉，这是她的第一部小说且非常有前景。她在第二本书《大地》中，以超乎人们最乐观期望的精彩绝伦实现了这一承诺。不考虑地域问题，《大地》是一部优秀的小说。它有风格，有力量，有连贯性，有一种无处不在的戏剧现实感。在更深层次的意义上，与其说它是对中国生活的写照，不如说是对全球任何地区任何时代的生活意义与悲剧的写照。尽管在行为方式和传统上存在根本的差异，但在读了开始的几页之后，人们往往会忘记故事中的人物是中国人而以为就是外国人。

毋庸置疑，巴克夫人了解她的中国。除了在美国上大学外，她大部分时间都在那里度过。但她描绘了一个普通读者不熟悉的中国，令人欣喜的是，这是一个有无尽的神秘或异国风情的中国。在她的书中很少有我们习惯的标签化"东方"特质，她对远东生活的描述一方面与拉夫卡迪奥·赫恩③的相去甚远，另一方面与来自好莱坞的相去甚远。

（英文原文见附贰：22. Kappa Delta Writes "Books of the Month"）

---

① 指美国。
② 赛珍珠1914年从伦道夫-梅肯女子学院毕业后，立即回到了中国。
③ 拉夫卡迪奥·赫恩（Lafcadio Hearn）是最早向西方世界介绍日本的日籍希腊作家。

《岩岛阿格斯报》（*The Rock Island Argus*），1932 年 5 月 4 日

[雷米尔·F. 帕顿]　在伦道夫-梅肯学院，珀尔·巴克，那时还是珀尔·西登斯特里克，在除去英语之外的其他所有科目都获得了高分。教授不喜欢她的英文作业，它不符合他的要求②。她有条顿人③血统，坚韧而执着。因此《大地》——顺便说一句，坚韧成就了史诗之作——普利策奖，盛誉都没能改变她的安静和意志坚强的生活。就像她作品中的王龙和阿兰一样，赛珍珠毫不动摇。

《岩岛阿格斯报》报影（1932-05-04）

赛珍珠小时候住在一个"幽州"古城④，当地人将干旱和不幸归咎于外国人家庭。一群暴动者来到了他们的房子前。她

---

① 本文标题由本书编著者加注，原文是报纸"Who's News Today"栏目中的文章。

② 赛珍珠在与同学们一起学习各门课程之外，还要额外地补习英语，修读 ESL——英语第二语言（English as a second or foreign language），直至大学毕业。

③ 罗马作家提到的一个古老的北欧部落。

④ 原文"幽州"（Yochow）可能形容当时的困境如幽州古战场。

的母亲准备了茶和糕点并把他们请了进来。这是一次美妙的聚会，来访者对他们受到热情款待深表谢意而鞠躬离去。在这样的接触中，小女孩了解到了中国人的性格。大学毕业后，赛珍珠花了数年时间阅读中国经典①，但她后来说，她发现自己的最主要的素材并不在其中。她说在她和旧中国的心灵之间没有中间人，这是不可征服的。

大学毕业后不久，她嫁给了康奈尔大学毕业生约翰·洛辛·巴克。《大地》吸收了他们两个人的思想认识，因为巴克写了一本书《农场经济》②，他现在是北京大学③农场管理系主任。

在她可爱的南京的家里，巴克夫人仍然耐心地继续着她的工作。在 1927 年的国内战乱中，巴克夫妇失去了家园和所有财产，但这并没有使她停止《大地》的写作。她会弹奏中国琴，乐于助人，并在她透彻了解的古老文化中找到满足感。她中等身材，三十出头，一头黑发，总是平和与内敛。

（英文原文见附贰：23. Who's News Today）

"The Good Earth" Wins Pulitzer Prize

PEARL S. BUCK'S "The Good Earth" is the Pulitzer prize novel of the year. In making the announcement of the awards, the judges' committee made the following comment on Mrs. Buck's book:

"Preference has been given to 'The Good Earth' for its epic sweep, its distinct and moving characterization, its sustained story-interest, its simple and yet richly-colored style. Also, so far as may be gathered, Mrs. Buck gives an undistorted picture of the life discribed."

Other literary awards by the Pulitzer Prize Committee are:

Drama—To the "book" of "Of Thee I Sing," by

BOOK CHAT

Europe no longer inspires America. The contrary is beginning to be true. —Andre Siegfried.

Dutton brings out a new edition of Tamara Karsavina's "Theater Street" at a new price, $3.75. This is the third large printing of the book.

Pearl S. Buck's "The Good Earth," chosen as the March "Book of the Month," is published by the John Day company. Like her earlier "East Wind: West Wind," it is a story of China."

Astrophysics have become enormously popular, perhaps because of the gorgeous mendacity to which they lend themselves.—George Bernard Shaw.

Young China Flames With Loves—Hates

1931 Pulitzer Prize Winner Writes a Novelet.

BY Zella Wallace, Des Moines.

THE YOUNG REVOLUTIONIST, by Pearl Buck (John Day $1.50).

FRIENDS and admirers of Pearl Sydenstricker Buck who followed the adventures of Wang Lung through the fascinating pages of The Good Earth, Pulitzer prize winner for 1931, will find an unforgettable evening in the reading of this new and slender volume The Young Revolutionist. This time Mrs. Buck has chosen for her medium that neglected form of American art—the novelet that Willa Cather and Edith Wharton have found so satisfactory. It is a form of expression that permits extreme concentration and illumination of a smaller

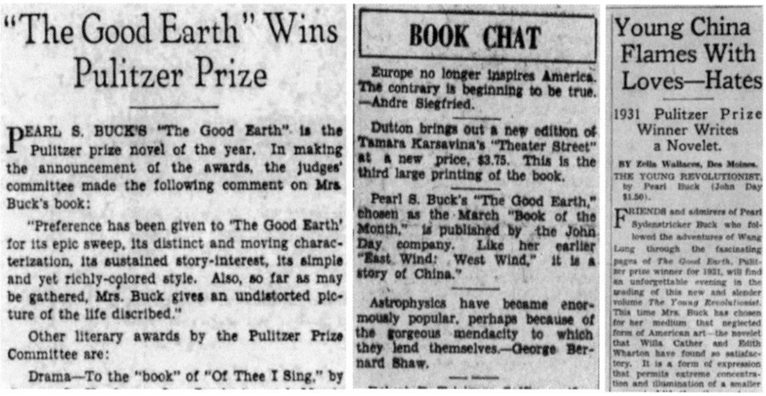

左图：普利策奖的新闻报道（英文原文见附贰：24. *The Good Earth* Wins Pulitzer Prize）——《时代殖民者报》（*Times Colonist*，1932-05-21）

中图：赛珍珠与 1925 年诺贝尔文学奖获得者萧伯纳齐名——《晨电》（*The Morning Call*，1931-03-14）

右图：爱与恨（英文原文见附贰：25. Young China Flames with Loves—Hates）——《得梅因登记册报》（*The Des Moines Register*，1932-05-22）

---

① 此处说的"经典"应指各种中国小说，包括四大名著。在赛珍珠到上海上学之前，私塾老师孔先生就开始教她中国文化的儒家经典了。

② 前文已经提到，赛珍珠跟着约翰·巴克在他考察的农村住过很久。那里的农民，正是王龙的原型。

③ 原文是 University of Peking，应该是 University of Nanking，即当时的金陵大学。

《布鲁克林时代联盟报》（*Brooklyn Times Union*），1932 年 5 月 4 日

ANNUAL PRIZE WON
BY BOOK ON CHINA

Pearl S. Buck Receives Pulitzer Award for Her "The
Good Earth."

Pearl S. Buck, author of "The
Good Earth," was awarded the
Pulitzer prize for the best American novel of the year, $1,000. The
rules of the award were changed
to enable the judges to honor this
writer.

《布鲁克林时代联盟报》报影（1932-05-04）

《大地》的作者赛珍珠被授予普利策年度最佳美国小说奖，奖金为 1,000 美元。评奖规则进行了更改，以使评委们能够表彰这位作家。

根据普利策遗嘱条款，评委有权更改评选的条件。该奖项原本是授予美国小说家的。该小说家的小说"应该最好地展现美国生活的健康氛围，以及最高标准的美国礼仪与男子人格"。《大地》出色地讲述了一个中国农民和他的兄弟的艰辛，以至于评委改变了奖项的授予条件。

---

① 本文标题由本书编著者引自报道文章。

WINS PULITZER PRIZE

Pearl S. Buck, whose novel "The Good Earth" won the 1932 Pulitzer fiction award prize.

(Associated Press Photo.)

MRS. PEARL S. BUCK.

上图:《阿格斯领袖报》（*Argus Leader*，1932-05-09）
下图:《早间新闻》（*The Morning News*，1933-04-13）

政治教育联盟晚宴

《伊萨卡日报》(*The Ithaca Journal*)，1933 年 1 月 21 日

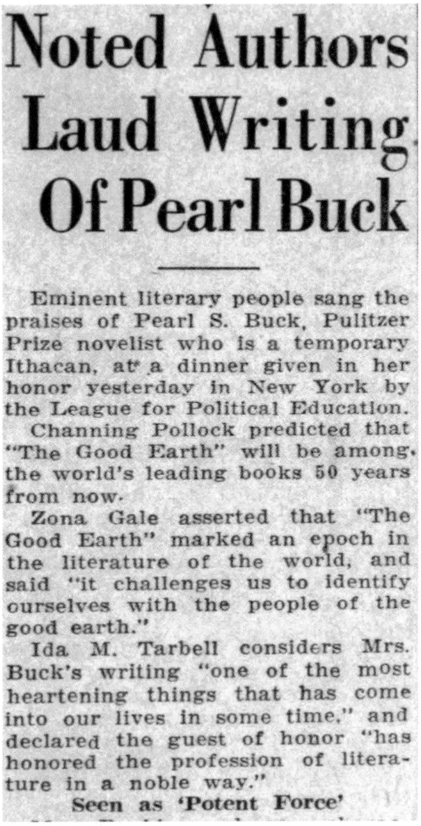

Noted Authors Laud Writing Of Pearl Buck

Eminent literary people sang the praises of Pearl S. Buck, Pulitzer Prize novelist who is a temporary Ithacan, at a dinner given in her honor yesterday in New York by the League for Political Education.

Channing Pollock predicted that "The Good Earth" will be among the world's leading books 50 years from now.

Zona Gale asserted that "The Good Earth" marked an epoch in the literature of the world, and said "it challenges us to identify ourselves with the people of the good earth."

Ida M. Tarbell considers Mrs. Buck's writing "one of the most heartening things that has come into our lives in some time," and declared the guest of honor "has honored the profession of literature in a noble way."

Seen as 'Potent Force'

《伊萨卡日报》报影（1933-01-21）

政治教育联盟昨天在纽约为赛珍珠举办的晚宴上，著名文学家对她获得普利策奖大加赞扬。查宁 · 波洛克（Channing Pollock）预测，《大地》将在 50 年后成为世界顶级书籍。艾达 · M. 塔贝尔（Ida M. Tarbell）认为巴克夫人的作品是“一段时间以来我们生活中最振奋人心的事情之一”。

关于政治教育联盟的这次晚宴的报道，左三为赛珍珠
——《温莎之星报》（*The Windsor Star*，1933-01-23）

左图：1932 年普利策奖授予普林格尔、赛珍珠、杜兰蒂和考夫曼——《使者报》（*The Messenger*，1932-05-05）

右图：纽约伊萨卡镇的报刊报道（英文原文见附贰：26. Pearl Buck to Live In Ithaca, Novelist Wrote "Best Seller"）——《伊萨卡杂志》（*The Ithaca Journal*，1932-04-07）

赛珍珠和女儿卡罗尔在南京的家中（英文原文见附贰：27. Popularity of *The Good Earth* Was a Surprise to Pearl S. Buck）——《堪萨斯城之星报》（*The Kansas City Star*, 1932-07-22）

左图：荣获诺贝尔文学奖的赛珍珠在新泽西州蒙特克莱尔的格伦里奇女子俱乐部讲演："我在中国的亲身经历"——《蒙特克莱尔时报》（*The Montclair Times*, 1935-03-29）

右图：赛珍珠在路易斯安那州门罗文兰高中讲演："我在中国的亲身经历"——《梦露新闻明星报》（*The Monroe News Star*, 1932-10-14）

《迪凯特每日评》（*The Decatur Daily Review*），1938 年 11 月 10 日

Pearl Buck Wins Nobel Prize

Award for Literature Based Principally on "The Good Earth," Pulitzer Novel

By Associated Press

STOCKHOLM — The 1936 Nobel prize for literature was awarded today to Pearl Buck, American author of "The Good Earth" and other novels dealing with China.

Mrs. Buck, formerly Pearl Sydenstrycker and now Mrs. Richard J. Walsh of Great Neck, N. Y., was born in Hillsboro, W. Va., in 1892 and has spent much of her life in China.

(Mrs. Buck's parents were missionaries in China and her first husband, J. Lossing Buck, was a member of the faculty of Nanking university. They were divorced in 1935.)

The Nobel award was understood to have been based particularly on "The Good Earth," which also won the 1932 Pulitzer prize for an American novel.

The Nobel literature prize amounts to 155,000 kroner, about $37,975.

Pearl Buck was the third American to win the Nobel award in literature, an honor she shares in this country only with Sinclair Lewis, who was awarded it in 1930, and Eugene O'Neill, who received it in 1936.

She joined the company of such literary greats as Maurice Maeterlinck, Rudyard Kipling, Anatole France, William Butler Yeats and George Bernard Shaw.

PEARL BUCK

She was the second woman of the decade to win Nobel recognition for her literature.

The first, in 1928, was Sigrid Undset.

"The Good Earth," probably best known of Mrs. Buck's works, won the Pulitzer award for the best novel of 1932. She also was awarded second prize in the 1933 O. Henry Memorial awards for her story, "The Frill."

《迪凯特每日评》报影（1938–11–10）

奖励主要产生在普利策奖小说《大地》基础上①

[美联社，斯德哥尔摩] 今天，1938 年诺贝尔文学奖授予了赛珍珠，这是一位著有《大地》及其他关于中国题材的小说的美国作家。

巴克夫人，以前是珀尔·西登斯特里克，现在是纽约州 Great Neck 的理查德·沃尔什夫人，1892 年出生于西弗吉尼亚州希尔斯伯勒，大部分时间都在中国度过。（巴克夫人的父母是在中国的传教士，她的第一任丈夫 J. 洛辛·巴克是金陵大学的

---

① 《迪凯特每日评》的这篇文章的副标题认为诺贝尔奖是特别基于获得了 1932 年普利策奖的小说《大地》，可能会让一些人产生错误认识，以为那一年的诺贝尔奖降低了标准，采用了一个美国普利策奖的标准。这是一个极大的误会，但是这个消极观点已经很难澄清。

教员。他们于 1935 年离婚。）

据了解，这一诺贝尔奖的主要根据是《大地》，该作品作为一部美国小说获得了 1932 年普利策奖。

诺贝尔文学奖奖金为 155,000 克朗，约合 37,975 美元。

赛珍珠是第三位获得诺贝尔文学奖的美国人，在美国只有辛克莱·刘易斯（Sinclair Lewis）在 1930 年和尤金·奥尼尔（Eugene O'Neil）在 1936 年获得过这一荣誉。

她进入了莫里斯·梅特林克、拉迪亚德·吉卜林、阿纳托尔·法兰西、威廉·巴特勒·叶芝和乔治·伯纳德·肖等文学大家的行列。

她是 10 年来第二位因文学创作获得诺贝尔奖的女性。第一位是 1928 年的西格丽德·昂德塞特（Sigrid Undset）[1]。

《大地》可能是巴克夫人最为人所知的作品，获得了 1932 年普利策最佳小说奖。她的故事《褶边》还获得了 1933 年欧·亨利纪念奖的二等奖。

（英文原文见附贰：28. Pearl Buck Wins Nobel Prize）

不想抹去的中国经历[2]

《圣路易斯邮报》（*St Louis Post Dispatch*），1938 年 12 月 11 日

《圣路易斯邮报》报影（1938-12-11）

---

[1] 西格丽德·昂德塞特是挪威裔丹麦小说家。

[2] 此标题是本书编著者所加，原报道题为"赛珍珠的双重身份"。

诺贝尔奖得主的兴趣始终是美国式的，但她的生活是中国式的

[弗吉尼亚·欧文，纽约] 与赛珍珠交谈就像服用了镇静剂，不是这位女士给你催眠了，而是她的平静具有感染力。她有一种惊人的平静的个性，一种超然的气质，这让任何与她交谈超过 10 分钟的人都能镇静，而她的声音，就像你最喜欢的小夜曲的旋律一样舒缓，令人信服。

最近，赛珍珠在她的出版商丈夫的办公室里，和我谈起了她因被授予诺贝尔文学奖而获得的荣誉，谈起了她未来的计划以及在中国已经长期持续的战争。她说话时，外面作为曼哈顿最繁忙的大街之一的麦迪逊大道上的噪音似乎逐渐消退，我们落座的房间似乎出奇地安静，赛珍珠身上好像有摆脱周围环境的能力，这并非精神上的力量。

"坦率地说，"我们谈到一个月前授予她的奖项时，巴克夫人笑了，不是表现在她的脸上而是透过她的眼睛，"这一切对我来说都是一个完全而巨大的惊喜。我甚至都不知道委员会会议是在每年的这个时候召开，而且我从来没有想过能够被认可。但现在我已经被赋予了这个荣誉，我感到责任重大。我当时的念头是，如果委员会再迟十年对我的工作给予这个褒奖也许会更好。但既然我赢得了奖项——不仅是因为我的《大地》，而且是因为我所有的工作，我决心做得更好。有太多的情节、太多的书在我的脑海里苦等着要写出来。"

作为第三位获得诺贝尔奖的美国人，这位相当腼腆、严肃的女性在这个国家仅与辛克莱·刘易斯和尤金·奥尼尔享受过这一荣誉，现在她进入了莫里斯·梅特林克、拉迪亚德·吉卜林、阿纳托尔·法兰西、威廉·巴特勒·叶芝和萧伯纳这些人物的行列。这个文学创作的国际认可被认为主要基于获得 1932 年普利策奖的《大地》，它使中国成为美国小说读者眼中鲜活的现实。

"许多人在看到任何有我签名的东西时都认定它必是另一个关于中国和中国人的故事。"巴克夫人在我们谈到她的作品时继续说道，"而且人们有这样的观点，即我在中国的岁月让我成了一名作家。其实我创作是因为我一直想写，而我的第一部作品是关于中国的，因这一点中国被解读为前提。我愿意在潜意识里作为一名作家来写美国人而不是写中国人，但我不想抹去我的中国经历。"

巴克夫人说，多年来她一直计划不将自己局限于只写有关中国的书籍，而她的最新著作《爱国者》是以美国为主题的。她的下一个故事将被称为"美国传奇"，并将关注美国给予她的英雄们的不可思议的爱。

"一个人碰巧独自飞越了大西洋，或者他比其他人打的棒球更多，对这种人的偶像崇拜泛滥是一种美国现象。"巴克夫人说，"偶像崇拜仅持续很短的时间，然后英雄就被遗忘了。世界上没有任何其他国家如此，在其他所有的国家，一个民族英雄是为国家的生活或者文化做出了某种确切的贡献的人，他的同胞会因这一贡献而给他荣誉和尊敬，这不是短暂的而是终生的，甚至是更久远的将来的。"

生于美国但在中国有 38 年的经历，赛珍珠认为自己过着双重生活。她说，她的关注点一直是美国人，背后是美国传统，但她的生活是中国的。她希望再次访问中国，但再也不会在那里安家。

"在来到美国之前，我从来没有过安宁的生活。"她平静地告诉我，"中国总是有内战，人们永远不知道明天会发生什么。现在那里的情况更糟了。"

巴克夫人认为，或许中国最终会屈服于日本。但她表示，真正的战争将在所有大战结束后发生——控制中国的精神及领土的战争。

"在这场战争爆发的两年前，中国人就已经预料到了这样一场战争。"巴克夫人解释道，"中国知道她永远不能指望以平等的军力来抵抗日本。中国当时和现在都知道可能会被迫屈服，但也知道自己永远不会在失败中被真正打败。对世界来说，中国可能是被占领的国家，但其文明不会改变。日本可能轰炸一个又一个大城市，控制沿海，但这一切都无关紧要，因为中国真正的文明是内在的。你知道中国百分之八十的地区是农村，中国不依赖外贸或贸易中心。她的社会是自给自足的，即使日本能占领中国所有的大城市，它也不能控制中国。控制中国和她的精神实际上都是不可能的。"

"中国从来没有被自己的官员控制过。因为中国人在认可家族控制的正当与公允的同时，他们从来没有也永远不会顺从政府的发号施令。中国家族将继续像他们几百年来那样地生活，管理只在自己内部进行，而拒绝家族以外的规则。正是这种对来自家族之外控制的拒绝，才让中国人的生活保持了强大。当人类的生活过于规范时，它就会变得虚弱而荒废。"

谈到希特勒迫害犹太人、天主教徒和德意志帝国，巴克夫人预测历史将把德国元首领导的运动视为文明史上"最可怕的污点"。"无论什么人为他的原则找什么借口，当然也没人能为希特勒的手段找到任何合理的辩解。"巴克夫人皱着眉头说，"毕竟，人根本不会掏空一个人的口袋后，看着他在这个世界上挨饿。"

直到 6 年前，赛珍珠在这个国家还没有一个固定的家。她出生在西弗吉尼亚州，很小的时候就被身为传教士的父亲带到了中国。在 15 岁进入上海的一所寄宿学校之前，她没有接受过正规教育。她说，在那之前，她都未曾意识到自己与中国人的不同。从 1921 年到 1931 年的 10 年间，她在金陵大学、东南大学和陈塔尔政府学校①任教。有五年的时间，她和第一任丈夫约翰·巴克住在中国北方一个偏僻的小镇，在那里他们有几个月没有看到过白人，并在那里了解和感受中国内地真正的美丽。

现在，赛珍珠自豪地拥有宾夕法尼亚州巴克斯县的永久性住宅。她和现在的丈夫、纽约出版商理查德·沃尔什与她的孩子们住在那里，并完成她的大部分工作。

"但我可以在任何地方工作，"她解释道，"我不像某些作家，他们必须有特定的一个房间，有那个房间的特定的地方，并且必须使用同一支笔。我随时可以在任何地方工作，因为我有能力专注于我要做的事。如果我在一个满是人的房间里，大家都在讲话，我可以继续思考一个情节，或者做任何我想到的最重要的事情。因为如果我不想听，我就不听。"

也许正是这种将她自己与周围环境分离的能力，使赛珍珠给人一种距离感，并增加了一种严肃的印象。在访谈期间，即使赛珍珠戴着时髦的帽子和穿着最时髦的服装，也无法将她严肃的形象从你的脑海中抹去。这种严肃在她柔和的蓝色大眼睛中表现得最为明显，让她看起来忧伤，只有当她微笑时，忧伤的神情才不见。赛珍珠经常微笑，但像中国人那样，她很少大声笑。

（英文原文见附贰：29. Pearl Buck Led Dual Existence）

记者弗吉尼亚·欧文完稿的 1938 年 12 月 10 日，正是诺贝尔奖颁奖的那一天。这一天，赛珍珠在斯德哥尔摩发出了"中国不会亡"的激昂声音。此时的赛珍珠已经清醒地看到，中国的抗日斗争主要依靠统一战线，将在广大的农村和山区消耗敌人，进而消灭敌人。同时中国也急需国际援助，以及国际上切断对日本的供给。沟通文明需要桥梁，捍卫文明需要斗争。这是赛珍珠"人桥"功能的典型例证。

赛珍珠因小说《大地》和传记等作品而获得诺贝尔文学奖。她写作的两本传记分别是记述父亲的《战斗的天使》（1936 年）和记述母亲的《异邦客》（1936 年）。

---

① 关于原文里的 Chental（陈塔尔）一词，同时期的其他转载报刊亦如是。是否指中央（Central）大学，有待考证。

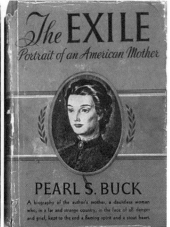

赛珍珠写作的两本传记《战斗的天使》和《异邦客》

　　杰出的瑞典作家、瑞典科学院院士塞尔玛·拉格洛夫（Selma Lagerlof）将诺贝尔奖选票投给了赛珍珠。她最近表示，在赛珍珠小姐的书中，她最喜欢的是《战斗的天使》。然而在瑞典，一般来说《异邦客》则更为流行。——《列克星敦先驱报》（*The Lexington Herald*，1939-01-01）

　　赛珍珠在写作上其实还有许多其他的荣誉。

　　1933 年，赛珍珠因其故事书《褶边》（*The Frill*）而获得欧·亨利奖纪念奖的二等奖。

　　1935 年，赛珍珠获得威廉·迪恩·豪威尔斯奖章。该奖是唯一授予具有特殊价值的短篇小说的年度奖项，每五年颁发一次，以表彰在此期间出版的最杰出的美国小说。

　　1938 年，赛珍珠获美国艺术学院金奖。

　　1938 年 2 月，尚未获得诺贝尔文学奖的赛珍珠名列当代最优秀十位作家的第二位。

　　1942 年 6 月 8 日，赛珍珠获得圣劳伦斯大学荣誉法学博士学位。

Honored For Words --- Spoken And Written

Selected as the three contemporaries who are most adept at the use of spoken and written English Lynn Fontanne (right), actress; Alois Havrilla (left), native of Czechoslovakia and radio announcer; and Pearl S. Buck (center), novelist. They were awarded gold medals by the American Academy of Arts and Letters at New York. Miss Fontanne for the most cultivated stage diction; Havrilla for the most cultural diction and pronunciation; and Mrs. Pearl S. Buck for her novel, "The Good Earth."

Q. Who are the best of the present day writers? E.L.

A. Dr. William Lyon Phelps has selected the following as the ten best living writers: Stephen Vincent Benet, Pearl S. Buck, Willa Cather, Robert Frost, Sinclair Lewis, Edna St. Vincent Millay, Eugene O'Neill, George Santayana, Booth Tarkington, and Dorothy Thompson.

左图：美国艺术学院金奖（中为赛珍珠）——《论坛报》（*The Tribune*，1938-11-12）

右图：1938 年当代最优秀的十位作家——《首都时报》（*The Capital Times*，1938-02-16）

The William Dean Howells Medal, awarded every fifth year by the American Academy of Arts and Letters, has been awarded to Pearl S. Buck for her novel, "The Good Earth," which won the 1931 Pulitzer prize. Reynal & Hitchcock announce a new novel by Mrs. Buck, "The Exile," to be published in February, while a motion picture film is being made of "The Good Earth."

Pearl S. Buck to Receive Doctorate

Canton, N. Y.—(AP)—Pearl S. Buck, novelist and first American woman awarded the Nobel prize for literature, is one of five persons who will receive honorary doctorates of law at St. Lawrence university's commencement June 8.

左图：赛珍珠荣获威廉·迪恩·豪威尔斯奖——《沃思堡星电报》（*Fort Worth Star Telegram*，1935-12-08）

右图：荣誉博士——《四城时报》（*Quad City Times*，1942-05-12）

PEARL S. BUCK

PORTRAIT BY FAMOUS ARTIST—The above portrait was painted by Sir John Quistgard, painter of presidents, kings, and other celebrities, who will exhibit a collection of his portraits and landscapes at the Woman's club. The exhibition will open Tuesday evening with a reception in his honor at 8 o'clock and will remain open until November 24.

Wins Nobel Prize of $40,000

PEARL S. BUCK, former American missionary in China and author of the novel "Good Earth" in addition to other novels and articles, holds the cablegram she received telling her that she had received the Nobel prize for literature in 1938. The announcement of the award, which did not mention specifically any of her works, is worth about $40,000.

左图：翰·奎斯加德爵士（Sir John Quistgard）绘赛珍珠肖像——《夏洛特观察家报》（*The Charlotte Observer*，1935-11-10）

右图：赛珍珠读完瑞典皇家学会通知她获得诺贝尔文学奖的电报，情不自禁地用汉语喊了出来："我不信啦！"图为赛珍珠手持通知她获得诺贝尔文学奖的电报——《公园纪录报》（*The Park Record*，1938-12-15）

1937 年《大地》被拍成电影，由著名演员保罗·穆尼（Paul Muni）和路易斯·雷纳（Luise Rainer）领衔主演。1940 年，赛珍珠成立中国紧急救援委员会时，路易斯·雷纳与赛珍珠共同募捐。

1937 年电影《大地》上映——密执安州本顿港（Benton Harbor）《先驱-钯报》（*The Herald-Palladium*，1937-08-05）

　　左图为电影《大地》1962 年重映海报，海报背面有主演保罗·穆尼的签名，右图为重映纪念活动卡上奥斯卡最佳女主角奖获得者、影星路易斯·雷纳的签名（火星云美术馆藏品）

赛珍珠多年的写作训练

《省报（加拿大）》（*The Province*, Canada），1939 年 1 月 7 日

Pearl Buck's Years of Training for Writing

By PROFESSOR W. T. ALLISON.

THE award of the Nobel Prize to Pearl S. Buck, recently, was probably based upon her novels of Chinese life. When "The Good Earth" appeared in 1931 it was received with applause in the United States, Canada, and Great Britain, and proved to be the world's best seller since Sinclair Lewis was lifted into fame by "Main Street."

It brought to Mrs. Buck not only a fortune in royalties but the Pulitzer Prize in 1932, a Yale M.A. honorary degree in 1933, and two years later from the American Academy of Arts and Letters the William Dean Howells medal for fiction. And now has come the crowning honor, the Nobel Prize, all the more acceptable because Mrs. Buck (now Mrs. J. Walsh) is the first American woman to be chosen by a committee of foreigners as worthy of this distinction.

Like so many successful authors, Pearl S. Buck rose to greatness because she was fortunate in her subject, her education, and her experience of life. When she was only two months old her father and mother went as missionaries of the Presbyterian church from Virginia to the interior of China. This was forty-five years ago when the people of the celestial kingdom looked upon white men and women as foreign devils.

Mrs. Buck's home was once mobbed in a city where the members of her family were the only foreigners; her father, who with the greatest courage went on lonely journeys throughout the district brought back stories of his narrow escapes from death and colorful descriptions of his mission work in villages along the Yangtse River. These stories and those related to the growing child by her old Chinese nurse who served the Buck family for eighteen years, laid a basis for her knowledge of native life.

Her Mother Her Only Teacher For Years

Her mother was her only teacher for many years. She taught Pearl to study the customs and institutions of her adopted country sympathetically and to see beauty everywhere; she also encouraged her to write, and gave her wise criticism.

When she grew up, Pearl married a young American professor and taught English literature on the staff of the University of Nanking. By this time she had become a deep student of Chinese literature. Over a period of ten years she read all the classic novels of China. This required infinite application, for she had first to learn between 10,000 and 20,000 Chinese characters.

Her formal study, added to her keen observation of the full tide of daily life at a time when China was being swept by the struggles of bandits and war-lords and by social and educational change, formed the abundant resources of a novelist who had learned to paint the thing as she saw it for people thousands of miles distant from the Nanking garden where she wrote "The Good Earth."

This novel which has won for its author such renown is a sincere and skilful interpretation of Chinese character. It discourses to us of "the still, sad music of humanity"; humanity, it is true, with a yellow skin and oblique eyes, and with ways and modes of thoughts far different from ours, but in its trials and temptations, essentially the same as those of the western world.

The western reader is, perhaps, most impressed by Mrs. Buck's characters, for they seem so understandable; there is nothing mysterious about them, nothing exotic, as in so many stories of the Orient. If it were not for the local color and the extreme poverty, the floods, droughts, pestilences and revolution, we might imagine we were reading about Canadian or English people.

"These people," as an authoritative critic has written, "are born, play, toil, suffer and dream as all humans have done, under whatever sun, or whatever patch of common earth."

《省报（加拿大）》报影（1939-01-07）

[威廉·塔尔伯特·艾莉森教授①] 赛珍珠最近获得诺贝尔奖或许是基于她写作关于中国生活的小说。当《大地》于 1931 年问世时，它在美国、加拿大和英国受到热烈欢迎，并被认为是自辛克莱·刘易斯因《大街》而声名鹊起后世界上最畅销的书。

它给巴克夫人带来的不仅有版税财富，还有 1932 年的普利策奖、1933 年的耶鲁大学荣誉文学硕士学位，还有两年后从美国艺术与文学学院获得的威廉·迪恩·豪威尔斯小说奖，现在得到的是最高荣誉——诺贝尔奖，所有这些都是顺理成章的，因为巴克夫人（现在的沃尔什夫人）是第一位因突出贡献而由外国人的委员会评选出来的美国女性。

像许多成功的作家一样，赛珍珠之所以成功，恰恰得益于她在工作、教育和生活各方面的经历。当她只有两个月大的

---

① 威廉·塔尔伯特·艾莉森教授（1875—1941）出生于加拿大安大略省尤宁维尔。他就读于哈伯德学院并获得了学士学位。1899 年至 1900 年在维多利亚学院学习并获得硕士学位。艾莉森随后继续获得耶鲁大学英语专业博士学位。他还学习了神学，并在 1902 年至 1910 年期间担任长老会牧师，同时完成了他的博士论文。

时候，她的父母作为长老会的传教士，将她从弗吉尼亚州①带到中国内地。45年前，天国之民视白人男女为异类。巴克夫人的家所在的城市曾经被围攻，在那里她的家人是城市仅有的外国人。她的父亲鼓起最大的勇气，孤独地穿行于整个地区，带回了他侥幸逃脱死亡的故事，以及他在扬子江畔村庄传教工作的生动描述。这些故事以及在巴克家服务18年的中国老佣人在孩子成长中的相伴，奠定了她了解本土生活的基础。

她的母亲，她多年来唯一的老师

多年来，她的母亲是她唯一的老师。她教珀尔以同情的态度研究接纳她的国家的风俗习惯和制度，并善于发现美，她还鼓励珀尔写作，并给予她睿智的批评。

长大后，珀尔嫁给了一位年轻的美国教授，并在金陵大学教英国文学。此时她已成为深谙中国文学的学生。十年间，她读完了中国所有的经典小说。这需要无限的应用，因为她首先要学习一万到两万个汉字。

她的正规学习，加上她对日常生活起伏的敏锐观察——那段时期的中国为土匪与军阀的争斗和社会与教育的变革所席卷——构成了一个小说家的丰富素材。她学会了以亲身经历的方式来讲述故事，并通过在南京花园里写作，将《大地》呈现给那些数千英里之外的人。

这部为作者赢得如此赞誉的小说是她对中国人品格的真诚而娴熟的诠释。它向我们讲述了"人类的定格的、悲伤的音乐"；这些人类是真真切切的，黄皮肤、丹凤眼，思考方式和思想模式与我们大相径庭。但在面对磨难和诱惑时，与西方世界基本相同。

西方读者也许对巴克夫人笔下的人物印象最深，因为他们看起来很容易理解。他们没有什么神秘之处，也不像许多东方故事那样充满异国情调。如果不是因为当地的色彩和极端贫困、洪水、干旱、瘟疫和革命，我们可能会以为自己是在阅读关于加拿大或英国人的小说。

正如一位权威评论家所写："这些人，无论生在哪片阳光下，或是身处哪片大地上，他们都像所有其他人一样（在同一个地球）出生、嬉戏、劳作、受苦和憧憬"。

（英文原文见附贰：30. Pearl Buck's Years of Training for Writing）

---

① 应为西弗吉尼亚州。

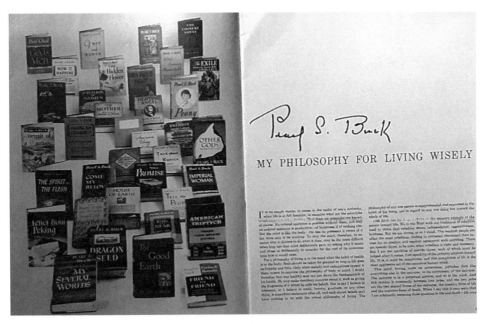

左图为赛珍珠出版的小说，其中有以笔名约翰·塞奇斯（John Sedges）出版的以美国人为题材的小说；右图为赛珍珠的文章《我明智生活的哲学》——《智慧》杂志（*Wisdom*，1959-05）

激情褪去，走向离婚

《每日新闻》（*Daily News*），1935 年 6 月 16 日

离婚：步入法院的沃尔什夫人和律师（中图）、赛珍珠和证人（右图）——《每日新闻》报影（1935-06-16）

　　[露丝·雷诺兹] 一位女性创造了现代离婚方式的一个新高度。在结婚 27 年后，她不仅同意将丈夫交给一个更漂亮的对

手，而且在离婚前各自建立住所期间，与她的继任者在内华达州友好相处了六周。

但白发苍苍的小妇人鲁比·阿博特·沃尔什（Ruby Abbott Walsh）坚决地走入里诺的瓦肖县法院时却是满眼泪水，她指控她那49岁的丈夫、纽约出版商理查德·J.沃尔什"残酷，我既不能原谅也不能宽恕他"。

……

当有时间时，赛珍珠写了她唯一真正了解的事物——中国和中国人。她的大部分手稿都随着拒稿单一起被出版社退回。最后，是约翰·戴公司的人看到了《东风·西风》，觉得很好。第一部小说卖得很少。她的第二部小说《大地》获得了1932年的普利策奖。就在那时，巴克夫人成了名人，成了鲁比和迪克·沃尔什夫妇的真正朋友。

……

另一方面，巴克对他在中国西北部为亨利·摩根索所做的政府工作太感兴趣了，以至于无暇顾及他的"旅行中的妻子"。当他最后听说她想要离婚时，默认了——认可了每个人都应该过自己的生活。至于孩子，巴克夫妇在1925年签订了一项着眼于长期的财产和监护权协议——将他们交给他们的母亲。

本着同样的精神——如果阻碍丈夫，则弊大于利——沃尔什夫人也同意离婚，他们的财产和监护协议于去年5月6日签署。

对这两个朋友来说，还有什么比他们在里诺（Reno）六周期间住在一起更自然的事呢？或者说还有比她们竟然聘请同一位律师乔治·A.怀特利更自然的吗？她们避开聚光灯。巴克夫人一直拒绝面对里诺妇女俱乐部讲话，沃尔什夫人的身份也没有被透露。

（英文原文见附贰：31. Divorce "Without" Passion）

肆

中国不会亡

作为反法西斯阵营的一员，作为大地的女儿，赛珍珠坚信中国不会灭亡。1938年12月10日，在瑞典斯德哥尔摩市政厅诺贝尔奖颁奖晚宴上，她在讲话中预言"中华不可征服"。

赛珍珠这次讲演的部分段落现代汉语译文大意如下：

> 如果我不是以自己的方式谈到中国人民，我就不能算是真正的自己。在过去的那么多年里，中国人民的生活也就是我自己的生活。而他们的生活也将永远都是我自己生活的一部分。我的养育国中国与我自己的国家有许多一致之处，其中最突出的就是对自由的热爱。今天，当整个中国正在从事人类最伟大的争取自由的斗争的时候，我们更能够看清楚这一点。我从来没有像现在这样更加敬佩中国。现在，中国人民正团结在一起抗击威胁她的自由的敌人。有了这种对自由的决心，这种决心深深地扎根于她的本性之中，我知道，她是不可征服的。[①]

赛珍珠获得诺贝尔文学奖的1938年底，中国的全面抗战进入相持阶段，当时的状况：日本占领了中国五个直辖市、九个省的全部和其他二十余个省的部分地区。日军所到之处，烧杀抢掠，中华大地河山破碎。中国军队的武器数量和质量与日军相差悬殊，而且日本还得到了工业大国的不断供给。正面战场上，中国军队虽然浴血奋战，但也只是由战略防御转入战略相持。在这样的背景下，在一个与战争毫无关系的文学奖颁奖晚宴上，赛珍珠发表了这一段与文学毫无关联的演讲——一份面向全世界的反法西斯宣言，足见她与中华民族血脉相通，视自己为其中一分子。对于挽救中华之危亡，她意志如钢且竭尽全力，因为她深深地了解中国的历史和人民的意志。她看到中国建立了广泛的抗日民族统一战线。她看到，中国的大多数人口在农村，而不是大城市或者主要县城。这是赛珍珠之所以成为"人桥"的原因之一，她认识和理解中国及其人民，也正是因为如此，她看到了希望。

《沙斯塔信使报》（*The Shasta Courier*），1951 年 4 月 19 日

> If we would know what the people of Asia are thinking and doing we should read the books of those who have gone out among them: Pearl Buck, Agnes Smedley, Harrison Forman, Edgar Snow, Israel Epstein, Anna Louise Strong, Gunther Stein, Joseph Stilwell and, of course, Mao Tze Tung. These people know what the people of Asia want and are determined to have after ages of repression. The subjugated peoples of the world have decided they will no longer be colonies. At their all-Asia congresses they have voiced this decision and they have the strength to enforce their demands.

读走出去的人的书——《沙斯塔信使报》报影（1951-04-19）

[克里斯汀·赫福德] 如果我们想知道亚洲人民的想法和行为，我们应该阅读走进他们当中的那些人的书：赛珍珠（Pearl Buck）、艾格尼丝·史沫特莱（Agnes Smedley）、哈里森·福尔曼（Harrison Forman）、埃德加·斯诺（Edgar Snow）、伊斯雷尔·爱泼斯坦（Israel Epstein）、安娜·路易斯·斯特朗（Anna Louise Strong）、冈瑟·斯坦（Gunther Stein）、约瑟夫·史迪威（Joseph Stilwell），当然还有毛泽东。这些人了解在经历了多年压迫后亚洲人民想要的并且决心去争取的是什么。世界上被压迫的人民已经决心不再被殖民奴役。在他们的全亚洲代表大会上，他们已经表达了这一决心，并且他们有实力履行他们的承诺。

---

① 《沙斯塔信使报》曾列出走出去并且真正了解亚洲（中国）的人物，其中，赛珍珠列居首位。她与名单中的艾格尼丝·史沫特莱、埃德加·斯诺、安娜·路易斯·斯特朗是好朋友。赛珍珠与史沫特莱和斯特朗的互动将在后续内容中介绍。

《沃思堡星电讯报》（*Fort Worth Star Telegram*），1935 年 6 月 2 日

Pearl Buck is a magazine book editor now, having signed up to conduct a monthly department, "Asia Book Shelf," in the magazine Asia. In the June issue Mrs. Buck reviews Anna Louise Strong's "I Change Worlds."

《沃思堡星电讯报》报影（1935-06-02）

赛珍珠现在是《亚洲》杂志的编辑，已签约在该杂志上每月开设"亚洲书架"栏目。在 6 月刊中，巴克夫人评论了安娜·路易斯·斯特朗的书《我改变了世界》。

斯特朗的自传《我改变了世界》（*I Change Worlds*）记述一名美国女性移居苏联并在那里接受了共产主义思想的故事，该书译成《我的世界变迁》或许更合适。

艾格尼丝·史沫特莱是美国著名的战地记者，1929 年出版了自传《大地的女儿》（*Daughter of Earth*），她在 1943 年出版的中国战地纪实《中华颂歌》（*Battle Hymn of China*）中有对于赛珍珠的评价。《商业诉求报》（*The Commercial Appeal*）1943 年 10 月 10 日刊登了《中华颂歌》中的游击队营地照片。根据该书的记述，我们了解到，史沫特莱在抗战期间跟随朱德和八路军游击队转战，她还接触了陈纳德、赛珍珠、斯诺等人。史沫特莱在英国去世后，其骨灰于 1951 年经友人转送至北京八宝山革命公墓安葬。

赛珍珠在回到美国之前，已经与宋庆龄、宋美龄、胡适等一些中国政界和文化界的人士建立了紧密的联系。她的援华活动均通过民国时期社会活动人士开展，同时由于受美国新闻报刊的舆论倾向性的影响，她很难获得来自延安的真实消息，因此对红军（八路军）的了解不多。赛珍珠对于此时的蒋介石领导的国民政府对日抵抗政策深信不疑。但是到了 1949 年，她对于国民政府的态度转变了。她认为：中国人民接受共产党，"是因为他们已经对蒋介石总统失望。"

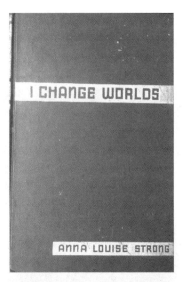

上图：安娜·路易斯·斯特朗自传《我改变了世界》1935 年第一版
下图：史沫特莱的战地纪实《中华颂歌》1943 年第一版

　　早在 1943 年，史沫特莱在《中华颂歌》中指出了赛珍珠对国民政府的态度已发生变化。《纽约客》评论员在 1939 年 4 月纠正了赛珍珠小说《爱国者》中出现的与中国前线事实不符的一段文字。

中国战争中，美国女性所了解的

英雄、匪徒和烈士

《商业诉求报》（*The Commercial Appeal*），1943 年 10 月 10 日

中国游击英雄在宿营——《商业诉求报》报影（1943-10-10）
《中华颂歌》书评

[作者：马克·克鲁特夫人] "他们的国家给予他们的只有悲伤和饥饿，寒冷和痛苦。但是，他们仍然为国家献出生命。他们成千上万地战死在荒凉的战场，幸存的人蹒跚地退居后方，悲哀地看着他们无人照顾的伤员，他们的眼睛搜寻着山路和公路，渴望着永不会到来的救援。"史沫特莱小姐如此描述英勇的中国军队。

史沫特莱小姐在个人信念上不属于共产党员，然而她对苏联给中国人施加的意识形态影响非常感兴趣。她发现中国红军的士兵比国民党的士兵更团结，更渴望教育，更具有不怕牺牲的精神。

实际上，这本书的作者是一位善良的记者，他有着一颗公平正义的心，这本书中记录的近代历史丰富详实。除此之外，这本书值得一读的原因还在于仅从一个视角我们就已看到了其

中有趣的个性。她毫不犹豫地批评了蒋介石，她敢于提出鲁迅是比林语堂更伟大的作家。她接触到了胡适、陈纳德、赛珍珠、乔治·索科尔斯基、史迪威将军、宋子文、埃德加·斯诺等各色名人。

她一次又一次地向读者强调美国允许将战争物资出售给日本所表现出的愚蠢和冷漠。她引用一位中国将军的话说："日本刽子手的手中没有武器，而美国给了他们。"

但是，本书主要关注的不是国际政治的错综复杂，这是一本关于人的书。她了解军阀和匪徒，还曾被迫逃离可怕的"蓝衫军"（Blue Shirt）帮派。她也深知广大中国普通百姓的勇气和忠诚，她努力为他们组织医疗服务。

（英文原文见附贰：32. American Woman in China's War Knew Heroes，Gangsters，Martyrs）

《爱国者》中的道听途说

《匹茨堡报》（*The Pittsburgh Press*），1939 年 4 月 16 日

* * *

With others joining my friends of "The New Yorker" in their war for the purity of dramatic criticism, I can see that my days are numbered, an so, passing over my liking for the tragic little country of Albania, where I once spent several pleasant days, I had better say a quick word again about China while I can.

It takes courage, too, because I intend to dispute so eminent an authority as Miss Pearl Buck. Nevertheless, I cannot resist calling her attention to two serious injustices in her new and entertaining novel, "The Patriot."

She shows her hero, an agent of Chiang Kai-shek, persuading the Eighth Route Army to give up its customs of killing its prisoners, and she suggests that the appeal for a united front came from Chiang, and not from the former Red Armies.

In both cases, I say dogmatically, she is mistaken. From the start of their war against Japan it has been the men of the Eight Route Army whose policy it was to spare prisoners in order to convert them, and the united-front policy came first from the same people.

As an ardent admirer of the soldiers of the legendary Chu Teh, I object to Miss Buck's otherwise interesting picture of a heroic struggle.

红军首先提出统一战线政策——《匹兹堡报》报影（1939-04-16）

随着其他人加入我的《纽约客》① 朋友圈参与纯粹的戏剧评论的辩论，我可以看到自己在《纽约客》的日子已经屈指可数了，于是表达一下对这个我曾经在那里度过了几天愉快时光的、悲惨的小国阿尔巴尼亚的喜爱，最好趁还有机会，我就简短地说几句中国。

这也需要勇气，因为我打算质疑的是赛珍珠小姐这样的知名的权威人士。尽管如此，我还是忍不住提醒她注意在其新创作的有趣小说《爱国者》中的两个严重的谬误。

她笔下的男主角，以蒋介石为原型，说服八路军放弃杀害俘虏的传统。她还认为是蒋介石呼吁建立统一战线，而不是之前的红军。

对这两种说法，我都要肯定地说，她错了。从抗日战争开始，八路军的政策就是优待俘虏，目的是转化他们，而统一战线政策也是由八路军率先提出的。

作为传奇人物朱德所带领士兵的忠实崇拜者，我不反对巴克小姐在其他方面对英雄战斗的有趣描绘。

1943 年，史沫特莱出版《中华颂歌》。关于赛珍珠，她在该书的第 234 页写道：

中外基督徒对赛珍珠的态度很有意思。其中她被注意到不仅是因为她有关中国的图书，还因为她离开了她的教会，离婚后再婚。正如许多政党经常攻击其前成员，传教士们对赛珍珠的看法也不以为然。他们暗示她会变坏，而当她显然没有变坏时，他们就非常不安。

许多中国人不喜欢赛珍珠的书，因为她并不总是让她的角色穿着盛装展现最好的一面。一位中国上校②曾经对我的一个朋友宣称赛珍珠"靠边站"了，因为她写了一篇关于八路军的文章，称八路军为"中国民主的枪"。他宣称赛珍珠从此被中国孤立了，被淘汰了。简直是胡扯！这就是憎恨她的人散播的谣言。

（英文原文见附贰：33. Comments on Pearl S. Buck in Agnes Smedley's *Battle Hymn of China*）

---

① 《纽约客》(*The New Yorker*) 周刊。

② "中国上校"即国军上校，他所说的赛珍珠"从此被中国孤立了，被淘汰了"应该理解为赛珍珠不再相信国民政府了。

《每日报》（*The Daily Journal*），1939 年 10 月 23 日

Pearl Buck Tells Audience That China-Japanese War Is Being Won Through Non-Resistance

After explaining the vast difference between the Chinese and Japanese peoples, Pearl S. Buck, noted writer, told a large audience at the Vineland High School auditorium, Saturday night, that the Chinese have adopted a new method of resisting the invasion of the Japanese, which is, by not resisting at all.

and geographical set-up, all of which, she indicated, are as different as day and night.

Japan is a world power, she said, imbued with a tremendous and fierce energy which she has poured into the war. She believes nothing is impossible to Japan in its present position, except to have faith in the Chinese ability to with-

《每日报》报影（1939 10 23）

周六晚上，在维恩兰高中礼堂，知名作家赛珍珠在解释了中日两国人民之间的巨大差异后告诉广大听众，中国人采用了一种新的方法来抵抗日本人的入侵，就是根本不抵抗。

这一观点让听众惊诧，直到她解释说，中国哲学认为"战争的胜利，属于战争结束后还活着的人"，她表达的观点是她不相信日本可以征服中国。

她向听众建议说，美国"在这个充满威胁的时代最好考虑一下这种中国哲学"，并补充说中国人正在让他们的敌人筋疲力尽，他们将游击战作为唯一的进攻手段——仅仅是骚扰日本兵。

巴克女士说，中国人民已经撤退到了广大的内地，因为日本人轰炸了中国大部分沿海城市，并占领了许多重要城市。她指出这些胜利根本没有影响到中国人的意志，因为他们在家园被毁后镇定地搬到了别处，并在内地建立了他们古老文化和文明的新中心。

她引用了一句中国谚语"三十六计走为上"来表达中国人对日本侵略的想法。她指出，中国人不是懦夫，而是对战争不感兴趣。

她含蓄地批评美国的出口是对日本的帮助，指出苏维埃俄国是唯一与中国友好的国家而俄国做得尚且不够。

巴克小姐预测，如果美国停止向日本出口产品，这个岛国将无法继续目前的战争。在回答问题时，她说自己相信今天的中国比以往任何时候都更不能被征服。战机对中国的轰炸已经

激起了人民对日本的仇恨，却并没有击垮他们的意志。"轰炸激发了中国人的愤怒。"她说。

……

巴克小姐指出，中国买不到美国的产品，因为他们没有渠道。……问题的公道由你们来判断。如果不是因为美国，日本是不可能维持对中国的战争的。

（英文原文见附贰：34. Pearl Buck Tells Audience That China-Japanese War Is Being Won Through Non-Resistance）

论持久战①

《索引报》（*The Index Journal*），1939 年 3 月 16 日

HOW CHINA CAN WIN

Mrs. Pearl Buck, author of "The Good Earth," and a recognized authority on Chinese affairs, doesn't agree with many of the war experts that Japan never will be able to whip China. She expresses the opinion that China has started a "tremendous trek" westward to revive her small industries as a means not only of relief, but of occupation for youth.

《索引报》报影（1939-03-16）

《大地》的作者、公认的中国事务权威珀尔·巴克夫人不赞同许多战争专家的观点，即日本永远无法欺凌中国。她表示，中国已经开始了向西的"长途跋涉"，以振兴她的小工业生产。这不仅是一种恢复的途径，也是为了青年就业的一种手段。

"中国无法靠武力赢得战争，她清楚这一点，"巴克夫人说，"因此尽管有战争，她决定她将不得不忍受战争。她的政策是撤退——不是逃跑，而是撤退。要长途跋涉到西部，中国的腹地，他们真正的根据地。"

---

① 赛珍珠的"三十六计"论虽然没有看出蒋介石消极抗日的目的，同时认为抗日民族统一战线是蒋发起的，但是赛珍珠开始对抗日战争的力量来自人民深信不疑。中国会亡吗？不会，最后的胜利是中国的。中国能够速胜吗？不能，必须打持久战。《论持久战》于 1938 年 9 月 24 日被翻译成英文版本 *How China Can Win*。

巴克夫人估计，日本占领了中国大约 70% 的大型工业，因此中国人转向了西部及其"几百年来在小型工业中的生产方式"，例如纺织和手工业。她说其目的是建立数千个地方合作产业。

　　"这让人松了一口气，但也让年轻人的大脑动起来了。"她在观察，"如果中国能守住她的原材料，激励她的人民投身小工业，并保持她的精神，她就会赢，尽管离战争结束还很遥远。"

（英文原文见附贰：35. How China Can Win）

赛珍珠发起五百万美元援华资金募集活动

　　《内布拉斯加州日报》（*The Nebraska State Journal*），1941 年 3 月 30 日

AIDING CAMPAIGN FOR CHINA RELIEF FUND: Wendell L. Willkie, writer on China, and Dr. Hu Shih, Chinese Ambassador to the United States, at the dinner in New York which opened the United, China Relief drive for $5,000,000. In his address, Mr. Willkie said China's fight is ours and "we must help the Chinese preserve their freedom."

《内布拉斯加州日报》报影（1941-03-30）

　　援助中国救济基金活动：温德尔·L. 威尔基（Wendell L. Willkie）①、中国主题的作家赛珍珠与中国驻美国大使胡适博士在纽约发起了五百万美元联合中国救济活动。威尔基先生在讲话中说，中国的斗争就是我们的斗争，"我们必须帮助中国人捍卫他们的自由"。

　　1940 年，赛珍珠成立中国紧急救援委员会并担任全国主席，宋美龄是救援委员会的联络人，相关报道刊登在 1940 年 11 月 28 日的《查

---

　　① 温德尔·刘易斯·威尔基（1892—1944）是一位美国律师，1940 年的共和党总统候选人。

塔努加每日时报》（*Chattanooga Daily Times*）上。此时的募集目标是一百万美元。1940 年 12 月 2 日的《汉福德哨兵报》 （*The Hanford Sentinel*）刊登了赛珍珠和主演《大地》的演员路易斯·雷纳共同募捐的照片。美国画家弗拉格为募捐设计的海报《中国期待着我们》刊登在 1940 年 12 月 30 日的《布鲁克林市民报》（*The Brooklyn Citizen*）上。

左图：赛珍珠与蒋夫人——《查塔努加每日时报》（*Chattanooga Daily Times*，1940-11-28）
右图：赛珍珠（左）和《大地》的演员路易斯·雷纳（右）共同募捐——《汉福德哨兵报》（*The Hanford Sentinel*，1940-12-02）

　　著名画家和插画家詹姆斯·蒙哥马利·弗拉格（James Montgomery Flagg）创作的一个中国婴儿裴雷葛的肖像出现在当时中国紧急救援委员会呼吁援华的海报上。它由弗拉格交给纽约州州长夫人赫伯特·H. 雷曼（Herbert H. Lehman），她是赛珍珠主持的、1940 年成立的国家委员会的成员。该作品用于为中国急需的医疗用品筹集一百万美元。左图为 1940 年 12 月 30 日《布鲁克林市民报》（*The Brooklyn Citizen*），右图为火星云美术馆收藏的《中国期待着我们》纪念章和邮票。

《查塔努加每日时报》(*Chattanooga Daily Times*),1939 年 3 月 5 日

远东局势——《查塔努加每日时报》报影(1939-03-05)

　　巴克夫人终止了她关于西方生活的并不完全成功的"再次为我们歌唱曼德勒"系列图书的写作,告诉我们更多的关于她最熟悉的生活环境,关于中国和中国人,以及这次写的中国与邻国日本的关系。在《爱国者》中,巴克夫人瞬间重获了她以前的精湛老练,她使读者完全沉浸在这陌生的异国情调的环境中,尽管跟过去相比,这种异国情调已经没有那么陌生,这得归功于赛珍珠,但更大的功劳属于战争,战争让书本和杂志表达对远东地区的新旧态度,给书本和杂志带来价值。读者阅读这些作品,就好像在阅读纽约、新奥尔良和洛杉矶的故事那样熟悉。不仅如此,赛珍珠回归了质朴甚至简单的写作风格,这些风格在她的早期作品,《大地》《母亲》等书中尤为突出。这种风格对西方读者来说有些陌生,但却非常有吸引力,读者感觉在听一位中国老者讲述故事,而不是在阅读美国人写的书。这绝对是一个有趣的故事。

　　在关于王家的系列书中,巴克夫人讲述了一个农民家庭的发展史,他们从贫穷无知到发家致富并开始接受一定程度的教育。通过这些叙述,巴克夫人也让读者了解了过去 50 年的中国历史,了解了传统中国向现代中国的转变,传统中国存续到本世纪,而现代中国作为一个被唤醒的年轻的中国,不只关注西

_____

① 此文是对赛珍珠小说《爱国者》的评论报道。

方的体制，而且关注西方的政治、经济思想。

《爱国者》不是关于王家的故事，但它从《分家》结尾的地方开始讲述。这一次，我们跟随吴氏家族的命运脉络，这是一个具有贵族和富裕背景的家庭。我们的男主角伊万是一个上海银行家的小儿子。伊万是一位革命理想主义者，如同他那一代东方和西方的许多其他人一样，他感到"在这个时代，团结一心比血缘联系更为深厚"。他对穷人和受压迫者的关注超越了大多数中国人所具有的强烈而传统的家庭归属感。伊万和他的朋友恩兰——上海运动的领袖，渴望蒋介石的革命成功。然而，令他们失望的是，他们无法摆脱对蒋介石在控制上海时屠杀革命者的愤怒。伊万被他的父亲送到了日本的一个朋友那里。在那里，他看到了生活中的新事物——秩序。"热爱自由的中国人习惯了无法无天、不拘一格。"在日本，他发现了一个"被责任感吞噬"的民族。在那里，他还遇到了 Tama 并与之成婚，他们建立了家庭，生了两个儿子。伊万开始忘记了他和日本人之间的差异，日本人开始认为他是他们中的一员。然后，有一天有报道说中国陷入了困境。士兵们被运送出国，新兵被征召。伊万开始对日本兵产生怀疑。最后，这种怀疑愈发强烈。他是中国人，所以他回去了。他发现中国终于团结了，共产党人和蒋介石的支持者以自己的方式与入侵者斗争。伊万还没想明白这一切是怎么回事，但是他决心战斗，故事到这里就结束了。

这部作品的文娱特征远没有被单纯叙事的手法所掩盖——在这方面，巴克夫人是非常睿智和伟大的作家，不只采用了常见的东西方对比，而且还有中日之间差异的呈现，其差异不亚于中国人与西方人之间的差异。巴克夫人尽力做到不偏不倚，她同情的毫无疑问是中国人，但这不会让她歪曲事实或纯粹是做宣传。在这两个方面她的素材是人，尽管差异明显，但本质上相同。日本给了伊万很多东西，"Tama 在一定程度上改变了他，在日常行为中她教会了他热爱秩序、正确的举止和文雅"。所以当他坐下来思考随后的结果时，他明白日本的军国主义是错误的，但是中国的混乱也存在问题。中国人诚实朴素，但"他们的朴素是不够的。启蒙和知识，秩序和文雅，这些也是生活必须具备的"。这是中国必须争取的。难道不是所有的民族应该争取的吗？①

（英文原文见附贰：36. In a New Novel About the Far East, Pearl Buck Writes of China and Japan Today）

---

① 可以看出，赛珍珠有明确的态度：蒋介石背信弃义，抛弃了孙中山"联俄、联共、扶助农工"的政策，杀戮同盟者，导致第一次国共合作宣告失败；封闭的中国人民需要知识，需要文明的交流，但是"文明国家"——日本却发动了对中国的侵略战争。

Love Amid Oriental Warfare

THE PATRIOT, by Pearl S. Buck (John Day, $2.50). **372 pages.**

IN "The Patriot" Mrs. Buck goes back to her first and most successful love—the Far East. Oddly enough, she is much more convincing when she is writing about Chinese than when she is writing about Americans. Her American women are just women, but O-Lan of "The Good Earth" is a masterpiece. Although there is no character here that approaches O-Lan, "The Patriot" is one of Mrs. Buck's better novels.

It is the story of I-Wan, the son of a wealthy Chinese family, who is sent to Japan in disgrace by his father when he becomes embroiled in a Communist plot. There he meets and falls in love with a Japanese girl. They marry and have children and are happy until the Japanese invasion of Manchuria crashes between them.

He leaves to fight for his country. She stays in hers. Their love for each other remains unchanged in the bitterness of the war. They are two individuals at the mercy of nations. They are symbolical of individuals the world over who, left to decide for themselves, would surely decide matters in a saner fashion.

左图：《爱国者》书讯——《每日新闻》（*Daily News*，1939-03-12）

右图：赛珍珠在小说《爱国者》1939 年第一版上的签名，图中是布莱尔学院（Blair Academy）废弃图书（火星云美术馆藏品）

Chinese Family in War: Pearl Buck's Vivid Novel

A Stirring Story Of Invasion and Heroic Peasants

"DRAGON SEED," by Pearl S. Buck. The John Day Co., $2.50.

Pearl Buck's Good Earth has now become the scorched earth.

'er new novel is once more of China, but this time it is a China which has been invaded and laid waste by the ferocious "dwarf men" from the "East Ocean." There have been several novels to come out of this war which is now in its fifth year, but none has depicted Japanese cruelty and barbarism and Chinese stoical resistance so vividly, so powerfully, and so feelingly as this one.

FAMILY FORTUNES

As was "The Good Earth," this is the novel of a family, and what happens to it is what has happened to uncounted thousands of Chinese families. It came to know death, despoliation and disease, but through the vicissitudes of war it remained adhered, and we are left in no doubt that heroic families like this one of Ling Tan will in the end conquer the conqueror.

Ling Tan lived in a village outside the gates of a city that is apparently Nanking. He was a simple, untutored farmer, but he and the others of the village were the inheritors of a rich and ancient culture. They could

PEARL S. BUCK

左图：1935 年的赛珍珠——《旧金山审核人报》（*The San Francisco Examiner*，1935-06-12）

右图：赛珍珠以南京大屠杀为背景创作小说《龙子》（英文原文见附贰：37. Chinese Family in War: Pearl Buck's Vivid Novel）——《费城询问者报》（*The Philadelphia Inquirer*，1942-01-21）

Pearl S. Buck, sitting on the arm of a chair in her modernistic New York apartment. She doesn't like to have photographs taken but, characteristically, made no fuss when asked to pose.

繁忙的作家——赛珍珠坐在她纽约现代派公寓的椅子扶手上。她不喜欢拍照，但被请求摆拍时，她一向不会大惊小怪（英文原文见附贰：38. "Mental Laziness" of Women in America Appalls Pearl Buck；Research，Writing，Editing and Children Keep Writer Busy）——《阿克伦灯塔杂志》（*The Akron Beacon Journal*，1940-02-18）

Tonight On The Air Waves

Broadcast Highlights

China Emergency Relief Committee: Mme. Chiang Kai-shek, speaking from China; Pearl S. Buck and Luise Rainer - WJZ at 7.45.
Hollywood Variety: Fanny Brice and Hanley Stafford, comedy; Dick Powell and Mary Martin, songs - WEAF at 8.
Variety: Music Maids, songs; Bob Burns, comedian; Bing Crosby, Connie Boswell and Joel McCrea - WEAF at 9.

WORK, 1320kc, York
6—Sports; Dance Melodies.
6.30—News; "Li'l Abner."
7—Fred Waring's orchestra.
7.15—Dance Time.
7.30—The Three Q's.
8 to 9.30—Same as WJZ.
9.30—"The War Front."
9.35—Same as WJZ.
10—Raymond Gram Swing.
10.15—Dance music.
11—News; dance music.

Pearl S. Buck, Nobel prize winner, whose latest novel is "Other Gods," the story of an American popular idol, reviewed today by Fanny Butcher.

左图：今晚 WJZ 广播预告：中国紧急救援委员会；蒋介石夫人将在中国讲话；赛珍珠和主演《大地》的演员路易斯·雷纳共同募捐——《晚报》（*The Evening*，1940-11-14）
右图：赛珍珠新书《又一个上帝》——《芝加哥论坛报》（*Chicago Tribune*，1940-02-21）

多萝西·塞琳·汤普森（Dorothy Celene Thompson）（1893—1961）是美国记者和电台的广播员，她也是 20 世纪 30 年代为数不多的电台女新闻评论员之一，被一些人视为"美国新闻界的第一女性"。1939 年《时代》杂志评价她与埃莉诺·罗斯福具有同等的影响力。Dorothy Thompson Lewis 是多萝西第二次婚姻后的姓名。汤普森和菲利斯·芬纳①一样，是赛珍珠和雅各布斯共同的朋友，她在1934年被纳粹德国驱逐出境。1932年，画家雅各布斯为汤普森画肖像，汤普森在肖像版画上签名。

左图是赛珍珠（左一）和芬纳（右二）——《曼彻斯特日报》（*The Manchester Journal*，1963-08-22），右图为雅各布斯所绘多萝西·汤普森肖像（1932年），上有汤普森的签名

根据《晚间新闻》1936年9月24日的报道，赛珍珠和汤普森都是罗斯福女士俱乐部成员，并且曾在一起工作。1942年9月23日《波士顿环球报》（*The Boston Globe*）曾报道罗斯福总统夫人埃莉诺·罗斯福、多萝西·汤普森、赛珍珠共同在电台就"纳粹入侵波兰三周年"发表演讲。

《晚间新闻》（*The Evening News*，1936-09-24）

---

① 见前言。雅各布斯通过好友菲利斯·芬纳将一本《我的中国》送给了赛珍珠。

8:00 P. M.

WCAE—American Forum of the Air.

The noted experts who will air their views on the topic, "What About India?" include Pearl S. Buck, famous authoress and Nobel Prize winner, who is an authority on the Far East; T. A. Raman, London editor of the United Press of India for many years; Louis Fischer, noted writer and lecturer who recently interviewed India's strong men, Gandhi and Nehur, and Bertrand Russell, internationally-known author.

9:45 P. M.

KQV—Dorothy Thompson. and

AIR ATTRACTIONS

AFTERNOON

REFRESHMENT TIME with Singin' Sam, songs; WBZ, 12:15 to 12:30.

SYLVIA MARLOWE, harpsichordist; WHDH, 3:45 to 4.

MRS. ELEANOR ROOSEVELT, Dorothy Thompson, Claire Booth, Mrs. Pearl S. Buck speakers on "Third Anniversary of Nazi Invasion of Poland; WCOP, 5 to 5:30.

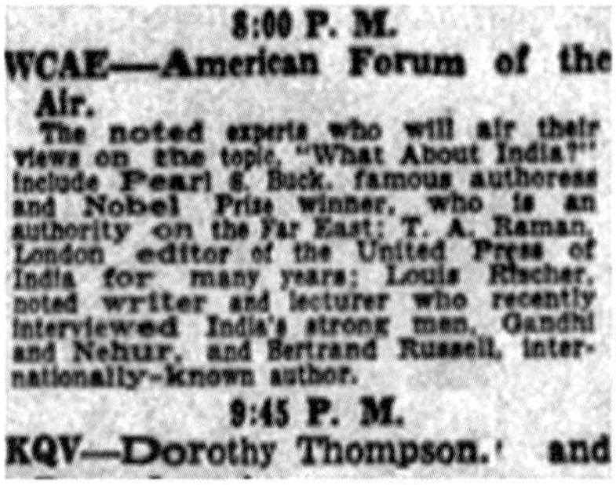

左图：赛珍珠、汤普森等知名人士在美国论坛节目谈印度——《匹兹堡太阳电讯报》（*Pittsburgh Sun Telegraph*，1942–10–11）

右图：《波士顿环球报》（*Thc Boston Globe*，1942–09–23）

national problems which don't make the headlines.

Columnists like Dorothy Thompson and Anne O'Hare McCormick have done the brain work for our distraught statesmen and have seldom taken the credit. Nobel Prize Winner Pearl S. Buck has the intelligence of ten male Pulitzer winners. In fact, let's face it, the written word is the special province of the ladies.

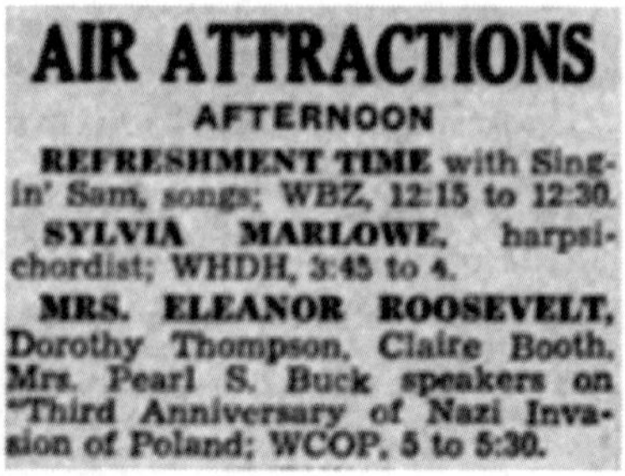

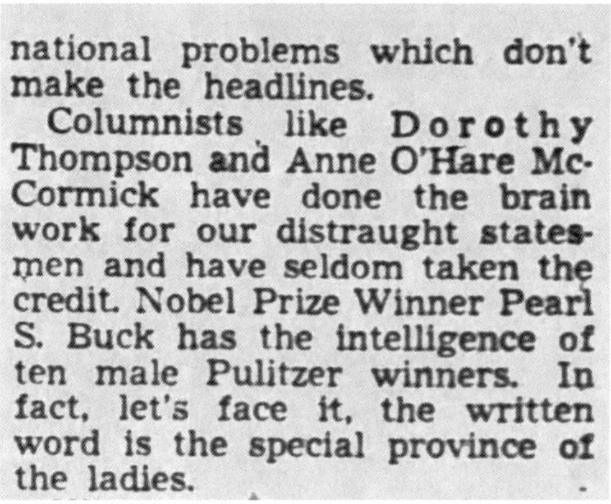

多萝西·汤普森和安妮·奥黑尔·麦考密克（Anne O'Hare McCormick）等专栏作家替我们浮躁的政治家们做了清脑工作，却很少获得表扬。诺贝尔奖得主赛珍珠拥有十位男性普利策奖得主的智慧。让我们面对现实吧，实际上，文字是女士们的特殊领域——《长海滩新闻电报》（*Long Beach Press Telegram*，1951–06–10）

Problems concerned with the advancement of mankind, achievements of women during the past 100 years and the present status of women will be studied by delegates to the Woman's Centennial congress late in 1940. Planning the New York meeting in November are (seated) Miss Josephine Schain, Mrs. Carrie Chapman Catt, Miss Henrietta Roelofs and Miss Mary W. Hillyer. Standing: Mrs. Helsey Wilson, Miss Alda H. Wilson and Mrs. Albin Johnson. Other leaders are Pearl S. Buck, Frances Perkins and Dorothy Canfield Fisher.

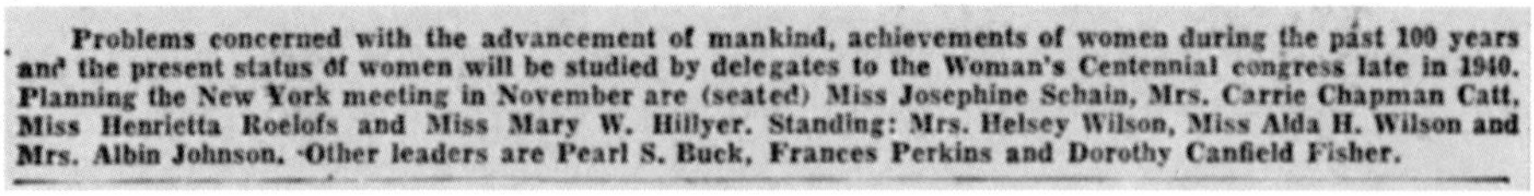

赛珍珠：妇女代表大会主席团成员——《博因顿指数报》（*Boynton Index*，1940–04–11）

《堪萨斯城时报》（*The Kansas City Times*），1940 年 11 月 15 日

OPEN CHINESE RELIEF DRIVE.

Fund of 1 Million Sought by New Emergency Committee.

(By the Associated Press.)

NEW YORK, Nov. 14.—A nation-wide drive to raise 1 million dollars for the relief of the war-stricken people of China was opened tonight by the newly-formed China Emergency Relief Committee, Inc., headed by Pearl S. Buck, author.

Miss Buck announced that Mrs. Franklin D. Roosevelt was honorary chairman.

As part of the opening ceremonies, the committee had planned to have Madam Chiang Kai-shek, wife of the Chinese generalissimo, speak by short wave radio from Hong Kong, but the National Broadcasting company was unable to make radio contact with that city at the scheduled time.

Miss Buck said that all money raised would be spent in the United States for medical and surgical supplies.

百万美元募捐——《堪萨斯城时报》报影（1940-11-15）

[美联社，11 月 14 日，纽约] 今晚，新成立的中国紧急救援委员会发起了一场全国性的、旨在帮助战乱中遭受不幸和灾难的中国人民的一百万美元募捐活动，该委员会由作家珀尔·巴克领导。巴克小姐宣布，罗斯福总统的夫人安娜·埃莉诺·罗斯福为名誉主席。

作为开幕式的一部分，委员会曾计划邀请中国特级上将蒋介石的夫人，从香港通过短波电台发表讲话，但全国广播公司（NBC）无法在预定时间与该城市建立无线电联系。巴克小姐说，所有筹集的资金都将用于采购美国的医疗和手术用品。

（英文原文见附贰：39. Open Chinese Relief Drive—Fund of 1 Million Sought by Emergency Committee）

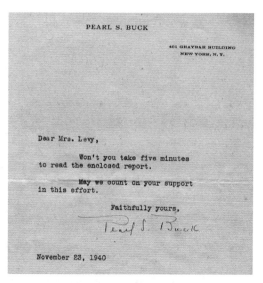

　　为了募捐，赛珍珠可谓呕心沥血。她不但要参加各种活动，还要写很多募捐信件。从她寄给利维夫人的信可见，她募捐的对象是各个阶层的人士。图为赛珍珠 1940 年写给利维夫人的募捐信（火星云美术馆藏品）

罗斯福总统夫人向中国捐款

《每日新闻领袖》（*The Daily News Leader*），1940 年 12 月 19 日中国救济募捐启动。紧急委员会寻求百万资金。

First Lady Helps China Fund

Pearl S. Buck, noted author, accepts a contribution from Mrs. Franklin D. Roosevelt, in Washington, for the fund for Chinese war victims. Miss Buck is chairman of the newly created China Emergency Relief Committee, which seeks to raise $1,000,000 for Chinese relief. Mrs. Roosevelt is honorary chairman.

总统夫人在白宫捐款——《每日新闻领袖》报影（1940-12-19）

昨天的里士满报纸上有一张照片，上面有标题"第一夫人援助中国救济——富兰克林·D. 罗斯福夫人向巴克夫人出示一百美元的支票"。

周日，新成立的中国紧急救援委员会主席、作家赛珍珠在白宫发起一项全国性活动，为中国的战争受害者筹集一百万美元用于购买医疗物资。

有意思的是，巴克夫人是 N. J. 道尔夫人和 C. S. 斯图廷先生的外甥女，也是 Mabel Ruth Doyle 小姐的表姐，他们是蒙特雷的知名人士。

巴克夫人是已故的 Absalom A. Sydenstricker 先生 和 Caroline Stulting Sydenstricker 夫人的女儿，他们曾是西弗吉尼亚州波卡洪塔斯县的居民，颇有名气，多年来一直在中国担任传教士，在那里他们的女儿花了很多年出版了多部关于中国生活和情况的书籍。就在几年前，她还因著述《大地》一书而成为诺贝尔文学奖的获得者。

巴克夫人还著有许多其他作品，这些作品都是关于她在中国生活多年后对中国人的观察和了解的。巴克夫人毕业于林奇堡的伦道夫-梅肯女子学院。她曾多次来这里探望亲戚。

她现在正忙着为她在父母传教期间接触到的，如今正遭受压迫和苦难的人筹集救济资金。

（英文原文见附贰：40. Richmond Paper Yesterday Carried a Picture，with the Caption "First Lady Aids Chinese Relief—Mrs. Franklin D. Roosevelt Presented a Check for ＄100. 00 to Mrs. Buck"）

《威斯康星州日报》（*Wisconsin State Journal*），1941 年 4 月 5 日

《威斯康星州日报》报影（1941-04-05）

　　在《皇冠》（*Coronet*）杂志 4 月刊的一篇文章中，获诺贝尔奖的小说家珀尔·S. 巴克把美国称为"瑞普·凡·温克尔式的国家"①，敦促美国"清醒过来，面对现实"，帮助中国人民。

　　如果日本征服了中国，"她也许会在一夜之间成为我们最危险的敌人"，巴克小姐断言，"但我们仍然没有从睡梦中醒来。我们对中国的帮助远远低于应有的水平，从政府贷款到红十字救济，我们提供的帮助太慢，而且也太少。"

　　巴克小姐谴责继续向日本出售战争物资。

　　"我们过时的思想没有让我们看到，在欧洲我们反对法西斯主义，而在远东却鼓励它，这有多么荒谬。这就是我们一直在做的。日本只比希特勒远几天的行程——如果把夏威夷当成美国的一部分②，那么日本到美国的距离，比希特勒到美国的距离更近。但是我们的落后思维没有抓住这个事实，我们继续无动于衷地出售弹药材料来支持那场战争，就如同现在我们竟然把希特勒需要的大部分钢铁、汽油和石油送给他，然后向英国

---

　　① 瑞普·凡·温克尔（Rip van Winkle）是美国的一个寓言故事。温克尔因躲避刁蛮彪悍的老婆，进山打猎，遇到了老友喝了仙酒，一睡就是二十年。温克尔因为贪杯误事，错过了一个时代。回到家后，一切都变了。这个故事比喻一个人落后于当前的时代。此文章发表仅数月后，1941 年 12 月 7 日星期日的早上，珍珠港事件爆发。

　　② 1919 年美国海军在珍珠港的第一个干船坞建成。1959 年 8 月夏威夷并入美国。

照会我们对她有多么抱歉，并且我们是多么喜欢英国人。这正是我们对中国所做的，因为这与今天英国和德国之间正在进行的战争完全相同。"

巴克宣称："中国永远不会屈服，但她越来越绝望，她非常了解她正在进行的战争。这是一场反对法西斯主义的民主战争。她的朋友在哪里？美国在哪里？……任何一天都可能为时已晚。中国需要帮助。她需要飞机，即使只有几架飞机也会心存感激。"

（英文原文见附贰：41. Any Day May Be Too Late）

《信使询问者报》（*Messenger Inquirer*），1941 年 5 月 28 日

Owensboro Churches Plan China Day June 8

American aid has not only helped bolster Chinese morale, it has cured the sick and fed the hungry. Here a group of formerly famished and broken down refugees line up for their daily clinic visit at an American supported hospital run by the American Bureau for Medical Aid to China, one of the member agencies of the United China Relief drive to raise $5,000,000 to extend and maintain such projects of civilian relief such as this.

《信使询问者报》报影（1941-05-28）

欧文斯伯勒教堂计划六月举办中国日

美国的支援不仅帮助中国提振了士气，还治愈了病患，消除了饥饿。在这里，一群以前饥肠辘辘的难民在一家美国支持的医院排队就诊，该医院由美国对华医疗救助局运营，该局是中国联合救济会的成员机构之一，旨在筹集五百万美元以扩展和维持这样的平民救济项目。

（英文原文见附贰：42. Questions China Aid Policy）

1941 年 12 月 7 日，珍珠港事件发生，美国立即对

日宣战。1942 年 6 月的中途岛海战美军取得标志性胜利后，日本开始丧失战争的主动权，此时的中国军队为配合盟军行动，更主动地与日本鏖战。这是 1942 年的反法西斯战争的大致情况。支援亚洲特别是中国的抗日，几乎是赛珍珠那几年所开展的全部社会活动。她呼吁政府，利用各种机会动员各个阶层的人士，她写稿件、发表讲演、写评论和创作小说，一切都是为了支援抗日战争。她似乎是在完成一项使命，是谁赋予了她这一使命？是她自己吗？

　　1942 年 6 月 27 日，身为美国东西方协会董事长的赛珍珠写了一封信给《费城询问者报》的电影评论员米尔德里德·马丁（Mildred Martin），向其征求介绍美国的影片清单，以便让亚洲更多的国家和人民了解美国。她写道：

亲爱的马丁小姐：

　　我写信给您，希望您能帮助制作一份电影清单推荐给太平洋彼岸的观众，这些电影可以真正代表美国的生活。近年来，这些国家的电影院数量大幅增加并且非常受欢迎。美国电影比任何其他电影都更频繁地放映，当然其中有很多并不是美国日常生活的好范本。黑帮影片、充满好莱坞奢华理念的影片、闹剧喜剧影片和西部片都在令东方人困惑。这将激发人们去了解美国人的好电影的兴趣——除了看电影，他们当中几乎没有人见识过美国。

　　因此您愿意帮助我们列出十部或更多的你想向不了解美国的人展映的电影吗？这些电影应该是 35 毫米的商业规格，但影片不必完全从最新的电影中挑选，因为过去五年左右的电影仍然在国外发行。我不想影响您的选择，但仅作为一个例子，我建议《迪兹先生进城》（*Dr. Deeds Goes Town*）或许可以作为一个合适的选择，但《大独裁者》（*The Great Dictator*）不适合，因为后者不涉及美国生活。

　　非常感谢您的合作，特别重视您的建议。

谨启　赛珍珠

（英文原文见附贰：43. A Letter from Pearl S. Buck）

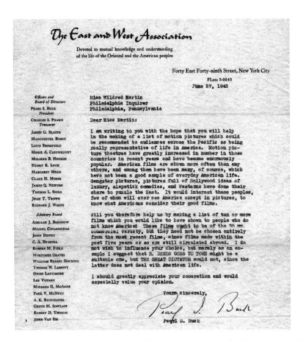

美国东西方协会董事长赛珍珠写给米尔德里德·马丁的信件（火星云美术馆藏品）

《每日通报》（*The Daily Journal*），1942 年 10 月 28 日

《每日通报》报影（1942-10-28）

女作家赛珍珠指导两个讲汉语的少年夏艾迪（Eddie Hsia）和林相如（Lin Meimei）录制广播节目，这是一个向中国孩子讲述她为东西方协会写作的节目。纽约中国研究院的 T. C. Hsiung 站在孩子们的身后。林相如是中国著名作家林语堂的小女儿。

（英文原文见附贰：44. Broadcast to Chinese Children）

《明星论坛报》（*Star Tribune*），1943 年 1 月 3 日

《明星论坛报》报影（1943-01-03）

[作者：赛珍珠] 致主编：我阅读了您在 12 月 13 日《明尼阿波利斯星期日论坛》报上的社论，很赞同。当您说出下面的话时就简明扼要地指出真谛。

"我们在太平洋地区最大的危险不是我们无法获胜，而是在获胜时，我们却会在不知不觉中做了我们最想要阻止日本做的事情——联合亚洲人民反对我们。"

"不知不觉"这个词用得很好。我相信无视亚洲人民和亚洲局势，已经成为我们错误的根源所在。

第一个错误是珍珠港事件。无视无疑是毫无准备的真正原因。

第二个错误是未能立即向中国保证，我们打算使太平洋地区成为与欧洲战线同等重要的前线。这种承诺本可以通过在战时议会和战争战略中平等对待中国来体现，至少给予蒋介石委

员长在华盛顿的个人代表与英国代表同等的待遇，并且至少在中国非常合理的要求范围内向其输送战争物资。

从来没有这样的平等。在华盛顿的中国代表被如此冷落，以至于蒋委员长直接派来的军事代表团几个月无果而终后被命令回国。实际上几乎没有（向他们）输送战争物资。

我们的第三个错误是在缅甸的败落。参加缅甸战役的中国人和其他人（我有第一手资料）的共识是，如果认识到太平洋战线的重要性，缅甸本不会沦陷。

造成这种损失的原因有两个：在首都仰光沦陷之前，拒绝让中国军队进入缅甸；英军的持续撤退导致英勇作战的中国最优秀的三个师被歼灭。

这种撤退不能归为胆怯，因为英国人不是胆小鬼。真实的情况似乎是，无论是士兵还是军官，英军都没有充分认识到缅甸在整个盟军战略中的重要性。英国士兵，甚至是军官说："我们在这里浪费生命有什么用？如果我们赢得了战争，缅甸无论如何都会归还给我们。如果我们输了，不管怎样，我们就失去它。"换句话说，他们没有想过因为缅甸在我们对日的战争中的至关重要而必须一步一步地再次夺回。

印度是战争补给通道，中国是空袭日本的唯一基地，而缅甸是连接中印的桥梁。

珍珠港事件后，中国人立即着手在他们的土地上建造许多机场供我们用来对付日本。他们认为我们当然要立即直接进攻日本，他们投入了成千上万的人建造这些必需的机场。这些人都是普通人，他们只有双手和农具，但却以惊人的速度建造了飞机场——从来没有使用的飞机场。

直到现在，希望我们为时不晚，我们才开始谈论夺回缅甸的必要性。如果我们早点认识到太平洋战线的重要性，付出的生命代价现在将得以减少。只有空军和陆军难以做到这一点，孟加拉湾必须有强大的海上支持。英国海军必须在那里帮助我们。

但愤愤不平的中国人表示，英国现在不想为缅甸进行真正的战斗，因为她想先结束欧洲战事，以便她可以在亚洲"杀戮"，然后恢复她的帝国，包括香港——中国人认为它再也不能成为大英帝国的一部分。

无论如何必须击败希特勒，我们没有认识到我们在亚洲损失的全部意义——不仅仅是军事损失，还有更严重的声望和善意的损失——不得不让我们付出沉重的代价。

任何了解事实的人，都不可能乐观

任何轻松乐观的时刻已经过去。我不会说希望的时刻已经过去，因为我相信热爱自由的美国人民的美好意愿。

但危险在于，美国人民甚至不知道正在发生什么。

现在是他们知道真相的时候了，我赞扬你正在承担的角色——说出我们在亚洲形势的真相。

R. F. D. No. 3，Perkasie，Pa. ——Pearl S. Buck. （赛珍珠的住址）

（英文原文见附贰：45. Pearl Buck Explains Why Allies Must Take Asia Initiative Now）

Pearl Buck Will Not Seek Seat In Congress

PHILADELPHIA. March 1. (Æ)—Denying a report that she might run for Congress, Pearl Buck informed Mrs. Harriet Hancock of the Democratic state committee today that she feels she can serve her country better as a writer and lecturer.

Earlier today, Dr. A. M. Peters, Lehigh county Democratic chairman, indicated that Miss Buck was considering the Democratic nomination for the Lehigh-Bucks district seat now held by Republican Rep. Charles L. Gerlach.

赛珍珠无意从政——《晨电》(*The Morning Call*，1944-03-02)

《蒙特利尔之星》（*The Montreal Star*），1943 年 8 月 21 日

《蒙特利尔之星》报影（1943-08-21）

[罗德尼·吉尔伯特] 现在我已经完全确信，那许多为这场运动做了受到高度赞赏的艰苦差事的人并没有意识到这些目的，也不会特意推进它们，而是通过呼吁他们的"自由主义"而被招募为公关宣传者。对此我深信不疑，例如，赛珍珠女士于今年 5 月 10 日在《生活》杂志上发表的一篇题为《关于中国的警告》的文章。然而，这篇文章刚登上报刊亭，就有两个不在中国政府担任任何职务的中国人——他们不是国民党人（蒋委员长一党专政背后的政党），也不效忠于宋氏家族——建议我带着巴克夫人显然受到了"左派"影响的无端见解去读它。我必须说，当时我不知道有任何"左派"发起的反对统治政权的抱怨，我本应该对此没有任何怀疑，因为巴克夫人所写的大部分关于孤立中国的阴郁和不祥的状态彼时都是完全准确的。

后来回顾她对蒋女士没有在这个国家为中国人民说话的暗示，她对在民主制度中消除蒋周围的官僚的建议，她斥责这场战争不再是一场人民战争，言论和新闻自由被"一个比民主国家的特务机关严厉得多的组织"所压制，学生和知识分子现在沉默不语，对中国民主的未来失去了信心——现在看来，不可避免的结论是，她要么纯属巧合为"左派"做了黑工作，要么间接受到了"左派"宣传的影响。

（英文原文见附贰：46. Belittling Gallant China's War Effort）

---

① 此文是从《蒙特利尔之星》（1943-08-21）所刊登的罗德尼·吉尔伯特的长文《贬低中国的战争努力》（Belittling Gallant China's War Effort）节选而来的，标题是本书编著者所加，以表明对报纸文章观点的理解。

关于中国的警告（节选）①

加利福尼亚州《圣贝纳迪诺县太阳报》（*San Bernardino County Sun*），1943 年 8 月 19 日

Unrest in China

China may be a land of just as mu
mystery as Russia, insofar as political d
velopments concerning the war are co
cerned.

Admiral Ernest J. King has publicly d
clared China must be kept in the wa
Since the heads of navies do not sa
things merely for the purpose of puttin
words together, it is necessary to look b
hind the scenes in an effort to determir

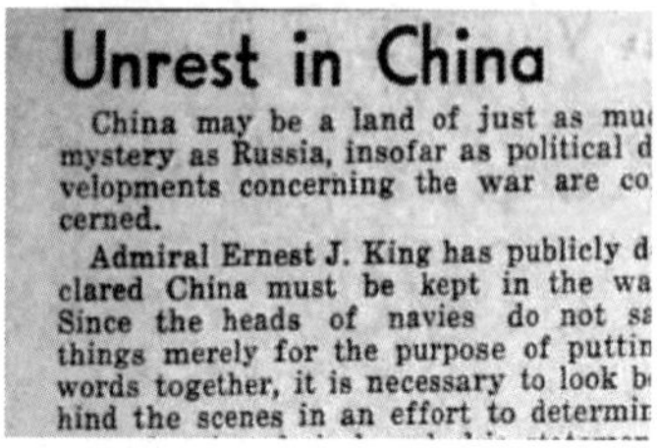

《圣贝纳迪诺县太阳报》报影（1943-08-19）

然而，有足够的硝烟表明中国国内并非一帆风顺。赛珍珠在 5 月 10 日的《生活》（*Life*）杂志上发表的《关于中国的警告》一文中说：

中国近期伟大的自由主义力量正在变得沉默。中国现在没有真正的新闻自由，没有真正的言论自由。官方的镇压工具是一个比民主国家的特务机构更严厉的组织。尽管都接受委员长为领袖，八路军和国军之间的分裂仍在继续。委员长周围有一些力量将现在本不应该分开的人民划为两大群体。

还有其他证据。传教士家庭成员克赖顿·莱西（Creighton Lacy）在他的著作《中国是民主国家吗？》中指出，“国民党内部的一些派别”非常“关心中国真正的民主派”。至少有两个团体被冠以“半法西斯”的绰号，因为他们“比反对日本更反对中国的共产主义，甚至可能更反对宪政民主。悲催的是，他们的成员包括一些最著名的内阁部长、将军和外交官”。

（英文原文见附贰：47. Unrest in China）

① 该报道原文标题为“中国的动荡”（Unrest in China），其中引用了赛珍珠的文章《关于中国的警告》（A Warning About China—A Great Friend of the Chinese People Points to Dangers That May Lose USA Valuable Ally）中的一段，本书收录了赛珍珠的这段文章，并使用原文标题。

《生活》（*Life*）杂志（1943-05-10）为赛珍珠的文章《关于中国的警告》配发的照片：
赛珍珠在书房研究宾夕法尼亚州佩尔卡西的乡间居民

《每日新闻》（*Daily News*），1943 年 10 月 19 日

《每日新闻》报影（1943-10-19）

日本从恐怖主义到和解的政策转变永远不会在中国成功。

赛珍珠，这位"用中文思考"的作家，在昨天为战争基金会演讲而抵达这里后不久，在查普曼公园酒店的一次新闻发布会上提出了这一主张。与她同行的是她的丈夫理查德·沃尔什，他也是出版赛珍珠图书的约翰·戴出版公司的总裁。

"多年来，日本在中国尝试了一场恐怖战役，但没有奏效。"这位作品曾获得诺贝尔奖和普利策奖的作家说，"如今他们试图在他们占领的土地上争取人民。在某些地方，这项政策已然奏效，但它永远不会得逞。"

"我无法想象，我的中国人民永远被征服了。"在说这些话时她的语气变得柔和了，"中国之前在等待良机，现在她正在对日本做同样的事情。"

巴克小姐说，即使中国军队受到饥饿与疲累的双重折磨，他们也不会倒下。然而我们（美国）不需要把粮食送到中国，因为那个国家的富饶的农业地区可以提供足够的食物——这是钱和交通的问题。

当被问及美国可以用何种方式最好地帮助盟友时，巴克小姐立即回答："她应该得到与其他盟国一样的平等待遇。我们应该像帮助英国一样帮助中国。"

在巴克小姐看来，目前我们对中国的所作所为与对英国的不同。

关于巴克小姐是否认为英国在一定程度上正避免在缅甸作战，因为他们想看到一个孱弱的中国，她回避了这个问题。她笑着说："我确信工党不会有这样的政策。"

说话低沉的巴克小姐说她并不想质疑军事战略，但她相信与日本的战争肯定不会被认为是次要战争，尽管在时间上它可能是次要的，但在重要性上它并不是次要的。

"没有一个欧洲国家能够赞同我们的立场，"她说，"这是我们美国特有的一种态度。"

这位作家认为美国人并未"人道地意识到"其他人民和民族的苦难。

"这不是我们的错——因为我们一向太安逸了。如果我们始终了解在我们自己舒适的国家之外发生的事情，这场战争就可能永远不会发生。现在没有人该这么想，因为他捐了50美元战争基金，他就做得够多了。"她愤愤地说，"诸如此类的救济只是开始，我们必须继续（援助）并了解那些人民和他们的文化。"

《大地》、《龙子》和《水浒传》等书籍让数百万的美国人对中国有了新的认识，他们以前认为中国是一个洗衣工和厨师的国度。巴克小姐刚刚完成了另一本书《承诺》。

"什么时候出版？"她问她的出版商丈夫。

"下个月。"他对记者说，"这本书是关于征战缅甸的。"

沃尔什还说，除了写作之外，巴克小姐还会抽出时间来管理他们居住的宾夕法尼亚州奎克敦的 200 英亩农场。

她发现在对"大地"的热爱和方式上，宾夕法尼亚州的荷兰农民与中国农民非常相似。

她也养牛，作为对战争的另一项贡献，但她宁愿"带着枪而不是织衣针"。

巴克小姐谦虚地否认通过她的写作促进了中美两国之间的关系，但她热情赞扬了中国作家林语堂在这方面所做的工作。

中文是巴克小姐的"第一语言"，她说一口流利的汉语。

新闻发布会结束后，巴克小姐和她的丈夫在大使酒店的"金房间"举行的招待会上受到了表彰，该招待会由中国联合救济会举办，该机构隶属于"战争基金"。

明天早上，巴克小姐将在大使酒店的大使厅向"战争基金"领导人的早餐会发表讲话。

（英文原文见附贰：48. Pearl Buck Here, Says Japs Can Never Appease Chinese）

左图：饥饿的中国人士气昂扬——《帕萨迪纳邮报》（*The Pasadena Post*，1943-10-19）
右图：援助中国的问题——《洛杉矶时报》（*The Los Angeles Times*，1943-10-19）

赛珍珠的民主呼吁打破了议员的问询——加利福尼亚州洛杉矶《每日新闻》（*Daily News*，1943-10-22，英文原文见附贰：49. Pearl Buck's Democracy Plea Derails Solons' Jap Inquiry）

　　有关赛珍珠从事援华抗日活动和开展时事评论的报道很多，很难在本章中尽数列举。她实际做的应该远比报道的要多。我们可以通过下面一段美国国务院的避重就轻的资料，体会当时的中国和赛珍珠所遇到的超乎想象的困难。

美国国务院历史资料"1937—1945 重大事件"之 "1937—1941 日本、中国、美国和珍珠港之路"①

　　1937 年至 1941 年间，中日之间冲突的升级②影响了美国与中日两国的关系，并最终推动美国与日本、德国全面开战。

　　一开始，美国官员对中国的事态发展抱有矛盾心态。一方面，由于对中国的长期深厚友谊和感情，他们反对日本入侵中国东北，反对日本军国主义在该

────────

① 译自美国国务院历史事件网站：https://history.state.gov/milestones/1937–1945/pearl-harbor.
② 应该是"战争"升级。这一场日本蓄谋发动的残酷的侵略战争，至今还被掩饰为"冲突"。

地区崛起；另一方面，大多数美国官员认为，美国在中国没有什么切身利益值得与日本开战①。此外，中国国民党和共产党人之间的国内冲突，使美国决策者不确定能否成功帮助这样一个内部分裂的国家。因此，很少有美国官员建议在 1937 年之前采取强硬立场。于是美国很少为中国提供帮助，以免激怒日本。1937 年 7 月 7 日，卢沟桥发生冲突，两国陷入全面战争之后，美国向中国提供援助的可能性增加了。当美国眼睁睁地看着日本军队席卷中国沿海，然后入侵首都南京时，民意坚定地支持中国人。当日军轰炸美国内河炮舰班乃号时，两国之间的紧张局势加剧。班乃号将美国公民从南京撤离，造成三人死亡。然而，美国政府继续避免冲突，并接受了日本人的道歉和赔偿。两国在 1940 年之前保持着不安的休战状态。

罗斯福签署租借法案

1940 年和 1941 年，罗斯福总统正式确定了美国对中国的援助。随着中国逐渐收紧对日本的限制，美国政府向中国政府提供了购买战争物资的信贷。美国是日本军队所需的石油、钢、铁和其他商品的主要供应商②。这种供需关系因中国的抵制而陷入困境，但在 1940 年 1 月，日本废除了与美国的现有通商条约。虽然这并没有导致立即的对日禁运，但这意味着罗斯福政府现在可以限制军用物资流入日本，并以此为杠杆迫使日本停止对中国的侵略。

1940 年 1 月之后，美国通过增加信贷和租借的计划，这项战略增加了对中国的援助，并逐步禁止对日本的所有军用物品贸易。日本政府在这两年做出了一些使局势恶化的决定。不知出于对军队控制的无能为力还是不情愿，日本政治领导人于 1940 年 8 月提出建立"大东亚共荣圈"来寻求更大的安全。由此，他们宣布日本打算将西方帝国主义国家赶出亚洲。然而，这个日本主导的计划旨在增加日本的经济和物质财富，使其不依赖西方的供给，也不"解放"长期受压迫的亚洲人民。事实上，日本本来要发动军事征服和统治的战役，其并不打算撤出中国。与此同时，日本与西方国家签订的几项协议只会让其对美国更具威胁性。首先，日本于 1940 年 9 月 27 日与德国、意大利签署了三方条约，从而将欧洲和亚洲的冲突联系起来，这使中国成为全球反法西斯斗争的潜在盟友。然后在 1941 年年中时，日本与苏联签署了中立条约，明确表示日本军队将

① 美国至少在日本有其切身的商业利益。
② 这里只提到了商业利益。

向美国利益更大的东南亚进军。与法国的维希政府①达成的第三项协议，使日本军队能够进入中南半岛，并开始他们的南方攻势。美国通过暂时停止与日本外交官的谈判、对日本实行全面出口禁运、冻结日本在美国银行的资产以及通过缅甸的公路向中国输送物资来应对这一日益严重的威胁。尽管美国在越来越多地对日本实施禁运后重新开始谈判，但进展甚微。华盛顿的外交官有几次接近达成协议，但由于美国的亲中情绪，很难达成不涉及日本从中国撤军的任何协议，这种情况对日本军方领导人来说是不可接受的②。

面对禁运造成的严重物资短缺并无法撤退，同时确信美国官员反对进一步谈判后，日本领导人得出的结论是他们必须迅速采取行动。就美国领导人而言，他们并没有放弃通过谈判达成解决方案，而且他们也怀疑日本是否有攻击美国领土的军事实力。因此，当1941年12月7日日本飞机在珍珠港轰炸美国舰队时，他们惊呆了。次日，美国对日本宣战，并很快与中国结成军事同盟。当德国站在盟友（日本）一边对美国宣战时，罗斯福政府在欧洲和亚洲都卷入了战争。

（英文原文见附贰：50. Japan, China, the United States and the Road to Pearl Harbor, 1937–1941）

---

① 二战时期的法国傀儡政权。
② 说明美方处于被动位置。

伍

中国最好的朋友

PEARL S. BUCK

Pearl Buck to Live
In Ithaca, Novelist
Wrote "Best Seller"

THE GOOD
EARTH
MUNI
RAINER
WALTER
CONNOLLY
TILLY LOSCH
CHARLEY GRAPEWIN
JESSIE RALPH

美国《排除中国人法案》简称《排华法案》，正式名称为《1882年移民法案》，是 1882 年 5 月 6 日通过的美国联邦法律。它是第一个，也是唯一一个明确暂停特定国籍移民的联邦立法，它禁止中国劳工即定义为"技术工人和非技术工人以及从事采矿业"的中国人进入美国。这一《排华法案》的出炉，不仅禁止中国劳工进入美国，而且在社会上助长了针对华人的暴力犯罪行为。

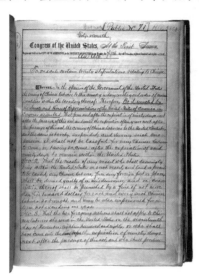 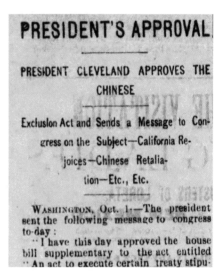

左图：《1882 年移民法案》的第一页（美国档案）
右图：克利夫兰总统批准《排华法案》

赛珍珠呼吁废除《排华法案》——《阿克伦灯塔日报》
(*The Akron Beacon Journal*，1943-04-02)

《迈阿密先驱报》（*The Miami Herald*），1943 年 4 月 10 日

Proving Our Friendship

CONGRESSIONAL action to eliminate a direct insult to China and other Oriental allies which has been included in U. S. immigration laws for 60 years will rob Japan of a most effective propaganda weapon. Influential groups are now sponsoring a measure to admit to the country and eventual U. S. citizenship Orientals from nations now allied with us against the Axis. It will not, however, permit the entry of Japanese.

《迈阿密先驱报》报影（1943-04-10）

国会消除已存在于美国移民法中达 60 年的对中国和其他东方盟友直接侮辱的行动，将解除日本最有效的宣传武器。有影响力的团体正在发起一项措施，允许来自目前与我们结盟对抗轴心国的东方人进入美国并最终获得美国公民身份。但是，该措施不允许日本人进入。

目前的美国移民法排除所有东方人，这为日本渗透和征服远东地区提供了舆论弹药。"你足够出色去为美国而战，并为美国而死。"日本告诉被征服的中国人、马来人和缅甸人，"但是你还没有出色到足以在美国生活。"针对这一宣传，最致命的是我们的限制在为其背书。

如果排除条款被废止，我们的东方盟友将被按照欧洲国家移民的配额基准管理。按照最多配额每年将允许 105 个中国人进入，根据同一规定，允许 100 个印度人、100 个菲律宾人和 100 个来自太平洋地区各自治或半自治地区的人进入美国，合法移民的总数可能比战前走私入境的人数少。

《排除中国人法案》的历史可以追溯到 1882 年，它是美国在西部铁路大规模输入中国苦力（劳工）的结果。美国劳动者无法与愿意每天为一碗米饭工作的中国人竞争。

美国劳动者不反对废除这个法案。今天 CIO 联盟（工业组织委员会）批准解除排除法案的禁令，并且 AFL（美国劳工联合会）可能采取类似的立场，两个工会联盟都承认了东方人的

西海岸工会会员资格。去年 6 月，汽车工人联合会呼吁废除《排华法案》并向日本人宣传其价值。

虽然蒋介石夫人在访问华盛顿期间没有公开讨论该提案，但众所周知，她希望美国能做出这种友谊的姿态。赛珍珠积极支持这一运动。

罗斯福总统不反对修订这一法律，尽管他更倾向于让国会行动。

众议员马丁·肯尼迪（Martin J. Kennedy）在国会提出了一项法案，允许中国人进入美国。众议员沃尔特·贾德（Walter Judd）正在准备另一项面向除日本以外的更广泛东方人的法案。国会和联邦政府应敦促尽快通过。

中国和我们的其他东方盟友正在与我们一道作战。欢迎他们进入我们的家园是起码的尊重。

（英文原文见附贰：51. Proving Our Friendship）

赛珍珠敦促废除《排华法案》

《记录探照灯》（*Redding Record Searchlight and the Courier Free Press*），1943 年 5 月 21 日

《记录探照灯》报影（1943-05-21）

[华盛顿，美联社] 中国主题的小说作家赛珍珠告诉众议院移民委员会，为了美国和中国的利益，《排除中国人法案》应该作为一项战争措施而被废除。

她作证说："所有中国人都知道这一法案禁止他们进入这个国家超过 50 年了。"

"我已在中国度过了五分之四的时光，并多次被问到这个问

题——为什么没有废除这一法案？这让我很尴尬。日本人在中国的宣传方案中利用了它。日本嘲讽中国人——'瞧！美国真的是你的盟友吗？你正遭受歧视！'"

（英文原文见附贰：52. Pearl S. Buck Urges Repeal of Exclusion Act）

Gossett Asks End of Chinese Exclusion Act

Contends Would Offset Jap Propaganda for Separate Peace

WASHINGTON (*P*).—To offset Japanese propaganda which he said "definitely is pointing toward a separate peace with China," Representative Gossett (D.-Tex.) yesterday urged repeal of the Chinese Exclusion Act as soon as Congress reconvenes next month.

Gossett, a member of the House Immigration Committee, declared the Japanese already have adopted separate peace tactics by "relenting on atrocities" in occupied China and by trying to win over the people of those territories, even to the extent of "passing out candy to Chinese children."

"And the Nipponese," he told an interviewer, "probably will offer liberal terms, including the delivery of Hong Kong to the Chinese government. They would hope by such a move to be able to prolong the war with us or to negotiate better peace terms with us."

戈塞特要求终止《排华法案》——《伯灵顿每日新闻》
(*Burlington Daily News*，1943-08-11)

《每日广告商人报》（*The Daily Advertiser*），1943 年 10 月 7 日

FAVOR BILL TO REPEAL CHINESE EXCLUSION ACTS

Will Allow Chinese Immigration To The U.S. On A Quota Basis

(By The Associated Press)

WASHINGTON, Oct. 7—In a surprise move today the House committee on immigration voted 8 to 4 in executive session to report favorably a bill to repeal Chinese exclusion acts and allow Chinese immigration to this country on a quota basis.

《每日广告商人报》报影（1943-10-07）

将允许中国人按照配额基数移民美国

[美联社华盛顿 10 月 7 日] 今天，众议院移民委员会出人意料地在执行会议上以 8 票对 4 票通过了一项议案以废除《排华法案》，并以配额为基础允许中国人移民美国。

这一迅速行动被认为是为下星期日中华民国国庆纪念而在本周通过法案的努力的结果。设定中国人配额的反对派领导人——众议员艾伦（D-La）没有出席今天的行政会议，据报道，他的代理人和其他几人没有投票。众议院可能在下周据此行动，废除可追溯到 1882 年的《排除中国人法案》，基于 1924 年的移民法案确定中国人配额，每年允许大约 105 人进入美国，并修改入籍法接受中国公民。

（英文原文见附贰：53. Favor Bill to Repeal Chinese Exclusion Acts）

《生活》（*Life*）杂志，1943 年 10 月 5 日

一个关于中国的警告①

A WARNING ABOUT CHINA
OF THE CHINESE PEOPLE POINTS TO DANGERS THAT MAY LOSE US A
by PEARL S. BUCK

Pearl Sydenstricker Buck, whose novels about the Chinese people won her the Nobel Prize in 1938, knows China as well as she knows America. She was brought up by her missionary parents in Chinkiang on the Yangtze, came back to Virginia to college (Randolph-Macon), and then returned to China to spend the next two decades. Her first husband, Dr. John Lossing Buck, taught rural economics at the University of Nanking; she herself taught English. In 1934, after the success of *The Good Earth*, she returned to the U. S. for good. She lives on a Pennsylvania farm with nine children and her second husband, Richard J. Walsh, who is editor of the magazine *Asia*.

Although Pearl Buck has not been in China since 1934, she still has a "Chinese self," and is one of the most understanding spokesmen the Chinese people have. Because she knows and loves them well, she has their confidence and can say things to and about the Chinese that would come most Americans with bad grace. For the frightening situations described here, however, she does not blame China, but puts the blame where it belongs: on America's failure to understand in time the necessity of helping China, so that China can help us.

《生活》（*Life*）杂志编者按（1943-10-05）

---

① 1947 年 10 月 5 日《生活》（*Life*）杂志刊发了一篇赛珍珠的文章《一个关于中国的警告》并配发了编者按。本文是编者按语的一段中文节译，英文全文另附。

尽管赛珍珠从 1934 年离开中国后就再也没有回去过，她仍然自我认知是一个中国人，而且是最了解中国的发言人之一。因为她了解并且热爱中国人，所以她得到了中国人的信任，可以对中国人说一些大多数美国人都不会说的话。而对于此处描述的恐怖情况（战争状态），她没有责备中国，只是将责备归于其应当的归属，即美国没有及时地认识到帮助中国的必要性，中国继而能够帮助美国。

（英文原文见附贰：54. A Warning About China—A Great Friend of the Chinese People Points to Dangers That May Lose US a Valuable Ally）

《布鲁克林每日鹰报》（*The Brooklyn Daily Eagle*）1944 年 10 月 22 日报道，作家赛珍珠将做客 YMCA（基督教青年会）发表演讲，配发的照片是赛珍珠与好莱坞米高梅影片公司的电影《龙子》的主演图尔汗·贝（Turhan Bey）和凯瑟琳·赫本（Katharine Hepburn）的合影。影片改编自赛珍珠的畅销小说《龙子》，小说以南京大屠杀为背景创作，是一本声讨法西斯、颂扬中国人民抗战不屈精神的可歌可泣的小说。

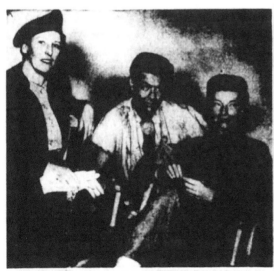

TO SPEAK HERE—Author Pearl S. Buck, who will be a guest at a Y. M. C. A. lecture, is shown here with Turhan Bey and Katharine Hepburn, who starred in Miss Buck's best seller, 'Dragon Seed.'

赛珍珠与《龙子》的演员——《布鲁克林每日鹰报》（1944-10-22），右图为小说《龙子》封面

Dragon Seed Playing at Majestic

Katharine Hepburn and Turhan Bey in a scene from Dragon Seed, based on the novel by Pearl S. Buck, which is playing now through Saturday at the Majestic theater, East Moline. The cast includes Walter Huston and Aline MacMahon.

电影《龙子》演员剧照——《派遣报》（*The Dispatch*，1944-12-07）

《林肯之星报》（*The Lincoln Star*），1945 年 8 月 14 日

Still A Change
Lincoln, Neb.
To the editor of The Lincoln Star: In the last number of Asia, Pearl S. Buck writes about "American Imperialism in the Making," deploring the fact that those who were supposed to represent Americanism at San Francisco and Potsdam were silent while Stalin insisted that all colonies must ultimately have independence. For some time she has also given word pictures of the achievements of the Russians under Stalin, making it plain that Russians accomplished more under Stalin than Americans did under Jefferson. Then, Russia, like Saul, now stands a head higher than all other Imperialisms in the

《林肯之星报》报影（1945-08-14）

致《林肯之星报》主编：

在《亚洲》的最后一期中，赛珍珠谈论关于"美国帝国主

仍然是一个变化

义正在形成"的问题，痛惜这样的事实，即那些本应在旧金山和波茨坦代表美国主义的人保持沉默而同时斯大林坚持认为所有殖民地最终都必须独立。一段时间以来，她得到的对俄罗斯人在斯大林治下所取得的成就的图文描述比对杰斐逊治下的美国的描述还要多。那么，现在俄罗斯像扫罗（Saul）一样，比所有在人类经历中的其他帝国主义都要高出一头。俾斯麦在路德的基础上建立了德意志帝国主义。"Ein Feste Burg 1st Unser Gott"① 以普鲁士军国主义为基石，而迪斯雷尔则在堡垒和战舰上建立了英国帝国主义。也许我们希望现在的胜利将导致以伍德罗·威尔逊的"自我决定"为基石的帝国主义。

（英文原文见附贰：55. Still a Change）

《威奇托鹰报》（*The Wichita Eagle*），1948 年 8 月 1 日

她的小说赢得了对中国的理解和广泛同情

1931 年，赛珍珠只是南京一所小学院的一位默默无闻的英国文学教师。一年后，作为《大地》的作者，她成为美国阅读量最大的作家之一、普利策奖的获得者和国际声誉的拥有者。这是一个灰姑娘的故事，但实际上，赛珍珠在默默无闻中一举成名并没有

"China's Best Friend . . ."

像这些对比隐喻的那样轻松。这是一次艰苦的攀登，充满了困难与波折。

巴克小姐的第 15 部成年读者的小说《牡丹》（纽约约翰·戴公司）一直是夏季小说排行榜上最畅销的图书之一。她于1920 年代在南京写了她的第一本书，1926 年完成了手稿并计划于次年春天将其送到纽约出版。

---

① 约翰·塞巴斯蒂安·巴赫为宗教改革日创作的合唱清唱剧。

化为烟雾的小说

1927 年 3 月，内战爆发，国民军猛攻南京，掠夺和杀害外国人。巴克小姐与她的丈夫和三个年幼的孩子①一起躲在一个山洞里，直到被一艘美国军舰救出。但他们的家被烧毁了，她的小说——五年的勤勉之作——消失在一缕薄薄的白色烟雾中。她最近说："我现在以我的第一部小说可能写得并不好来安慰自己。"

赛珍珠于 1892 年出生在西弗吉尼亚州的希尔斯伯勒，她身为传教士的父母在她 5 个月②大的时候就把她带到了中国。她在学习英语之前就学会了中文，就读于中国的学校，并在 1914 年从弗吉尼亚州林奇堡的伦道夫-梅肯学院毕业后回到中国任教。

在这些年里，她写作故事、小说、文章，所有这些都受到了纽约出版商们的冷漠对待。1923 年，她在《大西洋月刊》上发表了一篇文章，次年又在《论坛》上发表了一篇文章。接着，在她的第一部小说被烧毁后，她又写了另一部作品《东风·西风》，于 1930 年出版。1931 年的《大地》使她一举成名。

在她后来的小说中，只有一部除外，其他的都以中国为背景，她的声誉正是建立在这种关注之上。1938 年，她成为第一位获得诺贝尔文学奖的美国女性。在受奖时，她以"中国对我来说就像我自己的（祖国）"向中国致敬。

多年来，巴克夫人一直带有双面性。她创作的小说与她那个时代的任何作品一样，具有可读性，并且在小说中她为中国和中国人民高举着旗帜。对于数以百万计的美国人来说，赛珍珠书中的中国人已经成为他们的邻居和好友。

（英文原文见附贰：56. China's Best Friend）

---

① 此处报道应该有误，赛珍珠当时只有一个女儿和一个养女。

② 应该是四五个月大的时候。赛珍珠 6 月 26 日出生。据《教务杂志》(*Chinese Recorder and Missionary Journal*) 载，1892 年 12 月 14 日，赛兆祥夫妇抵达上海。

《星期六评论》（*Saturday Review*），1949 年 10 月 8 日

　　1949 年 10 月 8 日，赛珍珠在《星期六评论》杂志上发表文章，相信中国将仍然是一片继承传统文明的沃土。

It Still Is the Good Earth

Much of China is today in the grip of Mao Tse-tung and his power-hungry Chinese Communist regime, but Pearl S. Buck says it still is the good earth, and that we of the Western World need not conclude that all is lost in China.

"The people of the Chinese earth," she writes in the Saturday Review of Literature, "have power in themselves. Long ago, they were stripped of falsehood and foolish pride. Life has educated them and time has civilized them. Even poverty and distress, or the corruptions of governments and the tyrannies of war, cannot degrade them. They persist and will persist. A thousand years are a thousand years, and the Chinese people have lived many thousands of years. This present moment ... cannot destroy the foundations of the past."

To this canny observer of the most populous of countries, the Chinese people demonstrate the capacity of a determined people to survive whatever the vicissitudes. China's part in World War II she deems longer and more bitter than any, but "hundreds of millions stayed on the land and weathered it through."

　　左图：中国仍然是一片沃土——《星期六评论》（*Saturday Review*，1949-10-08）

　　右图：中国仍然是一片沃土——《布法罗晚报》（*Buffalo Evening News*，1949-10-28）

《里士满时报快讯报》（*Richmond Times Dispatch*），1950 年 6 月 30 日

Pearl Buck Counsels Calm in Korean Crisis

CAPE MAY, N. J., June 29—(UP)—Pearl S. Buck, Nobel prize-winning author and authority on Asia, said today that Americans should not worry about Korea, but should watch Formosa, "which is tremendously important."

"Don't take the Korean situation too seriously because Korea is too small a matter in the over-all world picture," she told 3,000 persons attending the general conference of the Society of Friends.

《里士满时报快讯报》报影（1950-06-30）

诺贝尔奖作家及亚洲问题专家赛珍珠今天说，美国不必担心朝鲜而应该关注更为重要的台湾。

"不要将朝鲜形势看得太重，因为在世界格局里朝鲜实在太小了。"赛珍珠向参加"友好协会"大会的3,000名与会者说。

对抗羞辱了赛珍珠

《图森每日公民报》（*Tucson Daily Citizen*），1950年6月30日

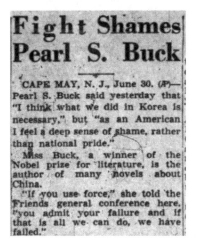

《图森每日公民报》报影（1950-06-30）

［美联社］赛珍珠昨天表示，"我认为我们在朝鲜所做的事情是必要的"，但是"作为一个美国人，我感到深深的羞耻，而不是民族自豪"。

赛珍珠小姐是诺贝尔文学奖获得者，也是多部关于中国的小说的作者。"如果你使用武力，"她在这里告诉"友好协会"大会，"你就承认了你的失败，如果这是我们所能做的全部，那我们就失败了。"

她说，美国向被入侵的南朝鲜（韩国）提供军事支持是必要的，因为"在某种意义上我们应当对朝鲜负责，原因在于我们的占领统治和朝鲜战后的国家分裂"。

但是，她补充说："台湾就没有我们的什么事了。如果我们保护台湾就意味着我们要保护整个亚洲。"

她告诉3,000名教友派教徒听众，她已经改变了对与中国

共产党建交的可能性的看法。

她说："我认为当下我们无法与中国人做朋友。这与我6个月前的看法大不相同。"

她断言，美国对华外交政策的错误"在我们两国之间制造了一个深渊"。

（英文原文见附贰：57. Fight Shames Pearl S. Buck）

Pearl Buck Tells Haddonfield Group U. S. Could Lose All Fighting China

By EDMUND N. WATKINS

If America should engage in a war in China proper, "we could lose everything we have and be taxed out of existence," Pearl S. Buck, world-famed author, said Tuesday night.

Speaking in the Haddonfield Memorial High school under the mended speaking the truth and acting on facts even if the Communists have said the same things.

Criticizing Chiang Kai-shek, Mrs. Buck said that if he had been able to do so he would have become emperor of China rather than president.

Terms Chiang Warlord

赛珍珠告诫，与中国开战将输掉一切（英文原文见附贰：58. Pearl Buck Tells Haddonfield Group U.S. Could Lose All Fighting China）——《信使邮报》（*Courier Post*，1950-10-18）

爱尔兰审查员禁止《目光》杂志

《沃思堡之星电报》（*Fort Worth Star Telegram*），1951 年 4 月 21 日

Irish Censors Ban Look

DUBLIN, April 20 (Reuter's). The government censorship of publications board Friday banned Look Magazine for six months. Nine other magazines and 69 books banned by the board included Pearl S. Buck's "The Patriot." The board gave no reason for its action.

《目光》杂志和赛珍珠的小说《爱国者》被禁——《沃思堡之星电报》报影（1951-04-21）

［都柏林，4 月 20 日，路透社］周五，政府的出版审查当局封禁《目光》杂志（*Look Magazine*）6 个月。当局封禁了其他 9 本杂志和 69 本书，包括赛珍珠的《爱国者》。当局未对这一举动给予解释。

A FEW weeks ago Pearl S. Buck, who knows Asia as few Americans do, wrote an article for LOOK Magazine entitled: "Why Asia Hates Us." The basic reason she gave was this:

"The Asians feel that we have taken sides against them. We have destroyed their ideal of us.

"The blow fell at the San Francisco conference (at which the UN was organized in 1945). What happened was reported in The New York Times in an article carrying the headline: 'United States will oppose colonial liberty—Americans indicate line up with Britain and France against an independence pledge'."

"What has happened since has been the inevitable consequence of an attitude of mind, a policy, which has denied again and again the true ideals of our people."

A billion and a half human beings who looked to us for leadership in attaining freedom and independence were bitterly disillusioned.

Pearl Buck: ASIA HATES US

左图：亚洲恨我们——《底特律自由报》（*Detroit Free Press*，1951-09-30）
右图：《目光》杂志（*Look*，1951-09）

作家赛珍珠谈美国在亚洲声望的降低

《布里斯托先驱信使报》（*The Bristol Herald Courier*），1951 年 3 月 2 日

Prestige Low In Asia, Says Writer

Gromyko To Help Set Big Four Agenda

《布里斯托先驱信使报》报影（1951-03-02）

"过去 5 年，美国在亚洲失去了相当多的威望，但是美国人只要努力理解亚洲人民对独立的深切渴望，仍然可以重新获得昔日的影响力。"昨晚，著名的美国作家赛珍珠对"布里斯托论坛"的听众说道。

面对苏林学院礼堂的一群听众，她说："美国在二战结束时拥有无与伦比的世界影响力和实力，但是我们犯了一个致命性的错误，我们没有宣布我们支持亚洲人民的民族独立。"

而后，她补充说："产生如此悲剧的原因，是那些因荷兰、英国和法国的殖民统治而极度羸弱的亚洲国家确信，美国会拥护亚洲人民争取独立，因为美国在1776 年已经摆脱了殖民统治而赢得了自己的独立。"

履行义务

"可是我们究竟做了什么，请告诉我?"她继续说，"我们宣称我们对亚洲的国家独立问题不发表任何看法或采取任何行动。我们之所以这样做是出于政治原因，担心我们可能会招致法国和荷兰的反感。然后，这一消息传到了亚洲，他们认为我们在背弃他们，而他们曾对我们的帮助寄予了很大的期望。"

巴克夫人说，我们在朝鲜犯的错误是将其一分为二。俄罗斯统治一半，我们统治另一半。因为像所有亚洲国家一样，小小的朝鲜最渴望民族独立。南朝鲜未能阻止北方的入侵，因为南方对我们派去占领他们国家的人失去了信心。在南朝鲜的美国人对朝鲜的历史和风俗一无所知，结果是我们做的工作相当窘迫。当入侵来临时，南朝鲜的士气很低落。

巴克夫人认为，美国应该改变对参与世界粮食组织、世界卫生组织、世界教育组织等联合国组织的态度。她说："我们拒绝与这些团体全心全意地合作，这已经让我们在世界上，尤其是在亚洲失去了很多声望。我们应该为这些组织活动投入数十亿美元，而不是继续制造一个又一个炸弹，从长远来看，炸弹不会解决任何问题。"

权力过大

她还认为，美国军人获得了过多的权力，而且在与朝鲜的军事行动有关的"杀手行动"等短语中，公关非常糟糕。她还对美国军方的"我们在朝鲜的'主要目标'是杀死尽可能多的中国人"等言论表示谴责。

巴克夫人说，佛教作为亚洲宗教之一，其教义强烈反对剥夺人的生命。"结果就是，"她说，"我们当局的这种言论势必会让亚洲人对美国人感到厌恶。如果我们在朝鲜有军事任务，我们应该在不破坏公共关系的前提下进行。"

谈到华盛顿正在考虑的立法，巴克夫人说，即将通过的《通用军事训练法》没有"每两年审查一次"的条款，而这一直是本国军事立法的惯例。"除非在新法律中加入这一条款，否则美国将面临一项永久性的征兵计划，这肯定与美国理想格格不入。"她说。

"我们陷入了一个非常糟糕的混乱局面，"巴克夫人说，"但如果我们优先实施一项积极的计划来改善世界的生存状况，停止过度依赖炸弹和战争机器作为解决亚洲问题的手段，就还有挽回的机会。"

（英文原文见附贰：59. Prestige Low in Asia，Says Writer）

—Photo by Ralph Morrissey
Pearl S. Buck and her husband, Richard J. Walsh.

赛珍珠和丈夫理查德·沃尔什（英文原文见附贰：60. Pearl S. Buck and Her Husband, Richard J. Walsh）——《田纳西人报》（*The Tennessean*，1951-06-10）

Woman's Club

Eighteen members of the Verona Woman's Club will attend the Seventh and Eighth District Federation of Women's Clubs Conference to be held Tuesday, beginning at 10 A M., at the Woman's Club of Montclair. Mrs. Pearl S. Buck, author, will be one of the feature speakers at the afternoon session, open to the public, to begin at 2 P. M. in the Congregational Church of Montclair on South Fullerton Avenue. Her topic will be "Children of Hope."

女子俱乐部：赛珍珠讲演"儿童是希望"——《维罗纳雪松林时代报》（*Verona Cedar Grove Times*，1950-10-05）

Pearl Buck Hopes Showdown Can Be Avoided In East

Atlantic City — Pearl S. Buck urged here Saturday that "the lay mind" rather than the limited "professional mind" make the decision in the present world crisis, the New York Times reported.

Describing the situation over Formosa as "terrifying," the winner of the Sobel Prize for literature said there were "two opposing rigidities and no way of bringing them together."

Miss Buck spoke at the opening session of the fourth annual forum of the Ventnor Foundation. The forum is a part of the German international exchange program for brotherhood and better international understanding.

The author who spent many years in China, explained that the Chinese people historically felt that Formosa rightfully belonged to the mainland. She noted, on the other hand, that the military minds of the United States felt there was no other course than to defend this island.

With the possibility that eventually "another way" to meet the problem might be found, she said lay persons should work and pray to prevent a decision from being forced now.

赛珍珠希望避免在东方摊牌——《公报和日报》（*The Gazette and Daily*，1955-02-07）

《每日快讯报》（*Daily Press*），1955 年 2 月 20 日

Pearl Buck Eloquently Disproves Saw Of The East And West Never Meeting

By WILLIAM D. PATTERSON

THE AUTHOR OF THE WEEK

The tragic truth in the jingling couplet "East is East, West is West, and never the twain shall meet" may still be true of most of the world today, but it could never reply to Pearl S. Buck. Two civilizations have fused in the distinguished author as seems humanly possible.

In her autobiography, "My Several Worlds", the Nobel Prize-winner writes with maturity and eloquence of her varied life and of the two worlds of China and the United States, in which she has lived her years almost equally.

This book may be her finest achievement. Certainly in humanity and craftsmanship have combined to make it stand out on The Saturday Review's list this week of books being most widely read and enjoyed around the country. Other best-readers were: "The Tumult and the Shouting," by Grantland Rice (Barnes). A lifetime spent covering sports all over the world is summed up in this informal but constantly in-

Born in West Virginia in 1892, Pearl Sydenstricker Buck grew up in the interior of China, where her parents were missionaries. She learned to speak Chinese before English.

Although she left China at the age of 17 to enter college in the United States, she returned to China on graduation. There she lived, married, taught and wrote until the turbulent march of history so transformed that friendly nation that she felt compelled finally to move permanently to the United States in 1932.

After the dissolution of her first marriage to a young

PEARL S. BUCK

东西方有共同点——《每日快讯报》报影（1955-02-20）

"东方是东方，西方是西方，孪生姊妹永远不会相遇"中的悲惨事实，可能在当今世界上的大部分地区仍然是真实的存在，但它永远不会适用于赛珍珠。在这位杰出的作家身上，两

赛珍珠有力反驳东西方永无聚合的观点

种文明融合得如此完美和优雅，几乎达到了人类可能的极限。

在她的自传《我的多重世界》中，这位诺贝尔奖获得者以成熟和雄辩的方式，描述了她多姿多彩的生活以及她在其中度过了相当时间的中国和美国这两个世界。①

这本书可能是她最好的成就。当然，人性和技艺相结合，使它脱颖而出，登上《星期六评论》本周畅销并广受喜爱的图书榜单。

（英文原文见附贰：61. Pearl Buck Eloquently Disproves Saw of the East and West Never Meeting）

Pearl Buck, Romulo Present Views On U.S.-Asia Relations

NEW YORK, NOV 13 (AP) — An Asian diplomat and a distinguished American woman whose affections reach deep into each other's parts of the world agree that the United States must work to restore Asian esteem.

Philippine Ambassador Carlos P. Romulo urged that America, by deeds, give new life to the basic clause of the 1776 U. S. Declaration of Independence, that "all men are created equal."

赛珍珠对东西方文明的见解在报刊中多有报道。
左图：赛珍珠评论中国画——《芝加哥论坛报》（*Chicago Tribune*，1949-05-01）
右图：赛珍珠评美亚关系——《关岛日报》（*Guam Daily News*，1958-11-14）

Pearl Buck Sees Red China As Reality U.S. Must Face

赛珍珠预见红色中国是美国必须面对的现实（英文原文见附贰：62. Pearl Buck Sees Red China as Reality U.S. Must Face）——《先驱新闻报》（*The Herald News*，1961-11-15）

---

① 在《我的多重世界》中，赛珍珠还回顾了少年时在上海租界看到洋人贴出"华人与狗不许入内"的辱华告示的经历。

陆

博
爱

作为一名社会活动家，从 20 世纪 50 年代开始，赛珍珠将注意力投向维护世界和平、消除贫困、消除种族歧视、保护妇女权利和关爱被遗弃儿童等亟待解决的问题，她以正义、博爱助推人类文明进步。

为黑人伸张正义

《中央新闻报》（*The Central News*），1941 年 10 月 23 日

Pleads For Justice For Negroes

With a real passion for justice for the colored Americans, Mrs. Pearl S. Buck, distinguished novelist who makes her home in Bucks county, asked that more than 200 professional women, representing Soroptimist Clubs from six Eastern States, make it a point to obtain real knowledge of the racial issue in connection with the colored Americans and then take strong, swift and courageous steps to have these oppressed peoples get their rights as American citizens.

Mrs. Buck, who spoke at the Fall conference of the North Atlantic region of the American Federation of Soroptimist Clubs at a luncheon meeting on Saturday at the Doylestown Inn, asserted it takes intellect and will to break down the instinct of race prejudice.

Mrs. Buck explained that she has written 12 outstanding American men and women, asking them to give of their time and talent to do something about the condition of the colored Americans.

《中央新闻报》报影（1941-10-23）

在伯克斯县安家的杰出小说家赛珍珠怀着为美国有色人种伸张正义的真正热情，要求代表东部六个州的职业妇女会俱乐部的 200 多名职业女性，要重视真正了解与美国有色人种有关的种族问题，然后采取强有力的、迅速的和勇敢的措施，让这些被压迫的人民获得他们作为美国公民的权利。

（英文原文见附贰：63. Pleads for Justice for Negroes）

《科文顿弗吉尼亚人报》（*Covington Virginian*），1950 年 11 月 4 日

Education Is Not Meeting Needs, Says Pearl Buck

RICHMOND, Nov. 4—(P)—Virginia Negro educators have been told that American education does not fit its youth for the needs of the world.

Mrs. Pearl S Buck, Nobel prize winning novelist, called for "complete revision" of the present school curriculum yesterday in an address before the Virginia Teachers Association here.

"What must we teach, and how can we teach it, when we don't have the materials?" Mrs. Buck asked some 3,000 Negro teachers and educators attending a general session of the convention yesterday.

Mo...ern textbooks, she said

学校缺乏关于黑人的教育——《科文顿弗吉尼亚人报》报影（1950-11-04）

[里士满，美联社] 弗吉尼亚州的黑人教育工作者被告诫，美国的教育不能满足世界对年轻人的要求。

诺贝尔奖获得者、小说家巴克夫人昨天在弗吉尼亚教师协会的演讲中呼吁"彻底修改"目前的学校课程。

"当我们没有材料的时候，我们必须教什么，又怎么能教呢？"昨天巴克夫人邀请了大约 3,000 名黑人教师和教育工作者参加集会。她认为现代的教科书"已经过时"。"你要教的东西，不会在教科书中找到。"女作家直言，"你必须告诉孩子们，他们必须以德报怨，为拯救和平而发声，让其他国家的人民知道他们可以成为我们的朋友。如果他们能记住做人的崇高的尊严和必要性，就能够做到这一点。"

（英文原文见附贰：64. Education Is Not Meeting Needs, Says Pearl Buck）

U. S. Race Bias End Seen by Pearl Buck

By CHARLES Q. FINLEY

Pearl S. Buck, world-famed novelist and Nobel prize winner, said last night time and American Democracy will overcome the race problem peacefully.

The author spoke at the 15th Annual Executives' Night Dinner of the Camden Chapter of the National Secretaries Association at which Dr. Reuben L. Sharp of Mount Laurel, Camden physician, received the Boss of the Year

Anna A. Martin, Camden High School graduate now studying business administration in Philadelphia.

Peggy Crossan, chapter president, extended a welcome. Veronica M. Kidder, dinner chairman, also addressed the secretaries and their bosses.

Miss Buck is chairman of the board of "Welcome House."

赛珍珠见证美国种族偏见的终结——新泽西州卡姆登（Camden）《信使邮报》（*Courier Post*，1963-11-14，英文原文见附贰：65. U.S. Race Bias End Seen by Pearl Buck）

BOSS OF THE YEAR, Dr. Reuben L. Sharp, Camden physician, receives a flower from Ginny Smith, his secretary, as Pearl S. Buck, famed novelist, looks on. It was the 15th Annual Executives Night of the Camden Chapter of the National Secretaries Association last night at Cherry Hill Inn.

在樱桃山酒店的全国秘书协会卡姆登分会的第 15 届年度之夜，年度老板、内科医生鲁本·夏普博士在著名作家赛珍珠的注视下接受他的秘书金妮·史密斯为其佩戴胸花——《信使邮报》（*Courier Post*，1963-11-14）

赛珍珠在家中和三个养女探讨下国际象棋——《新闻和太阳公报》（*Press and Sun Bulletin*，1964-05-15）

关注精神缺陷的成因，赛珍珠认为对于智力障碍儿童的教育远远不够——《米尔维尔日报》（*The Millville Daily*，1951-01-31）

十年后再次当选为残障儿童培训学校董事长的赛珍珠（左起第8位）和丈夫沃尔什（右一）与董事会成员合影。赛珍珠连任董事会主席——《每日通报》（*The Daily Journal*，1954-12-20）

OBSERVERS—The work of two Lebanon County Workshop trainees is examined by Dr. Charletta Weyland (standing, left), chairman of Mayor Richard D. Schreiber's Community Council for the Handicapped, and Pearl S. Buck (standing, right), noted novelist and chairman of the Governor's Committee for the Handicapped. The trainees are Frances Sheetel (left), Lebanon, and Helen Troutman, Myerstown. Dr. Weyland and Miss Buck watched the trainees package moth crystals before the dedication ceremonies of the LCWS on Monday.

市长理查德·施赖伯（Richard D. Schreiber，左一），残疾人社区委员会主席查莉塔·韦兰（Charletta Weyland）博士（左二），赛珍珠（右二）观看了两名黎巴嫩县残障讲习班学员演示包装飞蛾水晶的过程——《黎巴嫩日报》（Lebanon Daily News，1962-05-22）

SPEAKERS CHAT—Mayor John T. Gross talks with author Pearl S. Buck and Gov. Lawrence. Miss Buck and Lawrence spoke at a joint meeting of the Mayor's Committee on the Handicapped and the Lehigh County Community Council in Allentown's Lehigh Valley Club.

赛珍珠（左）、宾夕法尼亚州州长大卫·利奥·劳伦斯（右）和约翰·T. 格罗斯市长（后排）讨论残疾人问题——《晨电》（The Morning Call，1961-10-07）

孤儿的欢迎之家

《希博伊根报》（*The Sheboygan Press*），1962 年 5 月 7 日

沃尔什奶奶——更为人们所知的是作家赛珍珠——与前"欢迎之家"① 的一些孩子聊天，他们周日在宾夕法尼亚州多伊尔斯敦附近的农场参加了一次聚会。"欢迎之家"是一家收养机构。该机构已经为 300 名儿童找到了美国家长，其中大多数儿童是未被收养的亚裔美国人。

GRANNY WALSH, better known as Author Pearl S. Buck, chats with some of the 270 former Welcome House children who attended a reunion Sunday on her farm near Doylestown, Pa. Granny started Welcome House, an adoption agency, which has found American parents for more than 300 children, most of whom are of Asian-American descent and were regarded as unadoptable — (AP Wirephoto).

《希博伊根报》报影（1962-05-07）

赛珍珠为美军在韩国的 5 万私生子们辛劳；这些孩子以每年 3,000 人的数量增加，他们靠从垃圾桶中寻找食物度日——《新闻与观察者报》（*The News and Observer*，1964-10-16）

---

① 1949 年赛珍珠创立"欢迎之家"（Welcome House）。

《记录报》（*The Record*），1964 年 4 月 13 日

What You're Doing

Pearl Buck Finds A Miracle

By MIRIAM TAYLOR PETRIE
(Home and Family Editor)

Harry Holt, who runs an orphanage for children of Asian-American parentage, is a 1-man miracle, according to author Pearl S. Buck, who drove from her home in suburban Phila-

Mrs. Frank B. Hennessy, president of the juniors, introduced Miss Buck. Mrs. John Auld of Dumont was chairman, assisted by Mrs. Mathias O'Gorman, Mrs. George Deubel, and Mrs. Dominic Telesco.

* * *

Two other major social functions of the weekend were a

《记录报》报影（1964-04-13）

[米里亚姆·泰勒·皮特里] 根据作家赛珍珠的介绍，哈里·霍尔特（Harry Holt）经营着一家为亚裔美国儿童而设的孤儿院，他是一个奇迹般的人。周六晚上，赛珍珠从费城郊区的家中开车到霍沃斯的白山毛榉乡村俱乐部参加为霍尔特孤儿院举办的慈善舞会。

巴克小姐对特纳弗莱青年女子俱乐部的 250 名成员和宾客说，这是她第一次参加这个孤儿院的慈善活动。

巴克小姐说："这些被收容的孩子很幸运，其他数以千计的孤儿还在韩国和其他亚洲国家游荡，没有食物和其他生活必需品。"

她说："这些不受欢迎、不被爱的孩子，被他们的同胞（韩国人）称为美国人。自相矛盾的是，当幸运的少数人到达美国的家庭时，他们又被称为韩国人。"

巴克小姐指出，父母分别是美国人和亚洲人的孩子们异常美丽，而且智力普遍较高。

她说："至少对于那些被遗弃后幸存下来并住进难民营的孩子来说是这样。"

正是为了这些永远不会到达美国海岸或没有家的孩子，作家成立了赛珍珠基金会。该基金会正在与韩国政府合作，寻求解决这个持续性的问题。

巴克小姐在基金会执行董事西奥多·哈里斯的陪同下参加舞会。她说，下周六她将在费城会议厅为她的基金会举办一场慈善活动。

（英文原文见附贰：66. Pearl Buck Finds a Miracle）

赛珍珠荣获金贝尔费城奖和一千美元奖金——《费城询问者报》（*The Philadelphia Inquirer*，1964-01-10）

《劳德代尔堡新闻报》（*Fort Lauderdale News*），1964 年 11 月 16 日

《劳德代尔堡新闻报》报影（1964-11-16）

　　不，我对有多少人阅读我的书并不感到惊讶。我写这些书就是供阅读的。

　　当陌生人出现并告诉我，我为人类做了多少好事时，这也没有让我不知所措。帮助这些孩子是我想做的事，这就是我的生活方式——做我想做的事，无论以什么方式。

---

① 此文标题为本书编著者所加，原文标题为 Pearl Buck Lives Success。

获得赛珍珠救助的士兵后代：美韩混血儿
——《波士顿环球报》（*The Boston Globe*）报影（1964-06-12）

《每日新闻》（*Daily News*），1964 年 7 月 12 日

《每日新闻》报影（1964-07-12）

生父是冷漠 GI① 的数以千计的亚洲儿童流落在他们的家乡，面临着近乎绝望的未来。

---

① GI 指美军。20 世纪初，美国军用垃圾桶和水桶上印有 GI 两个字母，代表镀锌铁。后来，在第一次世界大战期间，它被用来指所有与军队有关的物或人。

Lost and Found

Abandoned by their GI fathers and unwed Asian mothers, thousands of half-American children (A) are living and dying in streets. Since U.S. government assumes no responsibility for these lost kids, novelist Pearl S. Buck (◄—) has set up private foundation to find and care for tots like two Korean-American boys she is shown entertaining.

level of food, clothing and opportunities for education that the Korean orphans get. We intend also to help them get jobs when the time comes."

If possible, Miss Buck said, the foundation will try to keep the children with their mothers. It will try to help the unwed mothers regain some sort of status and to find work so that they can make decent homes for their children.

The foundation's first project is already under way, Miss Buck

赛珍珠于 1959 年在国会委员会作证说，美国军人的子女在韩国孤儿院"正在像苍蝇一样死去"——《每日新闻》（1964-07-12）

［克里斯蒂娜·柯克］四年前，美国作家赛珍珠战后首次前往东方旅行时，韩国人满为患、满是泥泞的肮脏街道并没有让她感到震惊。身为传教士父母的女儿，她一半的时光在中国度过，非常了解贫穷的情景和味道。

就连那些拉着她的裙子乞求一碗饭的赤脚孩子们，都是令人心酸的相似——直到有一天，她偶然看到了红发流浪儿那双杏仁蓝眼睛。

"让人觉得很奇怪，"巴克小姐伤心地说，"一个乞讨的孩子伸出手来换一分钱，我低头看着孩子的眼睛，那无疑是美国人。"

（英文原文见附贰：67. The Babies）

Pearl Buck to Visit City

REUNION WITH Pearl S. Buck is big moment in life of Nancy DeWire, seventh-grade student at Fairview. Nancy, who came to Mr. and Mrs. Harry DeWire from Welcome House at age four months, also saw her benefactor on Miss Buck's 1960 visit to Dayton. (Staff Photo by Walt Kleine)

PEARL S. BUCK and her four adopted, half-American daughters—from left, Chieko, Johanna, Henriette and Theresa.

左图：见到了 1960 年救助的孤儿——《先驱》（*The Journal Herald*，1965-05-05）
右图：赛珍珠和她领养的四个女儿——《新闻和观察者报》（*The News and Observer*，1964-08-30）

左图：美军遗弃的孩子处境恶劣——《迈阿密先驱报》（*The Miami Herald*，1964-09-14）

右图：被遗弃的孩子在赛珍珠基金会的帮助下终于回到了家——《每日新闻》（*Daily News*，1964-07-12）

基金会新总部破土典礼：为了缅怀赛珍珠妈妈并在将来帮助更多的人，朱莉·亨宁[①]带着3岁的儿子彼得出席赛珍珠基金会新总部破土典礼（左）——《每日费城询问者报》（*The Philadelphia Inquirer*，1986-03-22）。右图为朱莉·亨宁的《小沟中的玫瑰——赛珍珠妈妈的女儿》。

---

① 朱莉·亨宁（Julie Henning）是朝鲜战争期间出生在朝鲜的美亚混血儿，一直不知其生父。13岁时，她被赛珍珠带到巴克斯县，如同赛珍珠自己的女儿一般被抚养长大。

　　左图：赛珍珠访问佛罗里达州彭萨科拉为儿童募捐——《彭萨科拉新闻杂志》（*Pensacola News Journal*，1964-08-02）

　　右图：赛珍珠逝世后的 1973 年 3 月 6 日，《彭萨科拉新闻》（*The Pensacola News*）刊登 1964 年赛珍珠到访时的照片

　　左图：赛珍珠获得亚利桑那州图森市荣誉公民铜牌——《亚利桑那每日星报》（*Arizona Daily Star*，1965-03-30）

　　右图：赛珍珠，72 岁，工作刚刚完成一半。赛珍珠和她的两个日裔养女，16 岁的 Johanna（右）和 17 岁的 Thereso（左），她们都是日裔美国人。赛珍珠有 10 个孩子，其中 9 个是收养的，4 个是混血儿——《公报》（*The Gazette*，1965-07-30）

FAMOUS WRITER HERE MAY 17

Pearl Buck to Visit

Pearl S. Buck, possessor of one of the most famous names in American letters and winner of the Nobel and Pulitzer prizes, will visit Binghamton May 17.

She will be guest of honor at the Arthur Murray Medal Award benefit ball, scheduled at 9 p.m. at the Arlington Hotel.

Proceeds from the ball will be donated to the Pearl S. Buck Foundation for the health, education and welfare of half-American children born of fathers in U.S. occupation forces in foreign lands.

The novelist is the only woman ever to receive both the Nobel and Pulitzer prizes for outstanding work in literature. She has published 58 best sellers and has three novels in the process of being released.

Among her books are "The Good Earth," "A House Divided," "Dragon Seed," "The Dragon Fish," "Peony," "The Living Reed," "Imperial Woman" and "What America Means to Me." Most of her books are set in the Orient.

Miss Buck, 71, lives in Dublin, Pa. She is well known for her work with retarded children, serving as the head of the governor's board for retarded children in the State of Pennsylvania.

The author is the daughter of Presbyterian missionary parents. She was born June

NOVELIST WITH A CAUSE — Award-winning author Pearl S. Buck is the founder of an adoption agency, "Welcome House," that places children of Asian-American parentage in good adoption homes throughout the U.S. She also raises money to help half-American children throughout the world obtain equal opportunities in the land of their birth.

赛珍珠获得亚瑟·默里奖章（Arthur Murray Medal Award）——《新闻和太阳公报》（*Press and Sun Bulletin*，1964-05-03）

MISS BUCK AND HOWARD CLARK PLAN THE BALL
. . . he'll lead the dance

PEARL S. BUCK, Pulitzer and Nobel prize winner Maj. Gen. James E. Roberts, commander of the Air for literature, is shown at Eglin Air Force Base with Proving Ground Center, on her whistle stop tour of 200 cities. Purpose of the tour, which will bring the celebrity to Tallahassee Nov. 1-4, is to raise funds for Pearl S. Buck Foundation.

左图：赛珍珠将在彭萨科拉举办慈善舞会——《彭萨科拉新闻杂志》（*Pensacola News Journal*，1964-10-29）

右图：赛珍珠在佛罗里达埃格林空军基地为基金会募捐——《塔拉哈西民主党人报》（*Tallahassee Democrat*，1964-10-28）

Pearl Buck Here For Drive

Help For 'Amerasian' Sought

By RUTH SMITH

When you look at the distinguished author, Pearl Buck — so gentle, so filled with kindliness, the old words rush to your mind: "Surely goodness and mercy will follow her all her days."

Mrs. Buck has been a guest in Orlando for three days in the interests of her most cherished project, The Pearl S. Buck Foundation, which was organized to help provide happy, useful lives for half-American children in foreign lands.

TONIGHT the Nobel and Pulitzer Prize winning author will be honored at a champagne reception at 7:30 p.m. at the Cherry Plaza Hotel, and will be present at the benefit ball following presented by the Arthur Murray School of Dancing. Mrs. Buck is particularly grateful to the Arthur Murray Studios in this country, for they have pledged $1 million to the great cause for which her foundation was organized.

Success Due

April 29, 1964 marked the date when the foundation began its activities, and so heart-warming has been the response, the cause is already destined for success. It was formed for the sole purpose of discovering and caring for those children whose fathers are

STUDENTS RALLY AROUND NOVELIST
... Mrs. Buck, surrounded by Edgewater students

Star Photo by Charles Foley

MRS. BUCK, CENTER
... With Harris and Ruth Smith

AUTHOR'S COMPANION — Mary Elizabeth Decorsey, four-year-old Korean child adopted through the Welcome House agency by John and Marjorie Decorsey, of Bucks County, is shown with Miss Pearl S. Buck, noted author, whom she accompanied to Wilson College when the novelist came here for an informal speaking engagement. (A. Simpson Photo).

左图：赛珍珠在佛罗里达州奥兰多为混血儿募捐——《奥兰多夜晚之星》（*Orlando Evening Star*，1964-11-27）

右图：巴克斯县的德科西夫妇通过"欢迎之家"领养了4岁的韩国孤儿——《公众报舆论》（*Public Opinion*，1964-02-21）

The Pearl S. Buck Foundation Chooses Winhall in 'Unprejudiced Vermont' As Transient Home for Education of 'Superior' Amerasian Children

By JACKIE BREEN

WINHALL — Selection of Vermont by The Pearl S. Buck Foundation as a transient home for Asian-American children, brought to this country for special training and education, was announced today as members of the foundation met at Miss Buck's summer homes here in the wilderness near Stratton Mountain.

"Vermont was chosen," said Miss Buck, world-renowned novelist and winner of both the Nobel and Pulitzer prizes, "because of the lack of prejudice here."

The president and executive director, Theodore F. Harris, and staff members of the foundation are now gathered in this secluded mountain valley to review the last year's work and to form plans for the future of the Foundation, created about 15 months ago, to care for and to educate children of American servicemen and Asian mothers in Korea, Japan, Okinawa, Taiwan, the Philippines and now Viet Nam, because of recent requests from that country.

Deeply distressed by seeing personally the pitiful plight of children fathered by American soldiers and scattered throughout occupied Asian coun-

MOUNTAIN MEETING — Members of The Pearl S. Buck Foundation trekked from Pennsylvania to the author's Vermont home for a conference in the wilderness near Stratton Mountain. Seated, from left, are Theodore Harris, president and executive director; Miss Pearl S. Buck and Don Anderson. Standing are Joan Toti, Constance Marquis, Wendy Parks, John Wood, Betsy Smith and Pat Alan. Missing is latest elected active member of the board of directors, George Breen of Manchester, who has been business manager of Miss Buck's Vermont properties 15 years. (Breen)

the size of returning from the country of their origin to scintile citizens.

"This, I believe, is the most effective way to dispel prejudice," Miss Buck said.

The first steps toward helping the children, it was explained, is to send a search team into the countries involved for the purpose of understanding the attitude of their citizens toward the half-American child and to carry out a thorough search for the children. They are usually found in orphanages, villages, cities and areas surrounding American camps. Persons chosen to work on the search teams, as well as other foundation personnel, are primarily interested in the welfare

Book published by Miss Buck's late husband, publisher Richard J. Walsh of The John Day Company. For two days last spring of 1949, the whole family participated in all the stages of the magazine process, from gathering the sap to the grading and canning of the syrup.

THIS week, Miss Buck purchased first maple farm, bought the first same 19 years ago, for inclusion in the trust for the Pearl S. Buck Foundation.

Buildings in trust for the foundation are excellent to ancestors and remodeled which looks across the Stratton's ski area. The new acquisition from George B. Breen of Manchester will be called "Simm Dimm," and it, too, is fashioned in stone and timber. The name "Forest Farms" will be retained to designate all Vermont properties to the trust.

The Pearl S. Buck Foundation is the only organization to which I have ever given my name or ever will give my name," said the author said, adding modestly that she does this because she feels that it might be of "slight value" to Asia.

Members of the board of Governors of the foundation include such distinguished names as Robert F. Kennedy, Art Buchwald, Joshua Logan, Mrs. William W. Scranton, R. Sargent Shriver, Joan Crawford, Kathryn Murray and Sophie Tucker; also the Most Rev. Angier Biddle Duke, former Chief of Protocol, who is now U.S. ambassador to Spain.

OFF TO THE BALL — Highly successful fund-raising balls for The Pearl S. Buck Foundation are held throughout the United States and Canada at Arthur Murray Studios. Miss Huck, a graceful and agile dancer, often performs at these occasions with Theodore Harris, president and executive director of the foundation.

CCS Board Solves Busing Problems

CAMBRIDGE, N.Y. — The Cambridge Central School board, meeting Sept. 8, approved a bus contract for the residents of Buskirk to the satisfaction of all. Some parents having small children, as well as...

无偏见的佛蒙特州：赛珍珠基金会选择"无偏见的佛蒙特州"的温霍尔作为"优秀"亚裔美国儿童教育的临时住所——《本宁顿旗帜报》（*Bennington Banner*，1965-09-15）

《萨克拉门托蜜蜂报》（*The Sacramento Bee*），1965 年 4 月 8 日

Pearl Buck Has No Time On Hands

By Gay Pauley

NEW YORK — UPI — "Me tire? From what?", asked Pearl Buck.

At 72, the woman who has written close to 60 books and holds the Nobel and Pulitzer prizes for literature, is still writing.

"they're not treated the same by either side. They're outcasts without opportunity.

"We'd like to see that they get a chance in their own country."

Miss Buck estimated there are at least 50,000 children of mixed blood in Korea, that at the end of the United States

Sacramento next week during a full spring trip cross country which will find her in Honolulu by May 8th.

Meanwhile, two more of her books, Death In The Castle and The Big Fight will join A Joy Of Children and Welcome Child currently in the book stores.

《萨克拉门托蜜蜂报》报影（1965-04-08）

[盖伊·保利，纽约，UPI—联合新闻国际] "我累了？从何谈起？"赛珍珠（巴克小姐）问道。

现年 72 岁，已经写了近 60 本书并获得诺贝尔奖和普利策奖的这位女性仍在写作。

她还参与了数量如此之多的其他活动，这些活动足以令年龄仅赛珍珠一半的大多数女性筋疲力尽了。

她正在学习舞蹈，正如她所说，"如果必须，我可以跳恰恰"。她正在拍电影，而且她正忙于一个新项目，以帮助美国军人与亚洲母亲生养的孩子。

为此，她成立了赛珍珠基金会并担任该基金会的董事会主席和财务主管。她说，该基金会通过"欢迎之家"进一步推进她为亚裔混血儿童所做的工作，该收养机构自 1949 年成立以来已为数百人提供永久的家。

"但收养并不能满足所有的需求。"她在采访中说，"我最近访问了亚洲，有成千上万的人需要照顾。"

巴克小姐说，这些都是可悲的例子，因为"他们没有得到任何一方的同等对待，他们是没有机会的弃儿"。"我们希望看到他们在自己的国家获得机会。"

巴克小姐估计韩国至少有 5 万名混血儿，而在美国占领日本末期已有 20 万名。她说，美国军方将这个数字定为 5,000 人，而"冲绳和现在越南的数字不详"。

该基金会将通过亚洲国家的已有机构开展工作，但基金会的一名代表也将在场参与。她说："例如在韩国，我们将通过政

府的儿童安置服务机构开展工作。"

巴克小姐对跳舞的兴趣有助于基金会筹集资金。在过去的两年里，她一直在一家舞蹈工作室学习，她已经推动350家隶属于该连锁店的工作室举办舞会，所得款项将捐给基金会。

该公司总裁哈里·埃文斯解释说，工作室已承诺在未来5年内将向基金会筹集至少100万美元。巴克小姐在活动中进行客串。

她定于下周在萨克拉门托进行一次全程的横跨美国的春季越野旅行，行程定于5月8日到达檀香山。

同时，她的另外两本书《城堡中的死亡》和《大战》将加入目前在书店的"儿童的喜悦"和"欢迎儿童"活动。

"我怎样才能为每件事划出时间？"她回答说，"嗯，我从不考虑时间，而且儿童读物写起来很容易。"

然后她谈到了她对斯特拉顿制片公司的兴趣，该公司的最新电影是在印度制作的《指南》。巴克小姐是这个电影公司的共同所有人，也是该电影剧本的合著者。

（英文原文见附贰：68. Pearl Buck Has No Time on Hands）

Pearl S. Buck Will Discuss Asia's Fatherless Children

Children deserted in Asia by American servicemen will be discussed Monday by novelist Pearl S. Buck in a lecture sponsored by the Wichita Child Evaluation and Advisory Foundation.

when their fathers return to the United States and Miss Buck has named the fatherless ones "Amerasians."

Being fatherless is particularly bad in Asia, according to Miss Buck, because there the child

赛珍珠将谈亚洲无父儿童——《威奇托鹰报》（*The Wichita Eagle*，1967-03-19）

1967年的多家报纸报道，在赛珍珠75岁诞辰前夕，她决定捐赠七百万美元给赛珍珠基金会以救助美亚混血儿（主要在日本、韩国、越南）。1976年美国的国内生产总值是0.861万亿美元，人均收入是4,336美元。赛珍珠的捐赠包括她的农场、房产、影视及电台收入和稿费，她还将捐赠身后的全部稿费。

Pearl Buck Gives $7 Million Fortune to Help Amerasians

PHILADELPHIA (AP)—Novelist Pearl Buck, about to celebrate her 75th birthday, is giving her estate and most of her earnings—more than $7 millions—to her own special welfare

until 1933. She has 10 children, nine of them adopted Amerasians.

"In a way the foundation is like adopting these children, who have no Asian fathers, no

... but what else would I do?" Her comments on the Asian military situation and Vietnam were few: "China is a 'formidable' power. She is quite assured about her place in the

Pearl Buck Donates $7 Million For Child Aid

WASHINGTON — Mention the name of Pearl Buck and the average American immediately thinks of "The Good Earth" and Paul Muni. The association is not entirely fortunate. A woman who has given away more than $7 million to square the American conscience deserves to be known for more than a movie that some sophisticates

"Sons" and "A House Divided." But she received the Nobel Prize for literature in 1938 primarily for the biographies she had written of her parents, "The Exile" and "The Fighting Angel."

"The decisive factor in the Academy's judgment," wrote the critic Anders Österling, "was, above all, the admirable

Pearl Buck Gives Estate To Project

PHILADELPHIA (AP)—Novelist Pearl Buck, about to celebrate her 75th birthday, is giving her estate and most of her earnings—more than $7 million—to her own special welfare project for half-American children living in Asian countries.

Miss Buck announced the gift to the Pearl S. Buck Foundation on Sunday as she prepared to leave on a tour of Asia.

She said she has signed over her television and movie royalties worth some $6 million, her suburban Bucks County farm and Vermont property and all future book royalties to the foundation effective immediately. Upon her death, all royalties from past books would also go to the foundation.

The Nobel prize-winning novelist, whose life and writings have been devoted to the ways of the Asians, explained simply in an interview, "I am giving my life to my work."

Miss Buck, who began the foundation in 1964, said "like my writing, its basis came from my experiences. I was in Asia, making a movie and I saw the children of American men and Asian mothers. And I was really quite ashamed."

"As an American, I don't like to see a half American problem in an Asian country. I'm too proud an American."

In some ways the foundation is an extension of her own life

左上图：赛珍珠捐赠七百万美元来帮助亚裔美国人——《星报》（ Star Gazette， 1967-05-22）

左下图：赛珍珠为援助儿童捐赠七百万美元——《西北阿肯色时报》（ Northwest Arkansas Times， 1967-06-22）

右图：赛珍珠将遗产交给基金会——《星报》（ Star Gazette， 1967-05-02）

不灭的期待

《底特律自由报》（*Detroit Free Press*），1960 年 8 月 27 日

Red China, U.S. Tie Seen

Two Nobel Prize winners had their say about various world events Friday.

● Author Pearl S. Buck said in Tokyo that the barriers between Communist China and the United States may be broken down in the next five years. "It is to their interest and to ours," said the American woman author of "The Good Earth," who has spent more than 40 of her 68 years in China. "Human nature has a way of overcoming ideologies in favor of more practical ways of living."

Pearl S. Buck

● Dr. Albert Schweitzer warned in New York that

《底特律自由报》报影（1960-08-27）

作家赛珍珠在东京预言，在未来五年内，共产党中国与美国之间的障碍有可能被排除。这位写作《大地》的 68 岁美国女作者，在中国生活了四十多年，她说"这符合他们的利益和我们的利益"，"人的本性有克服意识形态的一面，以利于更实际的生活方式"。

Women's Meet Urges UN Admission of Red China

NEW YORK (UPI) —A group of women leaders from the United States and Russia have agreed upon a number of proposals designed to ease cold war tensions. One is the admission of Communist China to the United Nations. Nine Soviet and 12 U.S. women

lege, Bryn Mawr, Pa., Nov 21-27.

In a statement released Tuesday, the women called upon their respective governments to work toward disarmament, a nuclear test ban, and the admission of Red China into the United Nations.

赛珍珠和一些妇女领袖呼吁裁军、禁止核试验以及联合国接纳中华人民共和国——《奥尔巴尼民主党先驱报》（*Albany Democrat Herald*，1961-11-29）

1962 年，中国国内和国际的形势都发生了巨大变化。中国准备以四亿美元购买美国粮食，可能是有意开通与美国的贸易往来，为实

现两国关系正常化铺路。赛珍珠呼吁美国总统肯尼迪取消禁止向中国出售价值四亿美元谷物的决定。

关于中国购买四亿美元粮食的报道有不少。据报道，赛珍珠呼吁将美国的余粮卖给中国，可以为其设两个条件：一是不能将粮食转售给其他国家；二是告诉中国人民粮食来自于美国人民。她的呼吁遭到了反对，并被指责是在援助"红色"敌人。

On Feeding China

In regard to Pearl S. Buck, who in Letters from the People voiced a plea that the United States sell surplus wheat to Red China:

Miss Buck seems to ignore or conveniently forget the grim lessons of the past bloody years; she seems not to remember our selling of scrap-iron and other materials to Japan, she seems to be suffering from total amnesia in regard to the folly of the Marshall Plan and other ridiculous schemes resulting in the spending of billions of dollars to help "poor" nations of the world.

Miss Buck forgets a simple lesson in psychology, namely that—to a certain extent—people are products of the culture in which they are born: their thinking is shaped according to the culture in which they mature.

Food and Mainland China

President Kennedy denies that the Communist Chinese government has formally approached the United States in an effort to purchase $400,000,000 worth of surplus wheat, although he indicates two firms have sought export licenses without giving evidence that they act as agents for Peiping. Some sort of approach was reported by Pearl S. Buck, author of novels with a Chinese setting, in a letter published on this page Sunday. Mrs. Buck advocated selling the food to China under two conditions: that it not be resold, and that the Chinese people should be informed of the source.

There have been previous reports that the Chinese have sought United States aid, but they have never been confirmed. But if the United States should let it be known that such a request would be entertained, it might be made. Preliminaries could be handled privately through the continuing ambassadorial conferences at Warsaw.

There would be no point in offering food to Red China unless Mrs. Buck's conditions were met, which seems unlikely. But the United States has a historic record of aid to the Chinese people, in flood and famine, and it might be advantageous to let them know that this country still has a high regard for them, despite its disapproval of their government. If approaches are made they should be considered on this basis.

FOOD FOR RED CHINA

To the Editor of The Inquirer:

However humane may be her reasons, Pearl S. Buck (letter March 11) in my opinion, does not serve the national interest in urging sale of grains to Communist China.

Miss Buck sets up two conditions for sale: (1) That no food be resold to other countries, and (2) that the Chinese people know the food comes from the American people. Both are wildly unrealistic. There is and can be no way of control over foods once sold to Red China.

Miss Buck argues that a seriously undernourished people will not have the will to revolt. It is even more unlikely that a well fed and contented people would have the will to revolt.

Against Miss Buck's weak arguments are the facts. No nation in this world is as violent

左图：呼吁将美国的余粮卖给中国——《圣路易斯邮政速递报》（*St Louis Post Dispatch*，1962-03-14）

中图：四亿美元购买粮食——《圣路易斯邮政速递报》（*St Louis Post Dispatch*，1962-03-16）

右图：粮食援助红色中国——《费城询问者报》（*The Philadelphia Inquirer*，1962-03-15）

be beastly to criminals. Who gives a damb about law-abiding citizens?

★ ★ ★

PEARL S. BUCK has urged the U. S. to sell Red China 400 million dollars worth of wheat. China has been hit by a food shortage ... Miss Buck is a gifted novelist and a humanitarian. She is also completely unrealistic. Red China is dedicated to the destruction of the U. S. In a real sense the Chinese Communists are at war with us. In Korea they were responsible for the death of many Americans. In war the choice is always grim. It is never between good and evil. It is fight or fall. If we help

Red China in any manner we are helping the Chinese Reds to destroy us.

★ ★ ★

LABOR leader Quill's final indignity: He's now a bore.

★ ★ ★

THE N. Y. TIMES correspondent in West Germany reported on March 11, 1962: "Almost without exception the West Germans believe that in the past year or two there has been a noticeable shift in American attitudes toward their country, that this has been stimulated by what are always tartly called 'certain circles' and that it is unfair at this distance from World War II."

Pearl S. Buck
...aid a Red enemy?

her was an informer.

呼吁卖余粮——《迈阿密先驱报》（*The Miami Herald*，1962-03-20）

中国：东方神秘的新视角[①]

《杰克逊太阳报》(*The Jackson Sun*)，1977 年 6 月 19 日

China: New Perspectives On Oriental Mystery

The Committee Of One Million; "China Lobby" Politics 1953-1971. By Stanley D. Bachrack. Columbia University Press: $14.95.

dling on the Hill — apparently they have simply copied the experience of other Asiatics — the Nationalist Chinese — who for years held the Congress and country captive to

《杰克逊太阳报》报影（1977-06-19）

［富兰克林 · 库玲］很长一段时间，很多美国人像赛珍珠一样关注着二战前的中国情况，他们担心中国政权会落入他人之手（中美双方彼时仍保持来往）。现在，我们开始讨论朝鲜战争结束以来的后续矛盾：是谁在游说让中国加入还是不让中国加入；是谁支持了台湾，又是什么神秘力量合谋将游说者、中情局特工和政府高官联系在一起，以实现美国在亚洲大陆的最新目标？对于一个认为其潜在最大敌人位于欧洲的国家来说，我们确实花了很多时间来担心中国人。

斯坦利 · D. 巴赫拉克进行了一些有意思的调查报道，以追踪所谓的“百万委员会”的影响。“百万委员会”是一个反共、反中华人民共和国的右翼组织，多年来一直致力于将红色中国——就正常的美国关系而言——排除在联合国以外。

（英文原文见附贰：69. China：New Perspectives on Oriental Mystery）

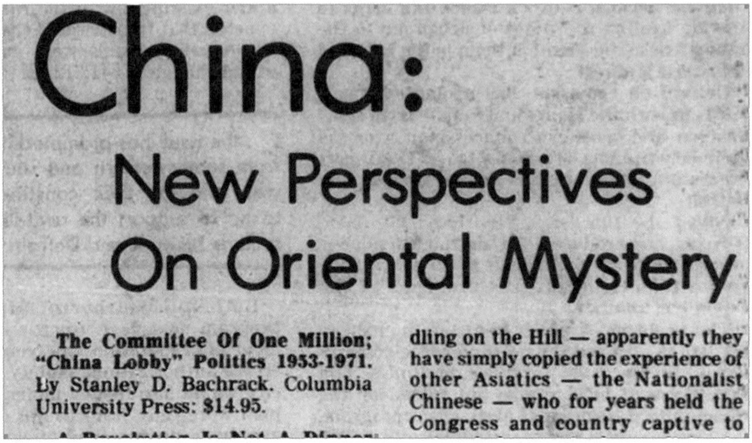

① 这是一篇关于斯坦利 · D. 巴赫拉克所著、哥伦比亚大学出版社出版的《百万委员会：中国游说政治（1953—1971）》(*The Committee of One Million*：“*China Lobby*” *Politics* 1953—1971）的报纸评论。

《奥尔巴尼民主党先驱报》报道中写道，赛珍珠积极参与推动红色中国重返联合国的运动，这是一次耗时 18 年的艰难历程，也是赛珍珠作为沟通中西方文明的"人桥"的一次历史性贡献。有关赛珍珠的最早的相应报道是 1955 年 7 月《杰克逊太阳报》介绍斯坦利·D. 巴赫拉克的著作《百万委员会：中国游说政治（1953—1971）》，该书提供了自 1953 年起反对中国重返联合国的各方势力的资料。其中明确地记载，在任 18 年的民主党不老松级别的参议员保罗·H. 道格拉斯（Paul Howard Douglas，1892—1976）被质询是否接受了蒋介石政府和孔、宋的献金时，道格拉斯坚决地否认了。但是道格拉斯去世后，他的后代于 2006 年低调委托拍卖行拍卖的一件嵌有"大清乾隆御制"款的国宝级剔红雕漆盒，里面留下的字条证明了这件器物的来路不一般。美国拍卖行的电子邮件证实这件漆器由已故参议员保罗·道格拉斯的孙女玛丽·道格拉斯卖出。玛丽的父亲约翰·道格拉斯被肯尼迪总统任命为司法部副部长，时任部长是肯尼迪总统的弟弟罗伯特·肯尼迪。此事例间接说明当时的背景之复杂，以及赛珍珠等美国亲华、主持正义的各界人士和群体的努力之艰难。

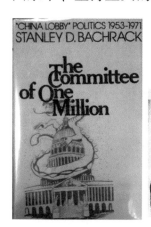

斯坦利·D. 巴赫拉克著《百万委员会：中国游说政治（1953—1971）》（*The Committee of One Million："China Lobby" Politics* 1953—1971），右图为第 191 页的记述

道格拉斯家族收藏的嵌有"大清乾隆御制"落款的国宝级剔红雕漆盒（局部）及漆盒里面留下的字条

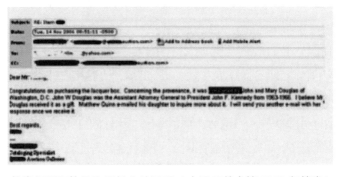

拍卖行关于拍品和委托人的记录（火星云美术馆 2006 年档案）

中
国
人
不
会
炸
毁
世
界

《劳德代尔堡新闻》（*Fort Lauderdale News*），1964 年 11 月 16 日

《劳德代尔堡新闻》报影（1964-11-16）

在今天第 1B 页的赛珍珠简介中，特约撰稿人爱丽丝·麦基（Alice McKee）讲述了为什么（中国原子弹试验）成功不会让这位著名的人道主义和诺贝尔奖作家感到惊讶。

[比尔·比肖夫，特约撰稿人] 著名小说家赛珍珠今天在这里说："我不相信中国人会炸毁世界。这样做不符合他们的利益。"巴克小姐一生大部分时间都在中国度过，她说她相信拥有

核弹会给中国人带来新的前景，这对世界和平来说是个好兆头。

这位作家说："中国人是一个自豪的民族。""任何人都不能阻止科学发展，"巴克小姐补充说，"现在中国人有了核弹，他们将不得不被纳入所有核协议中，否则这些协议将毫无用处。"

巴克小姐相信这将使中国人对世界文明的人民产生新的归属感，从而产生新的责任感。

巴克小姐在佛罗里达州的劳德代尔堡发起赛珍珠基金会，组织帮助世界各地数以百万计的亚裔美国儿童，这些儿童的生父是派遣在世界各地的美军。

她将出现在今天下午 5 点的鸡尾酒会，以及明天晚上 7 点举行的香槟酒会上。这两项活动都安排在州长俱乐部酒店举行。

作为她的基金会希望帮助解决的问题的一个例子，巴克小姐指出，韩国有50,000 名没有父亲的混血儿，而且每年都有 3,000 名这样的婴儿出生。这样的孩子面临着无望的未来。他们被亚洲人拒绝，也被他们的美国父亲抛弃。他们的母亲也被亚洲社会排斥。她们唯一的避难所是妓院。

巴克小姐指出，营救这些孩子并不是一项施舍计划。相反，她说该基金会的工作将是努力让孩子们被他们自己的社会所接纳。她说，军事政策加剧了这个问题。"美国军人一旦得知自己被调走，那个女孩则不得不自己搬家。"

巴克小姐说该基金会还在努力改变政策，使美国军人能够承担起他们对亚裔美国孩子的责任。她说，许多被调来的美国男性曾与她接触，他们希望得到帮助，以便回到他们的孩子身边，并与孩子的母亲结婚。

Associating herself with various humanitarian movements, Mrs. Buck is well-known for this dedication in Asia. With the entrance of Red China on the world scene as an atomic power, Americans must know more about the peoples of China.

Doubts Deadly Red China Blast

Fort Lauderdale, Fla. (AP)—Pearl S. Buck, Nobel and Pulitzer prize winning author, says she doesn't think Red China will use its nuclear potential to blow up the world.

"It isn't in their interest," she said.

Asked if she thought Red China and its leaders would be as responsible with a nuclear potential as are the Western nations, she said, "yes."

No nuclear agreement, she said, is worth anything unless Red China is included.

"As long as you have one member with nuclear power without control of international public opinion, then you are lost," she said.

Pearl S. Buck

左图：巴克夫人将自己与各种人道主义运动联系在一起，她在亚洲以这种奉献精神而闻名。随着红色中国作为核大国进入世界舞台，美国人必须更多地了解中国人民——《彭萨科拉新闻杂志》(The Pensacola News Journal，1964-11-14)

右图：世界和平——《堪萨斯城时报》(The Kansas City Times，1964-11-18)

赛珍珠抨击美国的对华政策：自己的 74 岁中有近 40 年在中国度过，"美国从未了解亚洲的总统" ——《比林斯公报》（The Billings Gazette，1964-12-02）

赛珍珠将在佛罗里达州州立大学做最新、最权威的亚洲时事分析 ——《彭萨科拉新闻杂志》（The Pensacola News Journal，1964-11-14）

《檀香山星报》（*Honolulu Star Bulletin*），1965 年 6 月 12 日

Among the national and honorary sponsors of the Women's International League for Peace and Freedom are singer Marian Anderson, authors Erich Fromm and Pearl S. Buck, Socialist leader Norman Thomas, Vijaya L. Pandit, Bertrand Russell and Albert Schweitzer.

....

"The Women's International League for Peace and Freedom believes that the continued escalation of the Vietnam war increases greatly the danger of a third world war. Since nuclear bombs will kill people of all political persuasions, all people, regardless of their political beliefs or personal histories, have an equal right and duty to speak up on behalf of reason

Critics of U.S. foreign policy to help pull the world away from disaster.

《檀香山星报》报影（1965-06-12）

作为一位杰出的社会工作者，亚当斯小姐是 1931 年诺贝尔和平奖的共同获得者①。国际妇女和平与自由联盟的国家和荣誉赞助商包括歌手玛丽安·安德森，作家埃里希·弗洛姆和赛珍珠，社会主义领袖诺曼托马斯、维贾亚·潘迪特、伯特兰·罗素和阿尔伯特·史怀哲。

联盟夏威夷分会主席玛丽恩·凯利夫人表示"致约翰逊总统的公开信"并不是当地联盟第一次发表抗议活动。凯利夫人说，发表这些越南信函所需资金是以信件方式向 450 人募集而来的，这些人都支持和平运动并反对约翰逊总统的行动。

她说，当地联盟只是赞助组织，但这封信的 62 位联署人不一定是成员。《星报》联系到的几乎所有联署者都表示，在名单公布之前，他们都不知道还会出现其他哪些名字。

然而，签署者确实申明他们同意这封信的内容，信中除了拒绝越南政策外，还敦促立即停火并召开所有有关国家的会议，以谈判来达成和平解决方案。

凯利夫人在给《星报》的一份声明中写道："国际妇女和平与自由联盟认为，越南战争的持续升级大大增加了第三次世界大战的风险。因为核弹会杀死各种政治信仰的人。所有人，无论他们的政治信仰或个人历史如何，都有平等的权利和义务代表理性发声，帮助世界摆脱灾难。"

（英文原文见附贰：70. Critics of U.S. Foreign Policy）

---

① 简·亚当斯于 1919 年创立了国际妇女和平与自由联盟，一直致力于争取妇女、黑人移居的权利，1931 年与巴特勒共同获得诺贝尔和平奖。1965 年，美国新闻界选出 10 位在世的杰出女性，其中有简·亚当斯、赛珍珠、罗斯福总统夫人、莫西奶奶。

How Communism Came to China
by Pearl S. Buck

(Editor's Note: Pearl S. Buck, Pulitzer and Nobel prize-winning author, is writing a 19-part series on the Far East exclusively for The Pensacola News-Journal and its affiliated All Florida News newspapers. Miss Buck is founder of the Pearl S. Buck Foundation, which seeks to aid unadopted children of American GIs left in Asia. Miss Buck lived in Asia for many years and is a recognized authority on that part of the world. (Second of a Series)

Let us remember first of all that communism cannot assume power in a country where the economy is stable and the government is not corrupt. The two go together. When the economy is unstable any government becomes corrupt. Officials protect themselves by corruption. In China the instability of the government and the economy began about a hundred years ago, when the Manchu Dynasty was entering its last phase.

Chinese history can be divided into 24 dynasties. Of these, two were not Chinese. The Mongols seized power at one period, and the Manchus at another. I was born and taken to China at the end of the Manchu Dynasty, when the last ruler was the great Empress Tzu Hsi, one of the most spectacular figures of human history. I have told her story in my novel, "Imperial Woman."

It was in her lifetime that the downfall of the Manchu Dynasty took place, and in the traditional Chinese manner. As a ruling house became weak through a succession of declining figures, it was usual in China that among the people strong young men arose to contend with each other for the throne, a process curiously democratic, for these young men usually came from humble beginnings. Gathering their personal armies of young men like themselves, discontents and rascals most of them, these rebellions men fought each other until one was the victor. Then by

common consent he took the throne and founded a new dynasty. It might not have proved as successful government, had it not been for the strong civil service organization which continued to govern during the period of change.

This ancient Chinese civil service deserves some attention now, for it too was democratic in its origins. The Imperial Examinations, upon which, incidentally, the British Civil Service was later based and then ours, based upon the British, was an astute and effective way of discovering the best brains in the country and thus giving them the administration of the government. The examinations covered the whole field of Chinese culture and included history, philosophy, poetry and mathematics. Only the best brains could pass, although anyone could try. In a village, for example, there might be a bright boy in a poor family. He would be discovered young, for the people were always looking for someone to bring them honor, and the whole

village would contribute funds for his education. However lowly his family, he could go up for examinations, and if he passed, he would be given a government post, his rank depending upon his achievement. In this way government continued, whatever the change on the throne.

China was proceeding in this traditional fashion toward the end of the last century. It was obvious that the Tsing Dynasty was ending with the old Empress Dowager. In the normal course of events, various young contenders would have appeared to offer themselves as candidates for the next dynasty. An new force had appeared in the nation, however, an unexpected disturbance. The force was Christianity. The Christian missionaries had in the course of the last 30 or 50 years come into China and there had started a new kind of school. These schools taught Western subjects instead of the old Chinese subjects. This meant that the graduates of

(CONTINUED ON PAGE 8A)

赛珍珠认为，如果中国（指国民党统治时期的中国）经济稳定，政府不腐败，共产党不会谋求夺取政权——《彭萨科拉新闻杂志》（*Pensacola News Journal*，1964-10-26）

追逐流逝的光芒

所有的图像都印在脑子里

《新闻和太阳公报》（*Press and Sun Bulletin*），1964 年 5 月 18 日

A First Lady Has Her Say

—PRESS PHOTO BY JOHN SOLAS.

Pearl Buck Ranges Over Wide Spectrum of Subjects in Interview.

《新闻和太阳公报》报影（1964-05-18）

公民权利、黑人问题、亚美混血儿、女性思想……所有的议题都不断出现在赛珍珠的头脑中。在 1964 年 5 月 18 日的《新闻和太阳公报》的报道里，赛珍珠在接受记者们采访时，对于广泛的议题侃侃而谈。在记者心目中，赛珍珠对于过往的事情，都印在脑子里，从来不记笔记。她认为，中国与其他旧殖民国家形成了鲜明对比。"虽然中国下定决心从西方学到很多东西，如语言、教育和治国之道，但是他们从来没有像现在这样向外展示自己是世界上最大的国家。"赛珍珠认为所有美国人可能都需要花时间来认真地审视自己。

实时观察：赛珍珠庆祝她的75岁生日

《圣约瑟夫新闻公报》（*St Joseph News Press Gazette*），1967 年 6 月 22 日

Timely Observations

PEARL BUCK observes he
75th birthday anniversar
Monday. Mention the name o
Pearl Buck and the averag
American immediately thinks o
The Good Earth and Paul Muni
The association is not entirel
fortunate. A woman who ha
given away more than $7 mil
lion to square the America
conscience deserves to be know
for more than a movie tha
some sophisticates like to down
grade.

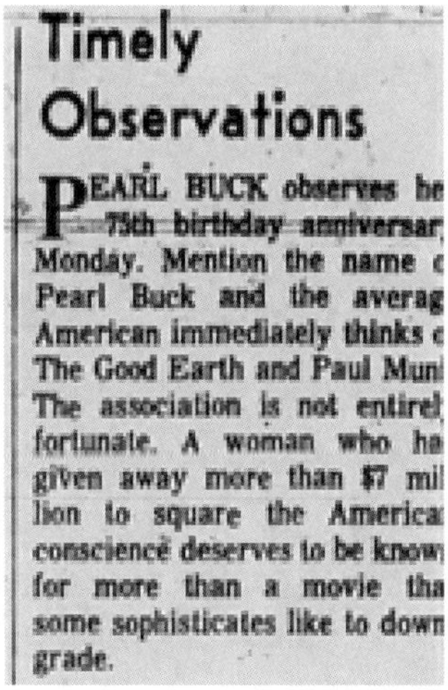

《圣约瑟夫新闻公报》报影（1967-06-22）

提到赛珍珠的名字，普通美国人会立即想到《大地》和保罗·穆尼（Paul Muni）。很遗憾会造成这样的联想。一位捐出七百多万美元来挽回美国人良知的女性，不应该仅仅因为一部时常被那些居心不良的人所贬低的电影而为人所知。

在她的自传《我的多重世界》中，赛珍珠写到，由于她早期的教育——早上跟她的美国母亲上课，下午跟中国家庭教师上课，她变得“精神上是双焦点的”①。

据报道，她在说英语之前先会说汉语。直到九岁时，她的家人被迫在义和团起义中逃亡，她才突然意识到自己是在中国的外国人。当和平恢复时，他们回到了在镇江的家。

珀尔·康福特·西登斯特里克（赛珍珠）于 1892 年 6 月 26 日出生在西弗吉尼亚州的希尔斯伯勒。她的父母曾是中国长老会的传教士，她在五个月大的时候，就随父母回到了中国。

传教士的传统也许是了解赛珍珠一生的关键核心。她最出名的是《大地》及其三部曲的其他两卷——《儿子》和《分

① 以两种视觉和思维方式看待事物。赛珍珠也说过，她先用汉语思考，再用英语交流。

家》。但她在 1938 年获得诺贝尔文学奖主要是因为她为父母写的传记《异邦客》和《战斗的天使》。评论家安德斯·奥斯特林（Anders Osterling）写道："评委会评判的主要因素首先是关于她父母那些令人钦佩的传记。这两卷似乎达到了经典级别，并且值得深入解读和反复欣赏。"关于小说，诺贝尔委员会在其引文中指出，它们因"对中国农民生活的丰富而真实的史诗描绘"而出类拔萃。

赛珍珠于 5 月 21 日——在她准备启程前往亚洲旅行时宣布，将把她的财产和超过七百万美元的大部分收入，用于她自己的特殊福利项目，该项目为生活在亚洲国家的美国混血儿童提供帮助。她已经签署了协议，将价值约六百万美元的电视和电影版税、她位于宾夕法尼亚州巴克斯县郊区的农场、她在佛蒙特州的财产，以及未来的所有图书版税捐至赛珍珠基金会。她的解释很简单。"我当时在亚洲拍电影，"她说，"我看到了美国军人和亚洲母亲的孩子。我真的很惭愧。"军营的追随者和士兵的故事是传奇。荷马写道："士兵离不开性欲。"赛珍珠基金会在某种程度上是她自己生命的延伸。她有 10 个孩子，其中 9 个是收养的美亚混血儿。

巴克夫人能够以理解和爱，清晰地看待两种文化。她于 1933 年出版了中国经典小说《水浒传》的英译本，题为《四海之内皆兄弟》。标题为庆祝她的生日提供了恰当的文案。

（英文原文见附贰：71. Timely Observations）

爱荷华州德雷克大学将举办中国周，赛珍珠将给学生推荐七位红色中国问题专家——《得梅因登记册报》（*The Des Moines Register*，1967–11–05）

1971 年 9 月 7 日的《沃思堡星电报》（*Fort Worth Star Telegram*）披露了一份涉及 12 万人的基于政治观点或倾向而被认为涉嫌有颠覆性危险的个人和组织名单的秘密报告。显然，赛珍珠由于自己对中国的态度和对美国政府对华政策的抨击而被列入这份名单，该名单里还有钱学森。

125,000 'Risks' to U.S. Listed in Secret File

By RICHARD HALLORAN
© 1971, New York Times News Service
WASHINGTON — A secret collection of reports on 125,000 allegedly subversive persons and organizations, the product of an extensive but unofficial intelligence operation that ranged across the nation

is Rep. Emanuel Celler, D.-N.Y., the chairman of the House Judiciary Committee. He was listed as a "Jew playing the Reds."

A staff aide here said the Brooklyn congressman was probably unaware that his name was in the Van Deman

be heavily infiltrated by Communists.

But by the late 1010s, the general's interest shifted to the civil rights movement. He was said to have thought the racial unrest in the nation was largely fomented by the Communist party.

125,000 名对美国的危险分子入列秘密文件——《沃思堡星电报》报影（1971-09-07）

据《沃思堡星电报》报道，这份秘密报告来源于一场非官方的情报行动，该项行动覆盖了全美，不仅范围广泛，而且持续时间长达 23 年，现被封存在参议院内部安全小组委员会。回看赛珍珠在那个年代与中外朋友交往的报道，也就不难推测她入列秘密名单的背后原因了。

《佩塔卢马阿格斯信使》（*Petaluma Argus Courier*）1949 年 6 月 8 日发布美联社报道，萨克拉门托州参议院美国境内活动委员会将数百人列为"斯大林主义圈子内的典型人物"，其中有几位是知名人士。该委员会 1949 年的报告无一例外地称，这些人"在很长一段时间内明显地遵循或姑息了一些共产党的路线纲领"。

Many Prominent Citizens In State Are Listed

SACRAMENTO, June 8. (AP)—The state senate committee on un-American activities today listed several hundred persons, several of them prominent, as "typical of the individuals within the various Stalinist orbits."

赛珍珠和安娜·路易斯·斯特朗被列在斯大林派名单内——《佩塔卢马阿格斯信使》（1949-06-08）

《奥克兰论坛报》（*Oakland Tribune*）转发 1945 年 12 月 8 日美联社发自重庆的报道，埃德加·斯诺的入华申请仍被搁置。此前，国民政府已经禁止了达雷尔·贝里根和哈罗德·R. 伊罗生的签证。

即使进入了 20 世纪 80 年代，西方媒体仍普遍患有涉新中国话题的"综合征"。新闻和影视的传媒机构只允许报道"可以接受的"话题。

左图：国民政府禁止左翼记者入华——《奥克兰论坛报》（*Oakland Tribune*，1945-12-08）
右图：新中国话题"综合征"——《孟菲斯报》（*The Memphis Press Scimitar*，1980-05-23）

赛珍珠与埃德加·斯诺是好朋友。斯诺曾经指出了赛珍珠小说《爱国者》中关于八路军"虐待俘虏"的错误。

赛珍珠与哈罗德·伊罗生长期交往共事。伊罗生从 1948 年起，经常与赛珍珠共同主持有关亚洲的讲座。1972 年，伊罗生在其文章中写道，随着尼克松总统即将访华，赛珍珠关于中国的评述在《纽约时报》重新出现。可见伊罗生与晚年的赛珍珠关系仍然密切。

赛珍珠与哈罗德·R. 伊罗生（Harold R. Isaacs）共同就亚洲局势发表广播演讲——《记录报》（*The Record*，1948-10-22）

关于赛珍珠与哈罗德·R. 伊罗生的报道——《合和新闻》（*The Hopewell News*，1950-08-04）

"East-West" Lecture Series---Each Wednesday Night---Roosevelt High School

A "post-graduate course in public affairs"—an integral part of the Hobby Night Program at Roosevelt. A three dollar fee covers the cost of the series. Single admissions are one dollar. 5 Consecutive Wednesdays at 8:30.

PEARL BUCK "The Rising Peoples" ROOSEVELT HIGH OCTOBER 29TH — Author of "The Good Earth," "Dragon Seed" and many other best sellers. Pulitzer Prize and the Nobel Prize winner.

P. E. DUSTOOR "India Takes the Lead in Asia" ROOSEVELT HIGH NOVEMBER 5TH — Dr. Dustoor is on the staff of the University of Allahabad in India, and a leading authority on Indian situation.

H. TAVARES DE SA "Whither Latin America" ROOSEVELT HIGH NOVEMBER 12TH — Dr. Tavares is a brilliant and eloquent Brazilian educator and author. His latest book is "The Brazilians."

HAROLD ISAACS "No Peace in Asia" ROOSEVELT HIGH NOVEMBER 19TH — News-Week Asian correspondent. Author of "The Tragedy of the Chinese Revolution" and "No Peace in Asia."

W. E. B. DU BOIS "Color and Democracy: A World Challenge" ROOSEVELT HIGH NOVEMBER 26TH — Authority on prejudice and race. Well known author, latest book "The World and Africa."

"东西方"系列演讲报道中的赛珍珠（左一）、伊罗生（右二）——《得梅因登记册报》（*The Des Moines Register*，1947-10-26）

JUST THE OPENING

So this is how the column of mirrors turns. A few days after Mr. Nixon announced his trip to Peking, almost as though on cue, Pearl Buck—a major source of a whole generation's favorable view of the Chinese—reappeared, in the pages of the New York Times, to tell us again how wonderful it was to be good friends with the wonderful Chinese. In theory, at least, all the way back to the warmly marvelling admiration of Marco Polo.

哈罗德·R. 伊罗生撰文认为赛珍珠的中国论述重新出现在《纽约时报》"只是个开始"——《波士顿环球报》（*The Boston Globe*，1972-02-16）

《科罗拉多斯普林斯电讯报》（*Colorado Springs Gazette Telegraph*），1972 年 11 月 2 日

《科罗拉多斯普林斯电讯报》报影（1972-11-02）

　　这些天，我一直在等待——等待那封信。在等待的过程中，我一直在回忆比自己的国家更了解的中国，更了解的人民。是的，因为我们是外国人，是白人，我和我的家人被这些人赶出了那个国家②。然而我了解中国人，了解他们的历史，即使在我被迫离开的时候，我也理解他们害怕成为西方帝国的一部分。他们遭受了不公正的对待。

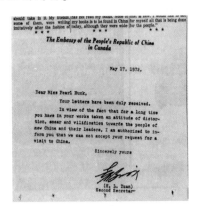

　　中国驻加拿大大使馆在拒绝赛珍珠访华申请的回函中写道：鉴于您长期以来在作品中对新中国人民及其领导人采取歪曲、抹黑、诽谤的态度，我经授权通知您，我们不能接受您访问中国的要求。——《科罗拉多斯普林斯电讯报》（1972-11-02）

---

　　①　此文是由《科罗拉多斯普林斯电讯报》转摘的赛珍珠《中国：过去与现在》的部分内容，本书进行了节译。

　　②　赛珍珠在回忆少年时期。

......

当然，我的整个生命和人格都不可避免地受到我在中国的童年和青年时期的影响。我的父母几乎只在中国人中交朋友。我的父亲是一个不屈不挠、有点正统的人。他在中国学者和知识分子中找到了朋友。我母亲的私人朋友也大致相同，但她很热情，对农民的妻子或饥荒难民的同情就像她对富裕家庭的女士们一样。所有人都属于中国人，因为我们生活在华人社区，所以都是中国人。尽管如此，我们是知识分子，我们最亲密的朋友是中国知识分子，因此也是精英。这有助于我理解当下中国革命中知识精英的困境。

大学毕业后，我回到中国，准备在那里度过一生。我又回到了中国年轻知识分子中的老朋友那里。我们讨论了天下的一切，但主要是讨论新文学，以及我们作为作家和创作者而能够或应该在其中扮演的角色。我的一些朋友在模仿西方作家的风格写作。我认为在我们身边的中国农民中，有一个全新的精彩生活素材领域。我发现我的建议很不受欢迎。他们反驳道，谁会对中国农民感兴趣呢？"我会！"我回答道。于是，我开始了自己的写作，从《大地》开始，写了一系列小说。

......

我承认，当我在 1943 年收到周恩来的一封信，一封简短的信，他邀请我回中国看看八路军在做什么，我很动心。我还保存着那封信。我最近在给已身为中华人民共和国总理的周恩来写信时，提到了那封信。说现在，自从我们的总统访问中国后，我想亲眼看看"新"中国，以便我可以用我尚未写成的书，作为我们两国人民友谊的新源泉。

这篇 1972 年 11 月 2 日《科罗拉多斯普林斯电讯报》的报纸内容转摘自纽约约翰·戴公司 1972 年出版的赛珍珠《中国：过去与现在》一书，是书中一系列文章中的最后一篇。该书出版后还被《林肯杂志之星》（*Lincoln Journal Star*）连续刊载。

《林肯杂志之星》（1972 - 11 - 11）刊登的《中国:过去与现在》书讯

Who in China Will Receive the Next 'Mandate From Heaven?'

First of Four
By PEARL S. BUCK
(c) 1972 Creativity, Inc.

The Great China Wall was built by forced labor.

谁是中国下一个受天命者？（《中国：过去与现在》之一）——《林肯杂志之星》
（1972-11-14）

'No Important Result From Nixon's Visit, But No Harm Either'

Second of Four
By PEARL S. BUCK

尼克松访华既没有重要结果，也没有坏处（《中国：过去与现在》之二）——《林肯杂志之星》（1972-11-15）

8 Lincoln, Neb. Journal, Thursday, Nov. 16, 1972

Premature Decline of West Left It Without Leaders To Help a Struggling Asia

Third of Four
By PEARL S. BUCK
(c) 1972 Creativity, Inc.

西方的过早衰落使其没有领袖帮助挣扎的亚洲（《中国：过去与现在》之三）——《林肯杂志之星》（1972-11-16）

China Letter Makes Pearl Buck Afraid for People of World

Last of Four
By PEARL S. BUCK
(c) 1972 Creativity, Inc.

《中国：过去与现在》之四——《林肯杂志之星》（1972-11-17）

由于不愿意加入尼克松总统的访华团，赛珍珠向中国驻加拿大大使馆递交了赴华申请。有一段日子，她每天都在焦虑中等待着回复。在等待回函期间，她还去了纽约霍尔马克画廊参观表现现代中国成就的摄影展览。

赛珍珠参观新中国摄影展——《迈阿密先驱报》（*The Miami Herald*，1973-03-07）

　　《中国：过去与现在》是赛珍珠非小说类作品中的最后一部，堪称封笔之作。从上述报纸转摘的部分内容中我们大致可以感觉到那段时间里她的心路历程，她提到了自己保留着 1943 年收到的周恩来邀请她访问八路军的一封简短的信，赛珍珠希望能重返中国以亲眼看看新中国并为两国人民的友谊谱写新作品，她还说到为此给周恩来总理写了信。赛珍珠还细述了自己穿着中式锦缎旗袍拜访中国驻联合国代表团时与工作人员对话的情景。也许是书中表达的特别期待的原因，赛珍珠赴华申请的被拒使其十分伤感。

《北山新闻记录报》（*North Hills News Record*），1972 年 2 月 23 日

《北山新闻记录报》报影（1972-02-23）

[特别撰稿人格里·K. 史密斯]

赛珍珠认为中国处于优势地位。

我认为赛珍珠是唯一有资格发表评论的人。这位获得诺贝尔奖的小说家在中国长大，并在那里生活了 40 年，然后又回到美国生活了 40 年。因此，她吸收了东方和西方两种文化的结晶。

在联合国投票恢复红色中国席位之后，我有幸在费城对巴克小姐进行了两个小时的私人采访。

从麦迪逊大街到主大街，中国的影响已经席卷全国。有关于针灸、歌舞伎袖和大陆项圈的讨论，家庭主妇们交流的新食谱（以及香港流感的补救措施！）等等①。曼哈顿精品店里卖的上海的筷子，远东的旅行社预订爆满（当总统去中国时，旅行者们会远远地跟在后面吗？）。

当我们一起坐在她私人书房里的壁炉前的时候，我问过巴克小姐："你如何看待总统去中国？"她慢慢地回答："这个主意很英明，但应该换个方式来处理。"

"我们要求去中国，这一点让我们处于劣势。我想知道尼克松先生是否知道这一点。但是，"她承认，"我的第一反应总是像亚洲人。当停下来从我的美国方面来考虑时，我知道他的意

---

① 原文：There was talk of acupuncture, of Kabuki sleeves and Mandarin collars. Housewives were trading new recipes for chop suey（and remedies for Hong Kong flu！）.

愿是好的。我们是一个年轻的国家，我们没有耐心。当我们期待某些东西时，我们现在就想要实现，而中国人知道如何等待。另一种见解是，制定总统前往中国的计划者，正是周恩来本人。"

Nixon's China Trip Risky, Says Miss Buck

赛珍珠乐见尼克松总统访华，但是她担心如果这是他个人意愿的话，会有政治风险——《后新月报》（*The Post Crescent*，1972-01-16）

China Still A Source Of Her Wisdom

Any Face You See Could Be Howard Hughes

中国仍然是赛珍珠的智慧源泉——《阿克伦灯塔杂志》（*The Akron Beacon Journal*，1972-01-16）

Pearl Buck at 80 Active, Looks Ahead

New Test May Head Off Stroke

80 岁高龄的赛珍珠仍然十分活跃，写作和基金会的工作排满了日程。她曾回顾 1927 年的经历，认为没有什么是放不下的，所有的经历都有意义，一切要向前看——《政治家杂志》（*Statesman Journal*，1972-01-25）

"Understanding" Is Nixon's Aim

David Lawrence

WASHINGTON — President Nixon has many things to talk about with Premier Chou En-lai, but the world will never get a detailed account of their conferences. The reports and communiques will probably cover only the merest generalities, which will reflect steps toward friendship if it is a successful mission or a continuance of the stalemate if the Peking regime is adamant in its present position.

For what the President is trying to achieve is an "understanding." This means a recognition of the problems of the government of Mainland China, the threats that confront it in the steady buildup of friction with the Soviet Union which could lead to war.

Apparently the biggest fear Peking has is that some day it will find itself not only faced by Soviet divisions across its borders but more and more encircled by countries under Moscow's influence, a group of the enemy allies.

The future of Taiwan is important, but it is by no means as pressing now as the changes going on in Asia which could compel Peking to spend more of its funds on armament and particularly on nuclear weapons.

Nixon emerges in a sense as a mediator. A detente between the 725 million people of Mainland China and the American people would be of great help to the Peking regime. In fact, there is every reason why Premier Chou En-lai should find a way to settle some of the questions that have brought disputes with the United States so as to pave the way for the attainment of the really far-reaching objective — restoring the friendly relations that used to exist between America and China.

As he left Washington, the President made it clear that he does not expect to deal with particular issues so much as he wants to provide evidences of friendship which would tell the world the governments of the United States and China are going to work together.

The President declared that he is under no illusions that 20 years of hostility between the Peking regime and the United States government "are going to be swept away by one week of talks." What he is undoubtedly seeking is a mutual willingness to cooperate amicably in dealing with the many problems that have arisen in Asia, some of which threaten larger wars.

Basically, Nixon does not go merely as a negotiator to take up specific subjects but as the representative of a country which wishes to show its good will to another nation and get the assurance that in the future the two governments will proceed with mutual trust and faith to try to maintain peace in Asia and thus help to preserve peace in the world.

Naturally economic questions will come up in the discussions, and there will be conversations about trade opportunities that China may obtain which have not been available before. This is of tremendous importance to Peking.

Developing ways for a country to become more productive and earn more money to improve the living standards of its people is one of the biggest political factors in the life of any government. The United States can be of assistance in such matters and has already opened some trade doors which have been closed in recent years.

If, as a consequence of the President's trip, trade relationships with Communist China become helpful to economic development there, this could have an effect on the attitudes of other nations, too. It could produce a more favorable feeling generally toward Peking.

(Publishers-Hall Syndicate)

Pearl S. Buck
American Writer, Nobel Prize, 1938
"The weakest people are often the most rebellious, finding in universal discontent their excuse for no positive and resolute agreement with anything."

增进理解是尼克松的目标——《钯金项目报》（*Palladium Item*，1972-02-25）

We Are Children

There surely is no better qualified person to comment on environmental abuse than the author of "The Good Earth", Pearl S. Buck. In the course of an interview with the editors of National Wildlife magazine, she commented rather caustically on the ill-mannered habits of Americans. She said, "We behave like careless children. We spoil the beauty of our superbly beautiful country by throwing trash wherever it suits us. I have traveled the roads and streets of many so-called 'underdeveloped' countries, and nowhere else have I seen the litter and trash that selfish, careless Americans throw out of their cars...."

However, Miss Buck is far from a pessimist with regard to the future. She believes our nation has done wonders, "But we are children.... We are scarcely two hundred years old. In China I lived in a city six thousand years old....in time we will grow old enough to be men and women, and to cherish our country enough to preserve its beauty." Miss Buck has expressed in words what many felt. The U. S. is suffering the growing pains of an adolescent. With any luck it should grow to sensible adulthood.

赛珍珠：我们的行为像个毫无顾忌的孩子。美国历史还不到 200 年，而在中国，我生活的城市有 6000 多年历史——《曼斯菲尔德广告商报》（*Mansfield Advertiser*，1972-03-02）

沟通东西方文化的桥梁——《迈阿密先驱报》（*The Miami Herald*，1973-03-07）

赛珍珠 1959 年 5 月在《智慧》（*Wisdom*）杂志上发表长篇文章《智慧来自于……》

赛珍珠在其自传《我的多重世界》中说："大学毕业后，我回到中国，准备在那里度过一生。我又回到了中国年轻知识分子中的老朋友那里。"在书中，出现了鲁迅、郭沫若、丁玲和冰心的名字。

The sickening romanticism purified itself gradually, however, and the strongest minds began to return to their own people. Chou Shu-jen, or "Lu Hsün," as he called himself, was perhaps the first to perceive that although his inspiration might come through Western literature, yet he could escape imitativeness only if he applied his newly found emotions to his own people. Thus he began to write sketches and stories and finally novels about the simple everyday people. Kuo Mo-jou became my own favorite and in spite of a cynicism that was sometimes only destructive. I think of that brilliant mind, whose habit was the utmost candor and whose passion was truth, and I wonder how he can live as he does nowadays under the Communist government in his country. Is he silenced, I wonder, or has he succumbed, as others have, to writing the extravaganzas of convulsive and surely compelled adoration of the new Magi? And I can scarcely believe that Ting Ling and Ping Hsin are changed, those two intrepid and fearless women writers, who used to make me so proud. But who can tell me? It is another world and one that I do not know. It is useless now to put down the names of all the brave young Chinese men and women who led the awakening minds of their compatriots, and who are either dead or in a living death, cut off from our knowledge by the present

赛珍珠自传《我的多重世界》，1956 年 Cardinal Gaint 版第 204 页

　　赛珍珠与宋庆龄关系密切，伊罗生 1933 年拜访宋庆龄时，除了有史沫特莱、萧伯纳参加外，还有中国新文化人蔡元培、鲁迅和林语堂陪同。

The lunch party at Soong Ching-ling's, Shanghai, 1933, before and after doctoring

　　左起：艾格尼丝·史沫特莱、萧伯纳、宋庆龄、哈罗德·R. 伊罗生、蔡元培、林语堂、鲁迅［选自哈罗德·R. 伊罗生《在中国——故交重逢》(Re-Encounters in China) 第 127 页］。萧伯纳 (George Bernard Shaw, 1856—1950)，于 1925 年获得诺贝尔文学奖。

图前排左起：周建人、许广平、鲁迅；后排左起：孙福熙、林语堂、孙伏园
（选自陈子善《关于孙伏园的〈鲁迅先生的小说〉》）

1924 年 4 月 12 日，1913 年诺贝尔文学奖获得者罗宾德拉纳特·泰戈尔（Rabindranath Tagore）应蔡元培邀请抵上海，在中国访问了50 天。泰戈尔在北京期间，受到梁启超、蔡元培、胡适、蒋梦麟、梁漱溟等人的热烈欢迎，雅各布斯为他画像。泰戈尔在南京讲学时，赛珍珠去听课。1944 年泰戈尔和赛珍珠为格特鲁德·爱默生·森（Gertrude Emerson Sen）的新版《沉默的印度》（*Voiceless India*）做介绍。蔡元培这次对泰戈尔的邀请，给予赛珍珠第一次接触诺贝尔奖获得者而开阔眼界的机会。

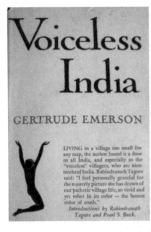

左图：1944 年泰戈尔、赛珍珠审阅并推介的《沉默的印度》
右图：罗宾德拉纳特·泰戈尔（雅各布斯绘）

1924 年，泰戈尔（右三）在北京与林徽因（右二）、徐志摩（右一）等人合影
（清华大学校史馆网站）

　　关于赛珍珠与中国美术界关联的报道比较少。1943 年 12 月至 1944 年 8 月，有几条关于赛珍珠介绍在美国访问的中国美术家张书旂（1900—1957，《艺风》杂志发起人之一）的报道。赛珍珠主持的东西方协会邀请张书旂做讲座。《艺风》杂志曾经在 1935 年第 11 期设立张书旂花鸟画专题。《艺风》杂志由蔡元培和鲁迅的学生孙福熙（1898—1962）主编。孙福熙长期跟随鲁迅，经蔡元培推荐成为民国最早的一批赴欧洲学习美术的学生之一。他回国后于 1933 年创办《艺风》杂志。

孙福熙为蔡元培绘的油画像

1945 年 11 月，约翰·戴出版公司出版了赛珍珠作序并注释的《中国版画集》（*China in Black and White*），其中选编了 30 多位艺术家的 82 幅作品。这本书的背景是 1939 年 4 月 6 日，中国全国木刻协会主办的"第三届全国抗战木刻展览会"在重庆举行。1939 年 7 月 1 日，鲁艺木刻工作团主编的《敌后方木刻》作为《新华日报》华北版的副刊，同年 11 月，浙江战时木刻研究社成立，孙福熙任社长。

　　从以上两条消息可以推测，赛珍珠与孙福熙之间至少有共同的朋友。

"赛珍珠为东西方协会贡献力量"报道了中国美术家张书旂——《里士满时报快讯》（*Richmond Times Dispatch*，1944-01-30）

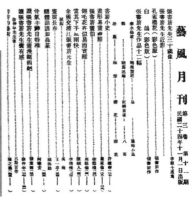

左图：《萨克拉门托蜜蜂报》（*The Sacramento Bee*，1944-08-24）对张书旂的报道
右图：孙福熙主编《艺风》杂志中设立了张书旂花鸟画专集（1935 年第 11 期）

The factual book is "China in Black and White," an album of Chinese woodcuts by contemporary Chinese artists, with a foreword and commentary by Pearl S. Buck. It is published by Asia Press. Many of the woodcuts are beautiful; all are interesting. The artists have provided a swiftly-moving story of wartime China.

China's Early Day Artist Was Best

CHINA IN BLACK AND WHITE. An album of Chinese woodcuts by contemporary Chinese artists, with a commentary by Pearl Buck. John Day Co. $3.

左图，蒙出版公司出版赛珍珠作序并注释的《中国版画集》。The Gazette Jul 3, 1948。
右图，赛珍珠评《中国版画集》：中国早期画家最优秀。The Daily Oklahoman. Jul 28, 1946。

赛珍珠评《中国版画集》：中国早期画家最优秀——《芝加哥论坛报》（*Chicago Tribune*，1945-12-02）

THE GAZETTE, MONTREAL, SATURDAY, JULY 3, 1948.

ARMY TRANSPORT, by Li Hwa, a typical example of the fine achievement in "China In Black and White" (John Day; 95 pages), a fascinating album of wartime woodcuts by contemporary Chinese artists, with a foreword by Pearl S. Buck. A visual commentary on China at war more moving and far more convincing than oceans of oratory or text.

《中国版画集》之"抗日队伍在行军"——《加拿大公报》（*The Gazette*，1948-07-03）

回看赛珍珠的一生，中国文化和中国思想已经融入她的内心世界。在《曼西晚报》（*Muncie Evening Press*）1973年3月10日的那篇《最后一次采访》里，赛珍珠坐在椅子上喃喃地说，佛蒙特州的这个村庄让她想起中国的靠近她"长大并且生活了40年"的地方。不仅在赛珍珠基金会的总部悬挂着"孔子行教像"，赛珍珠在自传《我的多重世界》中，也多次提及孔子和儒家思想。

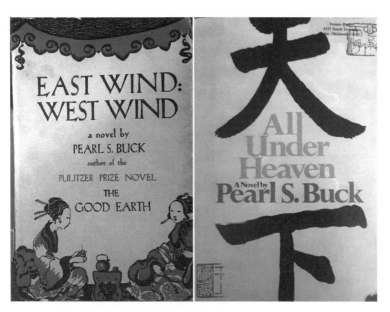

赛珍珠 1930 年发表《东风·西风》，1973 年 3 月发表《天下》

Pearl Buck, pictured in the Philadelphia headquarters of the Pearl S. Buck Foundation, is following recent developments in China with close interest—and with more insight than most. The authoress and Nobel Prize winner has split her lifetime almost equally between China and the United States, and that makes her a rarity among American writers. She's one of the few able to flavor current observations about China with a wealth of personal experience.

赛珍珠坐在"孔子行教像"前——《巴特尔克里克询问者报》（*Battle Creek Enquirer*，1972-01-16）

致力于东西方世界的文明交流是赛珍珠毕生践行的事业。如今哲人赛珍珠回归大地，留给天下的是永恒的精神，是永不消失的光芒。正可谓"大地分东西，天下为一"。

附壹

雅各布斯

本书将"追逐流逝的光芒"作为书名，旨在缅怀沟通东西方文明的"文化人桥"赛珍珠，探究历史过往中的"人桥"精神，承继新时代沟通中西方文明的"人桥"使命。我进入到赛珍珠研究这一领域，不能不提到美国的著名肖像画家利奥尼贝尔·优曼·雅各布斯（Leonebel Uhlman Jacobs），正是赛珍珠写给雅各布斯的一封信引起我的关注并指引我开启了对"流逝的光芒"的追逐。

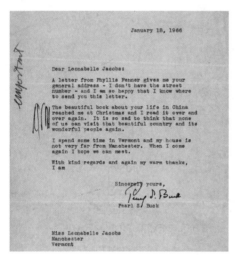

亲爱的利奥尼贝尔·雅各布斯①：

菲利斯·芬纳的一封信给了我您的大致地址——我没有您的街道门牌号码——我很高兴知道了这封信将如何寄给您。

圣诞节时我收到了您这本关于中国生活的美丽的书②，我一遍一遍地拜读。每当想到，我们都不再有机会去探望那个美丽的国家和那里优秀的人民，真的是令人痛心。

我在佛蒙特州待了一段时间，我的家离曼彻斯特不远。当我再来的时候，希望我们能见面。

谨致问候并再次表示热烈的感谢。

真挚的赛珍珠

一九六六年一月十八日

赛珍珠致雅各布斯的信（图片来源：俄勒冈大学图书馆馆藏雅各布斯档案）

认识雅各布斯

利奥尼贝尔·优曼·雅各布斯（1884 年 12 月 15 日—1967 年 4 月 15 日），美国著名油画和水彩肖像画家。她出生于华盛顿州塔科马市（Tacoma），出生时姓名为利奥尼贝尔·优曼，其生父优曼先生早逝。1900 年，利奥尼贝尔跟随母亲迁居到俄勒冈州尤金市（Eugene），住在位于威拉米特街 1200 号（1200 Willamette Street）的继父凯斯（Kays）家，并改名为利奥尼贝尔·凯斯。她在少年时期就显露出了艺术天分。利奥尼贝尔在俄勒冈州立大学（University of Oregon）学习两年，然后就读于加利福尼亚州旧金山霍普金斯艺术学院（Hopkins Art Institute in San Francisco）。1908 年结婚后她改名为利奥尼贝尔·雅各布斯。结婚后的利奥尼贝尔·雅各布斯（以下使用她婚后姓氏雅

① 利奥尼贝尔·雅各布斯的英文名字是 Leonebel Jacobs。赛珍珠将其误拼成 Leonabelle Jacobs。
② 即雅各布斯八十寿辰时出版的自传《我的中国》（*My China*）。2020 年，笔者向美国宾夕法尼亚州赛珍珠国际询问该书的情况，那里没有这本书的相关记录。赛珍珠手中的这本《我的中国》可能在丹比遗失了。

各布斯）就读于宾夕法尼亚美术学院（Pennsylvania Academy of Fine Art），师从乔治·德·福雷斯特·布勒斯（George de Forrest Brush）。她积极参与反法西斯战争的活动和慈善事业。从 1917 年开始，她的名字出现在公众面前。1918 年，雅各布斯为美国参加第一次世界大战创作了几幅宣传海报："现在打赢下一场战争"（Win the Next War Now）、"胜利果实"（The Fruits of Victory）、"美利坚女性为胜利而劳动"（Women of America Work for Victory）、"你为胜利制作罐头了吗？"（Are You a Victory Canner?）、"一定要回来"（Home Again）等。她的作品陆续被一些著名女性报刊及其他刊物选为封面图片。

雅各布斯为美国参加第一次世界大战创作的宣传海报（1918 年，左一由火星云美术馆收藏）

雅各布斯创作的期刊封面画：左图为 1919 年 2 月《人民之家》（The People's Home Journal），右图为 1919 年 3 月《妇女杂志》（The Woman's Magazine）

1919 年 1 月"巴黎和会"在巴黎凡尔赛宫召开,雅各布斯在那里为世界政要们画像。选用雅各布斯作品作为封面的杂志包括《人民之家》(*The People's Home Journal*)、《妇女杂志》(*The Woman's Magazine*)、《轮廓标》(*The Delineator*)、《设计者》(*The Designer*)、《读者文摘》(*The Literary Digest*)、《穆伦伯格周刊》(*Muhlenberg Weekly*)、《现代普里西拉》(*Modern Priscilla*)、《圣尼古拉斯杂志》(*St Nicholas Magazine*,儿童杂志)、《先驱论坛杂志》(*Herald Tribune Magazine*)、《太平洋月刊》(*Pacific Monthly*,时政杂志)等,可见她的作品受欢迎、被认可程度之高。

1922 年,《轮廓标》杂志社派遣她到首都华盛顿为名人画像,那里正在召开由美国总统哈丁(Warren G. Harding)召集的"华盛顿武器控制会议"(The Washington Arms Conference,也称裁军会议,The Washington Disarmament Conference)。在华盛顿,雅各布斯还结识了北洋政府驻美国大使顾维钧(Wellington Koo)夫妇。雅各布斯为顾维钧夫人画的肖像征服了大使夫妇。顾大使建议她去北京,并给予她签证。

1922 年雅各布斯为参加"华盛顿武器控制会议"的名人绘像的轰动消息——《俄勒冈每日卫报》(*The Eugene Daily Guard*,1922-04-22,左图)和《纽约先驱报》(*New York Herald*,1922-05-28,右图)

雅各布斯先后共为三位美国总统画像,他们是小约翰·卡尔文·柯立芝(John Calvin Coolidge,Jr)、赫伯特·克拉克·胡佛(Herbert Clark Hoover)和沃伦·盖玛利尔·哈丁(Warren Gamaliel Harding)。没有其他画家比雅各布斯画的名人肖像更多,雅各布斯的艺术成就获得普遍承认,罗斯福总统的夫人称她是杰出的画家。

My Day

By Eleanor Roosevelt

HYDE PARK—I stopped yesterday afternoon to see some friends of mine who have not had a very easy time the past few months. The man has lost part of one foot. Sometimes the pain leaves him entirely and he does not limp, and sometimes he endures acute suffering. No one looking at his face can doubt he has suffered, for the lines of pain are deep.

There are two small children in this family, and the oldest one, a boy, must be between 5 and 6 years old. When his mother told him that his father could not work and they must be careful of their money for a time, which meant he could only have ice cream on Sundays, he acquiesced solemnly. From that time on, she said, he would protest if they ever tried to buy ice cream any weekday. Which shows what can be done with youngsters if you give them a feeling of responsibility.

When one suffers, one must, if possible, keep busy, so, in his spare time, this man has been making models of ships. He had one of a sailing ship which must have taken endless hours of work, but which is really a most satisfactory achievement.

I listened last night on the radio to the concert given by Hans Kindler's orchestra in Washington at the Water Steps. The music was lovely and it must have been a beautiful sight.

I only hope it is as cool in Washington as it has been here for the last few days. It may inspire everybody to deliberate more calmly over whatever they do. I thought when I talked to my husband today that he sounded very cheerful. I always know that in summer the climate is responsible for everybody's attitude of mind.

The birds in my cedar tree flew away this morning. One of them hovered for awhile outside of my window, just as though he were saying goodbye, and now the nest is empty.

A letter has come to me from the church committee for China relief. This committee is composed of the Federal Council of the Churches of Christ in America, the Foreign Missions Conference of North America and the China Famine Relief, U. S. A., Inc. They enclose a most beautiful poster made for their appeal by the distinguished artist, Leonebel Jacobs.

The amount they say will feed a Chinese child for a year seems unbelievably small. When war is going on, I think it is the women and the children in both belligerent countries who suffer the most. All possible resources go into looking after the men at the front and the poor, who are never perhaps very well off, are worse than they would otherwise be. Those of us who are at peace, should do what we can to alleviate the suffering of those who do not fight, but who nevertheless reap the results of war.

美国总统罗斯福夫人埃莉诺·罗斯福《我的一天》——宾夕法尼亚《匹兹堡报》专栏
(*The Pittsburgh Press*，1939-07-18)

雅各布斯在中国

雅各布斯在中国度过了三年半①。笔者没有检索到她具体是哪一年来到北京。雅各布斯的文章《笔端观物》（*Seeing Things with A Pencil*）发表于 1922 年 6 月的《轮廓标》，雅各布斯为顾维钧夫人画的肖像已经出现在这篇文章中。她在文中的一句话 "While I was in Washington" 用的是过去时态，说明此时她已经拿到签证准备去中国了。1922 年末至 1924 年上半年有关雅各布斯的新闻空缺待考。根据 1924 年 9 月美国一些新闻媒体的报道，笔者推测她到北京的时间可能在 1923 年初。关于这段时间里雅各布斯的活动情况的了解，基本上来自于她的回忆录《我的中国》（*My China*）和一些报刊报道。

---

① 据新墨西哥州《阿尔伯克基杂志》（*Albuquerque Journal*，1927-04-07）。

雅各布斯的回忆录《我的中国》（*My China*）封面及书中雅各布斯穿着满族服饰的照片

有的报刊报道细节是不符合实际的，比如说她在紫禁城教溥仪学骑自行车。此时的雅各布斯已近40岁，步入中年。这可能导致以后的学者认为雅各布斯的绘画艺术成熟于从中国归来之后①。雅各布斯进过紫禁城，见过溥仪和"皇后"，画过"皇后"像，画过紫禁城的景致，还画过班禅。

下面是《我的中国》的节选：

> 《我的中国》其实是一本画册。它之所以重要，因为它是一段历史。我的肖像画是我在北京外国人群落中所经历的轻松和童话般生活中所遇到的人们的记录。
>
> 我的中国记忆是优雅和简单的。我的各个房间里摆满了一盆盆各种正在生长的花卉，有樱花、紫藤、小柠檬树、菊花。它也是美食美酒的记忆……房间里还有一架羚羊角…令人称奇的北京鸭和鸡绒。
>
> 我知道了东方柚子比橙子更大更好。山竹是一种非常好而且非常稀罕的水果，它与芒果没有任何关系。东方的芒果是最好的。新鲜荔

---

① 确实有些报道和文章称雅各布斯的绘画艺术成熟于其从中国归来之后。纽约博物馆学者认为，"雅各布斯早年在中国成长发展。她早期的许多肖像作品都集中于中国人。回到美国后，雅各布斯在纽约市定居，成为著名的肖像艺术家，并画了美国总统赫伯特·胡佛、安兰德和许多纽约社会精英的肖像画"（Aron Noble, Keith Swaney, and Vicki Weiss, *A Spirit of Sacrifice*, State University of New York Press, Albany, 2017，p238）。但这个观点是错误的。

枝的核很漂亮而且与荔枝粉相比大不相同。中国的柿子比在佛罗里达州可以找到的更大，更好吃。

我的储藏室里总是有一只中国野鸡。我有两个记忆：儿时，每到狩猎季节，都会有这种我最喜欢吃的鸟放在餐桌上；当我长大后，在纽约麦迪逊大道的超市买一只野鸡需要破开十美元，而在北京只要三十五美分。

在中国朋友家做客，女主人用皮影戏给我们讲中国的古老故事。她很擅长烹饪。一大罐鸡汤上面点缀几枚菊花瓣。见识中国晚餐，给我印象深刻。用碗装的酒、茶、米饭、汤，配一只盘子和两根细长的小棒（筷子）。精美的老瓷器是另一番天地。有的薄如蛋壳，有的与黄金等价。

我对胡同里的吆喝（叫）声印象深刻。各种商贩、工匠有各自特殊的吆喝法。我的院子里有一棵小柳树。树上有三个鸟窝。小鸟们使劲地唱，唱得它们的小心脏都要从嗓子里跳出来。

我的门前有一面传统的屏风形成一道墙，用以避邪。但是无论在哪个国家，这都是保护隐私的好办法。

我收集了许多中国风筝，准备给中国儿童画像时当背景。对于我来说，中国玩具比美国玩具更有趣。

真是妙极了，我在北京又见到了顾夫人。她告诉我，当我乘着发出嗖嗖响声的黄包车时，人们称我"画画女"！

我只懂一点点汉语，能够数到一百，可以吩咐佣人干活。

但是无论如何，结束一天有趣的工作生活，吸引人的是淘古董、打桥牌、打麻将和晚餐聚会。我一直期望能够为溥仪画像，我确信他将是中国最后的一位皇帝。我要记录一些旧中国，不要等到来不及了。然而，进入紫禁城看"天子"，可没那么容易。杰出的外国人，哪怕已经在北京住了一辈子，也从来没有进入这个门。更何况，在中国没有"一着急就能办成的事"。

我为旧宫廷的人和来访的外国人画像。最后的一幅特殊的画像是给溥仪的英文教师雷金纳德·约翰斯顿爵士（Sir Reginal Johnston）画的。他将此事告诉了溥仪。由于这个原因，紫禁城的大门对我开放了。

我画过很多中国通……伊莎贝尔·英格拉姆，一个俊俏的人，是"皇后"（婉容）的英语教师，她精通中国语言。……终于在好几个月后，我要见溥仪的日子到了。我们坐着雷金纳德爵士的车，开进了朱红大门……

　　皇帝相当亲切。他让我讲素描课，并给皇后画像。他送给我他的照片，有坐在宝座上的，有在花园里的，有做外国式骑术动作的。他给我看美国生产的自行车和在门槛上搭的（通行的）小桥，便于他骑车在各个庭院间穿梭。之后，纽约的一家报纸用一整页报道了我"教皇帝骑自行车"的不实新闻。

雅各布斯绘画的溥仪和婉容肖像（左图），以及梅兰芳肖像（右图），均摘自《我的中国》

左图：逊帝亨利溥先生——《里士满时代快报》（*Richmond Times Dispatch*，1931-12-06）
右图：纽约女士绘皇室肖像——《新闻民主党》（*News Democrat*，1927-01-16）

我看到一份预先印刷版本（一位朋友为此把一整份报纸带到了北京）。假新闻令我极其不悦。在我开始画溥仪像之前，中国基督徒将军冯玉祥将他驱逐出宫。后来（1925年）溥仪逃到了天津。在那里，我画了几幅溥仪和皇后的肖像。我们有了良好的友谊。皇帝有着某种年轻的孩子气的幽默。他有《木头兵》的唱片。因为知道我在纽约看过这部电影而且喜欢，他经常拿出来放给我听。与此同时，皇后拖着她苗条、柔弱而美丽的身段，走来走去。

当我离开北京时，溥仪送给我几卷丝绸和一百多颗珊瑚珠。（作为过去的纪念，我把它们送给了朋友们的孩子。每人送两颗珠子，做一对耳环，让她们对古老中国有一些了解。我剩下两颗。）我留了遗嘱，将来把他送给我的一对玉手镯，送给我的同名人①。

雅各布斯的肖像画曾在北京的美术专门学校（The Peking Institute of Fine Arts，今中央美术学院）展出。她在日记中写道，再次回到北京后，等待紫禁城的召见。她想再见到皇上和皇后以完成他们的画像。那些印象一直在脑海中像过电影一样。她在日记或者写给朋友和亲属的书信中，主要篇幅都是她在东方的经历，从来没有提及回美国。

雅各布斯除了给中外名人画像，也为普通民众画像。雅各布斯在北京肖像画的海报里有排队等待画像的场景，画师在用双手同时为三个人作画。可以想象，雅各布斯揽生意很在行，"著名北美美术家"、"五块钱"（WU K'UAI CH'IEN）的广告语，"梅兰芳"（MEI LAN FONG）的大名，"太太""奶奶""聪明孩子"等字样都出现在海报上，极度吸引人。可能是有所忌惮，海报里没敢写上皇帝和皇后。为名人画像的收入一定不能满足她的需求，为广开财源，需要大力提高绘画效率，只是画的质量肯定不会很高。她在《笔端观物》中说过，在华盛顿期间，有时一天要画两三人。但是被画的人足以用之来炫耀了，因为这位女画家是给大人物画画的。

雅各布斯的海报左上角"MEI LAN FONG, CHINA'S MOST POPULAR ACTOR TIFFITS WITH LEONEBEL JACOBS"，大意是"中国最著名的演员梅兰芳与利奥尼贝尔·雅各布斯吃便餐"。很有可能雅各布斯在中国期间，赛珍珠与雅各布斯通过泰戈尔和梅兰芳就互有耳闻了。但是没有检索到赛珍珠和雅各布斯在与梅兰芳交往过程中是否谈及另一方。

---

① 与她同名的晚辈。

雅各布斯在北京肖像画的海报，可以看到雅各布斯在用双手同时为三个人画肖像（俄勒冈大学图书馆提供）

1926 年末，为了躲避战争，雅各布斯同意大利驻华大使夫妇，取道苏联回国了。途经法国时，她在巴黎举办了个人画展。所谓雅各布斯在紫禁城教清皇帝骑自行车的假新闻不但在美国热传，第二天英国的《泰晤士报》也整版刊登了。这件事起码说明了雅各布斯的知名程度和她所具有的传奇色彩。这篇假新闻（1924 年 9 月 13 日）的标题是"一个纽约女郎在中国庄严的紫禁城"（A Yankee Girl in China's Sacred Forbidden City），副标题是"一段美国艺术家在封闭的大墙里，假小子般的她与绮年天子邂近并教他骑自行车的离奇故事"（Weird Experiences of a Young American Artist Behind Sealed Walls Where She "Tomboyed" with the Youthful "Heaven Born" and Taught Him to Ride a "Bike"）。画面中共出现了三排主要人物。第一排只有一个人，她是介绍雅各布斯去北京并给予特殊安排的顾维钧夫人。第二排左边的是溥仪，右边站在香炉之上玩耍的是雅各布斯。第三排人物形象基本是杜撰的：左边的是孩子气十足，邋邋遢遢追赶前面蹬车女郎的溥仪；中间是挑逗性十足的纽约女郎；右边站在石狮下的是与溥仪出来玩儿的雅各布斯。在《我的中国》书中，雅各布斯记述了许多中国通和中国名人的画像。不知名的中美百姓的画像，无法统计。

不准确的报纸报道——《奥兰多夜晚之星》（*Orlando Evening Star*，1924-09-13）

同样不准确的报道还出现在 1924 年的《汉弥尔顿晚报》（*Hamilton Evening Journal*）和《泰晤士报》（*The Times*）

　　雅各布斯至少在 1922 年 4 月来到华盛顿之前，已经在纽约成了著名画家。《时尚标》杂志社要猎取的重要人物，是美国政要和那些聚集在华盛顿参加"华盛顿武器会议"（出席会议的有九个国家：美国、日本、中国、法国、英国、意大利、比利时、荷兰和葡萄牙）的领袖们。她画了美国总统卡尔文·柯立芝和许多其他知名人士。雅各布斯为参加"华盛顿武器（控制）会议"的名人画像的消息，轰动了家乡俄勒冈州尤金市。去北京之前，38岁的雅各布斯艺术已经成熟，并已经从当时美国著名肖像画家中脱颖而出，不然她也不会受到顾维钧夫妇的特殊待遇。

赛珍珠与雅各布斯——相似的经历与共同的朋友

雅各布斯何时到达和离开中国，并没有明确的记载。1927年1月6日《晨报》报道，雅各布斯的肖像画于1926年11月12日在法国巴黎展出。"本月（1月3日）在纽约展览，明年在泊特兰和西雅图展览"。纽约《布鲁克林每日鹰报》也刊登了展览广告。从俄勒冈尤金《晨报》的报道可以推算出雅各布斯离开中国大概在1926年8月至10月。

EXHIBITION OF PORTRAITS
by
LEONEBEL JACOBS
January 3d to 16th
AINSLIE GALLERIES
677 Fifth Ave., New York

雅各布斯的画展广告——《布鲁克林每日鹰报》（*The Brooklyn Daily Eagle*，1927-01-03）

1926年巴黎个人画展上的雅各布斯（左图由俄勒冈大学图书馆提供，右图为火星云美术馆收藏）

雅各布斯回到美国后，马不停蹄地向美国公众宣传她在中国的所见所闻。她的画展定在新一年的第一个工作日。展览内容包括了许多她在中国创作的肖像和从中国带回去的中国国宝级绘画。我们无从考证她从中国带回了哪些古画。可以查到去向的有北宋赵令穰的青绿山水画《春山待客图》和明代林良的花鸟画。雅各布斯将赵令穰的青绿山水画送给了居住在宾夕法尼亚州伊斯顿（Easton Pennsylvania）的友人，将林良的花鸟画捐赠给了俄勒冈州波特兰美术博物馆（Portland Art Museum）。令人沮丧和惋惜的是，林良的花鸟画 2016 年被波特兰美术博物馆处理了而后不知去向。

北宋赵令穰的《春山待客图》

　　雅各布斯于 1926 年从中国带到美国的这幅北宋赵令穰（赵大年）的《春山待客图》，画面景色极似镇江山水。《春山待客图》的色调接近于自然，符合北宋山水画师造化，画中局部体现的是真山真水的规律。《宣和画谱》记赵令穰："使周览江浙荆湘，重山峻岭，江湖溪涧之胜丽，以为笔端之助，则亦不减晋宋流辈。"通过网络搜索镇江的山形地貌，发现有几处（比如圌山）与《春山待客图》的局部很接近。端王赵佶继帝位之前，就嗜好书画，与驸马王诜、宗室赵令穰等画家交往密切。赵佶与镇江更有渊源。北宋末年，金兵南侵，身为太上皇的赵佶逃离开封至镇江，众旧臣相随。赵令穰的另一位好友米芾（1051—1107）晚年定居润州（今镇江），他在《画史》中多次提到赵令穰。《画史》亦有记载："后数年，丹徒僧房有一轴山水与浩一同，而笔干不圆。于瀑水边题'华原范宽'，乃是少年所作。"丹徒僧房是米芾经常会友之处。故而，赵令穰有机会游历镇江丹徒圌山等地域山水。镇江的丹徒与美国的丹比（Danby），在赛珍珠心底有着同样的感受。

雅各布斯回到美国后的四十年的艺术生涯里，我们看到了她为中国在侵略者踩躏下挣扎的贫苦人民募捐而呼号；我们看到了她为援助英国的反法西斯战争，参加义务劳动；我们看到了她为支援奔赴抗击法西斯前线的军人鼓舞士气；我们看到了她为身受癌症折磨的病人募捐。艺术和善举伴随了雅各布斯的一生。

雅各布斯从中国回来后，住在纽约有三十年。1956 年她迁至佛蒙特州曼彻斯特镇（Manchester, Vermont）定居。1956 年 8 月 1 日的佛蒙特州《北亚当斯笔录报》（*The North Adams Transcript*）报道，雅各布斯为曼彻斯特镇居民所绘的 39 幅油彩和水彩肖像画，将在当地美术馆展出。当时雅各布斯 72 岁。

《北亚当斯笔录报》报影（1956-08-01）

1966 年 1 月 18 日，赛珍珠收到《我的中国》后写信给雅各布斯。雅各布斯没有想到，1971 年尼克松总统访华，重新开启了那个古老文明大国之门。她更没有想到，那里的人民已经远离了战争，远离了贫穷和饥饿。在那片充满阳光的土地上，独立自主，幸福地学习、工作和生活。

1967 年 4 月 15 日，雅各布斯在佛蒙特州的小镇本宁顿（Bennington Vermont）普特曼纪念医院去世，享年 82 岁，无子女。她被安葬在崇山环抱的佛蒙特州本宁顿县曼彻斯特镇的戴尔伍德公墓（Dellwood Cemetery in

Manchester，Bennington County）。2019 年 10 月 12 日，笔者夫妇驱车七百余公里，前去瞻仰墓碑，缅怀和平与艺术的使者、一代著名肖像画家雅各布斯。有一半的路程是在美国东部阿巴拉契亚山脉中穿行，满山遍野被红黄绿色的树木和草地覆盖，一条条溪水清澈见底。曼彻斯特镇（Manchester，Vermont）坐落于佛蒙特州的格林山脉的群山之中。格林山脉是阿巴拉契亚山脉的一部分。

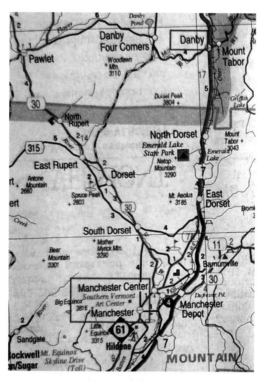

赛珍珠和雅各布斯晚年都住在佛蒙特州，赛珍珠的故居地丹比（Danby）与雅各布斯的故居地曼彻斯特（Manchester）相距的车程仅 25 公里

利奥尼贝尔·优曼·雅各布斯与赛珍珠有着不同的教育、成长背景和职业特征，赛珍珠是一位文学家、社会活动家，雅各布斯是美国著名的肖像画家，她们社会交往的群体自然不会类同，但是她们的经历却有许多相同之处。她们都曾在中国生活过，而且自从离开中国后，她们都时刻关注着中国和中国人民，并且她们在美国的家里都一直保持着中国的家居陈设风格；在中国的抗日战争时期，她们都竭尽全力帮助中国人民，而且她们的活动都获得了罗斯福总统夫人的支持；她们都交往了很多文学艺术家；她们都热心于慈善事业；她们都选择在与中国某地环境景致相似的佛蒙特州南部山区居住，直至去世。

雅各布斯家居陈设中的中国元素（俄勒冈大学图书馆提供）

雅各布斯（中）设咖喱鸡宴，室内装潢和陈设到处可见中国元素——《巴尔的摩太阳》（*The Baltimore Sun*）和《辛辛那提询问报》（*Cincinnati Enquirer*）1936 年 5 月 3 日同一天相同的报道

　　根据不完全的检索结果，我发现在赛珍珠和雅各布斯的各类社会交往关系中，存在着不少二人共同交往的朋友和重要人物。二者共同的朋友或许为研究赛珍珠拓展了一个新的视角，提供了一些新的信息。对于已经发现的十三位赛

珍珠和雅各布斯的共同的朋友，本书前面的章节已经介绍过的有安娜·埃莉诺·罗斯福、菲利斯·芬纳、多萝西·汤普森、罗宾德拉纳特·泰戈尔和梅兰芳，在此再来介绍其中的其他几位共同友人。

　　1938 年的当代最优秀的十位作家中，除了赛珍珠和汤普森以外，雅各布斯为其他两位画过肖像：1930 年获得诺贝尔文学奖的美国作家、剧作家辛克莱·刘易斯（Sinclair Lewis）；美国抒情诗人、剧作家，纽约著名的社会人物和女权主义者，1923 年获得普利策奖的埃德娜·圣文森特·米莱（Edna St. Vincent Millay）。

Q. Who are the best of the present day writers? E.L.

A. Dr. William Lyon Phelps has selected the following as the ten best living writers: Stephen Vincent Benet, Pearl S. Buck, Willa Cather, Robert Frost, Sinclair Lewis, Edna St. Vincent Millay, Eugene O'Neill, George Santayana, Booth Tarkington, and Dorothy Thompson.

Miss Adele deLeeuw Presents Authors To Pen and Brush Club

Miss Adele deLeeuw of Park Ave. was in charge of the annual Authors' Day program of the Pen and Brush Club in New York Thursday at which she presented the members of the club who have published books during 1939. Miss deLeeuw herself has published a book "Doll's Cottage" recently.

Among the authors whom she introduced were Ida Farell, president of the club, Pearl Buck, Malvina Hoffman, Dorothy Thompson, Faith Baldwin and Anne Bosworth Greene.

　　左图：1938 年当代最优秀的十位作家中，赛珍珠、刘易斯、米莱和汤普森都是雅各布斯的朋友——《首都时报》（*The Capital Times*，1938-02-16）

　　右图：赛珍珠和汤普森在同一个笔友俱乐部——《信使新闻报》（*The Courier News*，1940-01-13）

　　雅各布斯为辛克莱·刘易斯（左）、埃德娜·圣文森特·米莱（中）和多萝西·汤普森（右）绘的肖像，汤普森在其肖像画上签上自己的姓名

还有德国作家、剧作家、左翼政治家和革命家恩斯特·托勒（Ernst Toller，1893—1939），美国作家、魔术师和电影演员钱宁·波洛克（Channing Pollock，1926—2006）及美国作家、调查记者、传记作家和讲师艾达·M. 塔贝尔（Ida M. Tarbell，1857—1944）等。

　　左图：世界作家大会发言人有赛珍珠、托勒、汤普森和林语堂等——《守护者报》（*The Guardian*，1939-05-13）
　　右图：雅各布斯绘恩斯特·托勒《七场戏剧》（火星云美术馆收藏）

　　左图：纽约表彰著名作家午宴：塔贝尔（左二）、赛珍珠（左三）、波洛克（左五）——《温莎之星报》（*The Windsor Star*，1933-01-23）
　　右图：钱宁·波洛克自传《我多年的收获》（雅各布斯绘，火星云美术馆收藏）

左图：1937 年 2 月，塔贝尔和赛珍珠成为纽约笔友俱乐部成员——《信使新闻》（The Courier News，1937-02-27）

右图：雅各布斯绘的艾达·M. 塔贝尔肖像

　　赛珍珠的作品在 1932 年、1933 年与著名作家艾恩·兰德（Ayn Rand）的作品分别被列为小说和非小说类的最畅销书的第一名。1964 年，赛珍珠和兰德同在百丽书信俱乐部。雅各布斯大约自 1940 年后，经常为艾恩·兰德和她的丈夫弗兰克·奥康纳（Frank O'Connor）画像，她们经常有书信往来。参加 1942 年赛珍珠等人发起的为中国平民援助募捐三百万美元活动的人士，包括兰德的丈夫奥康纳。

Seeking Aid for Chinese Civilians

Piles of supplies donated by Americans through United China relief are shown (above) in front of a medical depot in western China. The undeclared war in China is one of the most destructive of human life in history. United China relief is attempting to provide a total of five million dollars for the aid of Chinese civilians who are now entering their fifth year of the war.

兰德的丈夫弗兰克·奥康纳参加了 1942 年赛珍珠等人发起的为中国募捐三百万美元的活动——《格林留声报》（The Greene Recorder，1942-01-14）

　　赛珍珠和雅各布斯共同的印度朋友，1913 年诺贝尔文学奖获得者罗宾德拉纳特·泰戈尔（Rabindranath Tagore）。1924 年，诗人泰戈尔访华，赛珍珠与泰戈尔在南京相识。1944 年一本书名为《无声的印度》的书，由泰戈尔和赛珍珠介绍，将由约翰·戴出版公司发行第三版。雅各布斯 1924 年在北京为泰戈尔画肖像。

左图：1913 年诺贝尔文学奖获得者罗宾德拉纳特·泰戈尔肖像（1924 年雅各布斯绘于北京）——《迈阿密先驱报》（*The Miami Herald*，1936-01-12）

右图：雅各布斯在北京画了泰戈尔、中国的末代皇帝和皇后——《伯灵顿每日新闻》（Burlington Daily News，1956-07-26）

1937 年，雅各布斯还与赛珍珠的挚友、中国作家林语堂（Lin Yutang）共同赞助纽约装饰家俱乐部举办的中国艺术、戏剧和建筑座谈会。尚没有考证出雅各布斯先认识赛珍珠和林语堂中的哪一位。

New York Sun
November 6, 1937
Three Symposia Planned by Club
Chinese Art, Theater and Architecture Covered.
Miss Waller Freeman of New York and Richmond, Va., chairman of the lecture committee for the Decorators Club of New York, has arranged a series of symposia to be held at the Cosmopolitan Club on November 8, November 22 and December 6. The first of the series is to be on Chinese art, with Chih Meng, director of the China Institute in America, speaking on Chinese architecture; C. F. Yau, eminent Oriental collector and authority, speaking on Chinese art, and Miss Sophia Han, associate professor of music at the University of Peiping, lecturing on Chinese music. His Excellency, Ambassador C. T. Wang, is a sponsor of this program. Other sponsors are Mrs. Francis N. Brownell, Mr. and Mrs. Ralph Polk Buell, Paul D. Cravath, Mr. and Mrs. Charles D. Hilles, Mr. and Mrs. Theodore Hobby, Mrs. Leonebel Jacobs, Miss Fania Marinoff, Mrs. R. Burnham Moffat, Mrs. William H. Moore, Mr. and Mrs. M. Parish-Watson, Alan Priest, Miss Pauline Simmons, Miss Mai-mai Sze, Carl Van Vechten, Mr. and Mrs. Dudley Wadsworth, Tsune-Chi Yu, Consul General, and Mr. and Mrs. Lin Yutang. Miss Ethel Lewis is chairman of the evening.

雅各布斯与林语堂共同参与赞助纽约装饰家俱乐部中国艺术、戏剧和建筑座谈会①

——————————

① 美国华人之眼：1921 年驻美大使施肇基的女儿施蕴珍（Mai-mai Sze）的往事。（http://chimericaneyes.blogspot.com/2014/09/mai-mai-sze.html）

1966 年雅各布斯通过好友将一本《我的中国》送给了赛珍珠。俄勒冈大学图书馆藏雅各布斯的档案，保存了赛珍珠写给雅各布斯的牵动我们肺腑的信，证明了赛珍珠与雅各布斯这两位伟大的女性之间存在着深厚的友谊和共同的悲欢。关于赛珍珠与雅各布斯之间有直接或间接联系的人士，应该还有很多，有待继续研究。尽量详细地整理参与赛珍珠社会活动的人物资料，有助于更深入、广泛和全面地分析和研究赛珍珠。

附贰

报刊报道原文

1. Pearl Buck: A Last Interview

Muncie Evening Press, Mar 10, 1973

Editors: The following is Pearl S. Buck's last interview. It was conducted in conjunction with the publication of her last work of non-fiction, *China: Past and Present*. Six days before her death on March 6, the John Day Company published her last book, a novel, *All Under Heaven*.

[Danby, Vt. (NEA), by Linda Way Richardson] When I was a little girl, I believed that Pearl Buck was an adventurer who had a special role in controlling all the decisions made in my concept of the world. I never quite realized whether she was a man or a woman; I only knew that Pearl Buck was a personage so great that no one could question her power or her ability.

I met Pearl Buck recently. I realized that my childhood vision was completely correct, except I am able to verify that she is very much indeed a beautiful, gracious woman.

Pearl S. Buck is the most translated author in the history of American literature, with published books equal in number to her age of 80. She is the recipient of the Nobel and Pulitzer Prizes and innumerable other honors. The world's greatest authority on China has also made unprecedented strides in the loving care and adoption of Amer-Asian children—those born of American fathers and Asian mothers in far-away places we know of in the context of war and poverty.

Pearl Buck now lives in a tiny New England town which is well into its second century of life. The village is Danby, Vermont, located just off state route 7, about 10 miles south of Rutland.

She received me in her sitting room, resplendent in a traditional Chinese robe of royal blue brocade. Her presence immediately put me at ease and I felt at once a friend, a confidante, a person of importance, if only for the time I would spend with her.

She sat regally in a comfortable chair and murmured that this Vermont village is situated in an area reminiscent of a mountainous region of China close to where she grew up and lived for 40 years.

She rarely moved while she spoke, even to gesture, and yet the vitality which was transmitted to me not as much by what she said—although her literate humor, and quick, well-phrased replies astounded me at the time and in retrospect—but by her obvious awareness of what life is all about.

Miss Buck lived in Japan for one year following her family's temporary expulsion from China during the revolution of 1926. I have just returned from living and working in Tokyo for three years. I am sure that my communion with Miss Buck was enhanced by my limited understanding of the Asian mind, for Pearl Buck is and will always be Asian.

Impossible to speak in this way of a woman who was born in the United States of American parents and who has spent the past 40 years of her life in this country?

No, not impossible, for as Miss Buck herself has admitted that she still thinks first in Chinese and then speaks in English. What she says is carefully weighed; there is no waste, no superfluousness in her conversation. The Asian subtlety which is her nature is so delicate that I felt myself seated beside a Confucian scholar, a Bodhisattva, a rare treasure of the mysterious Orient never to be completely fathomed by the Western mind.

When I gave Miss Buck my token present, a ritual observed when visiting an Asian home, she admired the wrapping at great length, believing the decorated paper to be the bookmark I had brought. When she discovered there was something within, she did not apologize for her error. She examined the simple woven strip of cloth from the mountains of Sapporo, Japan, and praised it with even greater extravagance, immediately placing it in the book she was currently reading.

The first floor of Pearl Buck's house is filled, nearly cluttered, with Asian treasures from her past. But her living and reception area on the second floor is decorated in cheerful tones in a style which might be called "dateless comfortable" with only a few reminders of China gathered about. And yet Miss Buck's presence in that western room changed it into a latter-day Imperial Court.

Taking my leave. I suppressed my overwhelming desire to bow, Asian fashion, and we lightly touched hands. I felt the sense of awe that one would expect, not because she was the immortal Pearl S. Buck, but because I felt she was the most complete person I had ever known. Pearl Buck has, in essence, the humility and grace of nobility born of a noble spirit.

2. Pearl S. Buck Dies; Author, China Expert
St Louis Dost Dispatch, Mar 6,1973

[Danby, Vt. (AP)] Miss Pearl S. Buck, the daughter of missionaries and winner of Nobel and Pulitzer Prizes for her writings on China, died today at her home here. She was 80 years old.

Beverly Drake, Miss Buck's private secretary, said the author died quietly. She had undergone gall bladder surgery last fall.

Miss Buck was born in West Virginia June 26, 1892, was reared in China and learned to speak Chinese before she learned English. It was that background, she said, that influenced not only the subject of her writing but her style as well.

She spent the first 17 years of her life in China, returned to the United States for a time, and then worked as a Presbyterian missionary in China from 1914 until 1935. The Chinese government refused her request to revisit the country last October.

She won the Pulitzer Prize in 1932 for *The Good Earth*, a book detailing the rise to power of a Chinese peasant. In 1938, she became the first American woman to win a Nobel Prize for Literature. The award made special mention of two 1936 biographies— *The Exile* and *Fighting Angel*.

Miss Buck had been in failing health for the last year.

Last July she entered a hospital after a pleurisy attack and spent nearly a month there. She was hospitalized again for two months for recuperation from gall bladder surgery in October.

A spokesman for the Pearl S. Buck Birthplace Foundation, Inc., in Hillsboro, W. Va., said today that private funeral services would be held in Bucks County, Pa., "in order to be close to her children."

Of her scores of books, the most popular was *The Good Earth*. It was translated into more than 30 languages. It was the basis of a play and a movie, which won an Academy Award for Luise Rainer in 1937 and also starred Paul Muni.

Miss Buck continued writing throughout her life, turning out three books a year. She published five novels under the penname "John Sedges."

Miss Buck said she found most contemporary writers "boringly preoccupied with sex." "I'm not moralistic at all," she said. "It doesn't shock me. It amuses me more than anything else."

Last June, looking forward to celebrating her eightieth birthday, Miss Buck reminisced about life, which included a brush with death in China at the hands of revolutionaries in 1927.

"I wouldn't have missed any of it," she commented. "Some was touch going, but everything seemed to have meaning."

Miss Buck's writings brought her wealth, much of which went to the Pearl S. Buck Foundation, an organization devoted to the support of Asian children fathered by American servicemen. The foundation, established in 1964, has helped more than 2,000 children in five countries.

The author was married twice. She divorced her first husband, John Lossing Buck, a missionary on the faculty of Nanking University, in 1935 after 18 years of marriage. She was married to her publisher, Richard J. Walsh. He died in 1960.

Miss Buck had one daughter by her first husband, a girl who suffered from a metabolic disorder and spent most of her life at a home in New Jersey. She adopted nine boys and girls and brought them up at her farm estate in Bucks County, Pa.

3. Pearl Buck Dies, Goes Home to "the Good Earth"

Longview Daily News, Mar 6, 1973

[Danby, Vt. (AP)] Pearl S. Buck, the daughter of missionaries, who won the Nobel and Pulitzer prizes for her writings on China, died today at her home here. She was 80.

Beverly Drake, Miss Buck's private secretary, said the author died quietly at about 7 : 25 a.m. today. She underwent gall bladder surgery last fall.

Born in West Virginia June 26, 1892, Miss Buck was raised in China and learned to speak Chinese before she learned English. It was that upbringing, she said, that influenced not only the subject of her writing but her style as well. She spent the first 17 years of her life in China, returned to the United States for a stay and then worked as a Presbyterian missionary in China from 1914 until 1935. The Chinese government refused her request to revisit the country last October.

She won the Pulitzer Prize in 1932 for *The Good Earth*, a book detailing the rise to power of a Chinese peasant which was cited for "its epic sweep, its distinct and moving characterization, its sustained story interest, its simple and yet richly colored style."

In 1938, she became the first American woman to win a Nobel Prize for Literature. The award made special mention of two 1936 biographies—*The Exile* and *Fighting Angel*.

Miss Buck had been in failing health in the past year, being hospitalized twice for extended periods.

Last July she spent nearly a month in the hospital following a pleurisy attack and in October was hospitalized again for two months as she recovered from gall bladder surgery.

Her secretary, Mrs. Drake, declined any comment on Miss Buck's death other than to say it had come quietly. She added that in accordance with Miss Buck's wishes funeral services would be private and would not be in Vermont.

She said the family did not plan to say where the services would be held, but did say members of the family were considering a West Virginia burial.

A family spokesman would not make any comment on Miss Buck's death other than to say it had come "quietly" and said in accordance with her wishes funeral services would be private and would not be in Vermont. The spokesman did not say where they would be held.

A spokesman for the Pearl S. Buck Birthplace Foundation, Inc., in Hillsboro, W. Va., said today that private funeral services would be held in Bucks County, Pa., "in order to be close to her children."

Of her scores of books, far the most popular was *The Good Earth*. Translated into more than 30 languages, it was the basis of a play and a movie, which won an Academy award for Louise Rainer in 1937 and also starred Paul Muni.

Miss Buck continued writing throughout her life, turning out three books a year. She published five novels under the pen name "John Sedges."

For years she was among the top-selling writers in America, but she said her largest public was in Europe.

In an interview in 1969, Mrs. Buck said that American critics tend to dismiss her "as a woman writer."

"American critics," she said, "accustomed to dealing with American writers, ought to face the fact that I am not a 100 percent American writer. My concept of the novel is based on the Chinese novel, which has a simple, direct style. I read Chinese novels almost exclusively until I came to America to go to college."

Miss Buck said she found most contemporary writers "boringly preoccupied with sex."

"I'm not moralistic at all," she said "It doesn't shock me. It amuses me more than anything else."

Among her interests in recent years was her foundation to aid Asian children fathered and abandoned by American GIs. It operated in seven Asian nations and last September opened an office in Saigon.

She contributed $1 million to the foundation herself.

Recently she purchased the house in Danby, Vt., a town which she had been trying to rejuvenate for several years by encouraging tourism, opening new shops and importing Asian gift items for local sale.

She said the admittedly commercial Danby project was motivated by a belief that "the life blood of a nation is fed from its villages."

Born Pearl Sydenstricker at Hillsboro, W. Va., she was taken to China as an infant by her Presbyterian missionary parents.

In 1917, she married Dr. John Lossing Buck, an agricultural missionary. They were divorced in 1935. That same year she married Richard J. Walsh, president of the John Day Co. Walsh died in 1960 at the age of 73.

Miss Buck had one daughter, a retarded child, by her first marriage. She told the girl's story in a magazine article and book, *The Child Who Never Grew*, in 1950, donating the proceeds to a training school and research into mental retardation.

4. Pearl Buck—"Human Bridge Between East, West"

The Press Democrat, Mar 7, 1973

[Danby, VT., (UPI)] President Nixon said Pearl S. Buck, first American woman to win the Nobel prize for literature, was "a human bridge between the civilization of the East and West."

Mrs. Buck died Tuesday at her home in this central Vermont community. She was 80.

Private funeral services will be held for her in Buckingham. Pa., later this week. It was not immediately determined when.

Mrs. Buck was author of *The Good Earth*, a portrayal of a Chinese couple's love of the soil in the face of hardship.

In Washington, President Nixon called her "a human bridge between the civilization of the East and West. Through her eyes, millions of readers were able to see the beauty of China and its people at a time when direct personal contact was impossible. It is fitting that Pearl Buck lived to see two peoples she loved so much draw closer together during her last years."

Shortly after her birthday last June 26, Mrs. Buck was stricken with a series of illnesses which hospitalized her several times. She underwent surgery for removal of her gall bladder in September. A native of Hillsboro, W. Va., Mrs. Buck grew up in China where her parents were Presbyterian missionaries. She learned to speak Chinese before English.

She won the Pulitzer Prize in 1931 for *The Good Earth*, later translated into more than 30 languages. She (The) book was the basis of a play and motion picture in which Luise Rainer won an Oscar as best actress of the year. Seven years after the Pulitzer she became the first American woman to be awarded the Nobel prize for literature. The citation read, "for rich and genuine epic portrayals of Chinese peasant life…"

China recently denied Mrs. Buck's application to re-enter that country on the ground that her works were considered "an attitude of distortion, smear and vilification toward the people of China and their leaders."

In all, she wrote 84 books, many reflecting her strong belief in the power of love to change men's lives.

5. Statement on the Death of Pearl S. Buck

March 06, 1973

In life Pearl Buck was a human bridge between the civilization of the East and

West. With simple eloquence she translated her personal love for the people and culture of China into a rich literary heritage, treasured by Asians and Westerners alike.

She lived a long, full life as artist, wife, mother, and philanthropist. Through her eyes, millions of readers were able to see the beauty of China and its people at a time when direct personal contact was impossible. It is fitting that Pearl Buck lived to see two peoples she loved so much draw closer together during her last years. Mrs. Nixon and I join all Americans in extending our sympathy to her family, and in mourning the passing of a great artist and a sensitive, compassionate human being.

(https://www.presidency.ucsb.edu/ocuments/statement-the-deathpearl-s-buck)

6. Danby to Be on Beaten Path Again Soon
Author Pearl Buck Behind Tourists' Cultural Center Development
Rutland Daily Herald, Oct 9, 1969

Four Danby Main Street buildings now being converted into a cultural center by a corporation headed by Miss Pearl Buck, the well-known author. At left is the Rosen Business Block, to be a Country Store. Houses were owned by Mr. and Mrs. Alvin Reed and Mrs. Mabel Stevens. At right is old tannery building, later used for town offices. (Herald photo—Merusi)

[By Aldo Merusi]

[Danby, Special] Danby, isolated when U.S. Route 7 was rerouted, will soon be on the beaten path again.

Several dilapidated buildings huddled together just north of Griffith Library on the west side of the narrow twisting Main Street are being rapidly restored by the Vermont Village Square Inc., whose principal stockholders are Miss Pearl Buck, noted author, and her biographer, Theodore Harris.

Harris, who has just completed his second volume on the life of Miss Buck, said Wednesday, a country store will be opened in the long vacant Rosen General Store, and an arts and crafts center, antiques shop and restaurant in the adjacent homes sold to the corporation by Mr. and Mrs. Alvin Reed and Mrs. Mabel Stevens who are in the process of moving out.

The original tannery building, owned by Mr. and Mrs. Philip Barnes of Greenville, Pa., which was once the town office, will also be utilized by the corporation in its ambitious project. Opening of the country store is scheduled for before the Christmas season, maybe as early as Thanksgiving Day.

The Vermont Village Square firm is a subsidiary of Creativity, Inc. which operated until it sold recently Old Mills Enterprises in Stratton where Miss Buck has a summer home.

The Rosen store, built in 1865 by Silas Griffith, Danby's lumber magnate, was at one time considered the tallest business block in southern Vermont.

It was purchased about 1910 by Abram Rosen from W. B. Griffith and sold to one of Rosen's daughters, Mrs. Michael Strauss of Danby and Ocenside, N.Y. Strauss is a sports writer for the New York Times.

A professional staff will operate at the center, bewhiskered Harris stated, including Mrs. Mary Pauls of Los Angeles, well known west coast artist. Manager will be Thomas Leypoldt of Stratton.

Mr. and Mrs. Alan Conklin of Livingston, Tex., will run a department of ceramics.

The corporation is in the process of extending its real estate holdings in the area. The old weather beaten tannery building stands on the south side of the bridge where the road leads to Danby Four Corners.

Danby is now a community of sidewalk superintendents as citizens in small groups watch the process of change. "We're going to be on the map again," voiced a farmer behind the smoke screen of his venerable pipe.

7. Pearl Sydenstricker Buck
Randolph-Macon Woman's College
Class of 1914

Pearl Sydenstricker Buck was born in Hillsboro, West Virginia, on June 26, 1892, to Presbyterian missionary parents. Her family returned to China when she was an infant, and she spent her early years in the city of Zhenjiang. Buck received her early education from her mother and a Chinese Confucian scholar, later attending missionary schools and a high school in Shanghai. She entered Randolph-Macon Woman's College in 1910. A philosophy major, she was active in student government and the YWCA and wrote for the college's literary magazine and yearbook.

Soon after her graduation in 1914, she left again for China, which she considered her true homeland. In 1917, she married John Lossing Buck, an agricultural specialist who was also doing missionary work in China. They lived for several years in North China, then moved in 1921 to Nanjing, where she was one of the first American teachers at Nanjing University and where her daughter Carol was born. In 1927 her family escaped a brutal anti-western attack through the kindness of a Chinese woman whom Buck had befriended.

Buck was deeply touched by the simplicity and purity of Chinese peasant life and wrote extensively on this subject. In 1931, she published *The Good Earth*, a novel about the fluctuating fortunes of the peasant family of Wang Lung. For this work, generally considered her masterpiece, she received the Pulitzer Prize in 1932. *The Good Earth* was followed by two sequels: *Sons* (1932) and *A House Divided* (1935). *The Exile* and *Fighting Angel*, biographies of her mother and father, followed in 1936 and were singled out for praise by the committee that awarded her the Nobel Prize in Literature in 1938.

She moved permanently to the United States in 1934. In the following year, she divorced Lossing Buck and married her publisher, Richard Walsh. For the remainder of her life, she wrote prolifically, producing a total of more than a hundred works of fiction and non-fiction. Her private life, too, was a full one, as she and Walsh adopted eight children.

She became a prominent advocate of many humanitarian causes. She was a founder of the East and West Association, dedicated to improving understanding between Asia and America. Her experiences as the mother of a retarded child led her to work extensively on behalf of the mentally handicapped and to publish the moving and influential book, *The Child Who Never Grew*. The plight of Amerasian children, rejected by two worlds, aroused her sympathy as well, and in 1964 she established the Pearl S. Buck Foundation to improve their lives.

She died on March 6, 1973, leaving behind an impressive body of writing and the memory of a life lived in service to tolerance and mutual respect.

This biographical sketch was written for the program of the Pearl S. Buck Centennial Symposium held at Randolph-Macon Woman's College on March 26—28, 1992.

(https://library.randolphcollege.edu/archives/Buck)

8. Pearl Buck in Her College Days
The Salt Lake Tribune, Apr 17, 1932

[By Alice Alden] It seems that Alexander Woollcott stirred up a bit of controversy when, in his sketch of Pearl Buck written as an introduction to her new novel, *Sons*, appearing in the *Cosmopolitan* for April, he described her college life in America, saying she was known as "that homesick girl with the funny name who came from the Far East somewhere and went about by herself so much."

Grace Adams, who as the daughter of a professor at Randolph-Macon Woman's College, knew Mrs. Buck as Pearl Sydenstricker through all her college career, draws quite a different picture of the girl now famous as the author of *The Good Earth*. Grace Adams says: "She was outstanding among her classmates for her competent and confident leadership in all their varied activities not only the serious duties of the Y. W. C. A. and the Student Governing Committee, but the more frivolous affairs of a social sorority and the cabalistic ceremonies of the most exclusive secret society." All of which doesn't suggest a "homesick" girl. At her graduation she was one of the most popular and prominent members of the student body.

One of her sorority sisters tells this story of her debt to Mrs. Buck, when at a time that the college's missionary came back for new recruits, "I was so carried away by Dr. White's stirring tales of her work in China that right away I signed up to be a missionary for three or five, I forget how many years—maybe my whole life."

"Well, I had just gone to bed feeling very virtuous... when the light went on in my room and I saw Pearl Sydenstricker standing beside me, with my pledge-card in her hand. I raised up expectantly, looking for fulsome congratulations, but Pearl said casually, 'Tess, I just found this and I'm mighty glad I did before it got to anyone else in the Y. W., because I know, even if you don't that after tonight you will never want to be a missionary again. So I just came over to let you watch me tear it up.' "

9. Pearl S. Buck—Student of China and Its People
Iowa City Press Citizen, Jun 3, 1932

To undertake a task for the sheer joy of accomplishing something, without thought of gain or fame, and later find that it wins the approbation of the whole world, means the attainment of one of life's great moments. But the wonderful woman who has written one of the greatest books of this generation found her greatest moment not in the signal recognition accorded her work, but in the actual work itself. To Pearl Buck the award of the Pulitzer Prize for her novel, *The Good Earth*, does not mean half as much as the knowledge that her book has helped the world to understand the Chinese, the people she knows and loves and with whom she has spent the major part of her interesting life.

Her Style of Simplicity

Millions of people are forever seeking rules that will enable them to become great writers. It is to be hoped that they will study Pearl Buck's style and learn that simplicity—the art of putting down clearly what one observes—is the secret of all great writing. When Pearl Buck painted in words and phrases a true picture of the people and the life about her, it was not with the desire to write a "best seller," but to show the world that there is intense drama in the lives of simple peasants, whether Caucasians or Mongols. Well may Mrs. Buck be happy that her great talent has been recognized in the signal honor of the award, but how much greater is satisfaction in knowing that the world's intense interest in her undistorted epic of peasant life in China has contributed to a better understanding among the races.

Pearl Buck was born in Hillsboro, West Virginia. Her parents, whose name was

Sydenstricker, were missionaries and took Pearl to China when she was still a little girl.

Pearl Sydenstricker returned to the land of her birth to attend college in the South, and her school companions recall that the shy girl from China became voluble only when she talked about the women of China and the unhappy conditions. After two years she eagerly returned to China, where a few years later she married John Lossing Buck.

Soon after Mrs. Buck's marriage they went to work in a city in which, for a part of the time, they were the only white people. And so her brilliant mind had ample time and uninterrupted opportunity to study the Chinese. Before she ever wrote a line she spent ten years in reading all the novels of China, which means that her knowledge of Chinese and the thousands of characters that make up the language is unsurpassed. She knows the Chinese classics, too, but feels that the real China, the pulsating heart of the people, is in their primitive naturalness, in the simple annals of a simple country family, not in stories of the scholars and sages.

The Pulitzer Award

So Pearl Buck set down a story of the life about her and sent it to America with the hope that perhaps some publisher would print it, so that the world could learn about China as it really is. To her amazement the book became a "best seller" overnight. And now has come the further recognition of the Pulitzer award.

10. Modern Christian Missionaries
Morning Tribune, Oct 26, 1924

[San Luis Obispo, California] The young pagan is not only very likely to be studying world history, geography and institutions, but he may also be studying modern science and thinking a lot for himself. Miss Pearl S. Buck, a missionary in Nanking, China, writing in the *New York Christian Advocate* of her experiences as a missionary, says: Today one has to stand before a crowd of hypercritical young students who know more about Darwin and Huxley and Russell and all the ancients and moderns than an old missionary can ever hope to know. Stand before some of those, and remembering the great war and the morphine traffic and indemnities and extraterritorial demands and other things that exist alongside Christianity in one's own country, and try to preach with the cocksureness of the old days and here is what happens:

"A backfire of a hundred questions comes rushing at you straightway. 'How do you explain the miracles?' 'Do you believe the divinity of Jesus was from within or without?' 'Explain Jesus' consciousness of divinity.' 'How can the death of one man really save anyone else from sin?' 'Are heaven and hell concrete or abstract, and how do you know, how can you prove it?' 'In the light of the present situation in the West, how can you prove the efficiency of Christianity in developing a moral and spiritual civilization?' "

" 'How can you prove—How can you prove' —the query comes at one from every angle from these restless, young Orientals. I think of the old, credulous, docile, street-chapel congregations, so comfortable to talk to, so unquestioning. These young folks are neither credulous nor superstitious, and certainly they are not comfortable."

From the above, and other recent declarations of missionaries that might be quoted, it is apparent that the task of the modern, Christian missionary is much the same as that which faces the modern, Christian minister in this country. It is useless to try to convince the young person who has just laid aside his microscope or has come from the biological laboratory or the study of geology or astronomy or anthology that the things he has seen and investigated for himself are delusions and false. No elucidation of Scriptural truth coming down from the far distant and shadowy past will cause him to throw away his own first-hand knowledge and his conclusions based upon it and make him accept a dogma formulated for him by someone who never had the knowledge or experience that he has had. One who would help such a person become a Christian must help him to make Christianity harmonize with all demonstrated, actual knowledge, as, when rightly understood, it does.

11. *Pacific Affairs* Out in New Form
Honolulu Star-Bulletin, Feb 5, 1930

The second number of *Pacific Affairs*, journal of the Institute of Pacific Relations, in its new form, is now upon the newsstands in Honolulu.

The issue for February contains three outstanding articles, all of particular interest to those of us living in the Pacific.

First of them is "China in the Mirror of Her Fiction," written by a woman, Pearl S. Buck, who has for years been making a special research into the origins of Chinese fiction and folk literature.

A native of China, Mrs. Buck was educated in both the written and spoken Chinese language, and, as she explains it, is more Chinese than western in her reactions to her native land and its people. Mrs. Buck is well known to American readers, as she has written for numerous American periodicals, and her first long novel of Chinese life, *East Wind, West Wind* is shortly to be published in New York.

12. *East Wind*, *West Wind* —Romance of the Orient

Oakland Tribune, Apr 13, 1930

The poetry of the East is in the writing of Pearl S. Buck's *East Wind*, *West Wind* and with it a gentle romance of a Chinese woman who marries a westernized modern husband.

Kwei-Lan, schooled in the old traditions, comes into conflict with the new. She finds her sorrows and her problems before the slow adjustment takes place and her story, told with a style suiting theme, becomes one to hold with its literary and human appeal.

It is easy to see charm in that which is strange. This writer has lived in the East, knows the Chinese so well that readers may accept the interpretations. But for the love and devotion of her husband Kwei-Lan would have found no rainbow at the end of her journey. There were so many things she could not understand. The author lets readers look through the eyes of this Chinese wife, questioning and bewildered, and allows them to share in the discovery.

East Wind, *West Wind*, by Pearl S. Buck: New York, John Day Co., $2.50.

13. Missionary "From China to U.S."

The Knoxville News Sentinel, Jan 11, 1933

Mrs. Pearl S. Buck, winner of the Pulitzer Prize for her book, *The Good Earth*, has been called a "renegade missionary" for her criticisms of the conduct of American missions in China. She is a missionary herself, home from Nanking on furlough. Her sister, Grace Sydenstricker, once attended Maryville College. Mrs. Buck attended Randolph-Macon.

Mrs. Buck has her ideas about American women. Having spent most of her life in China, she finds the women of her native land are just as dependent on what men think of them as ever.

Calls Mrs. Pearl S. Buck "Renegade Missionary" for Her Frank Writing Pulitzer Author's Words on Folk Church Sends to China Irritates Churchman; Maryvillians Shocked at Book.

About a year ago a young woman missionary, the daughter of missionaries, bore in America but reared in China since the age of four months and educated in Randolph-Macon Woman's College, Va., brought her two small daughters to her native land to spend a brief furlough.

This young woman is Pearl Sydenstricker Buck, daughter of Presbyterian missionaries. Her husband, John Lossing Buck, is head of the farm management department of the University of Nanking.

And besides her young daughters, she brought some ideas along and a talent for effectively expressing them.

And so during the years she has been here, she has proved a missionary from China to the United States.

Name Often Gets in Print

First, she published a novel, *The Good Earth*, which won the Pulitzer Prize as the best of the year. Then she wrote other stories and articles for magazines, then she lectured and was interviewed. Her prize novel was dramatized and produced on Broadway. One way of another, Pearl S. Buck's name has been in print much more than you might expect of a returned missionary.

The latest instance comes in a United Press dispatch from Philadelphia, where the Rev. John C. Monsma, general secretary of the Reformation Fellowship, told the Philadelphia Presbytery that Pearl Buck is a "renegade missionary."

"Mrs. Buck has been quoted as 'criticizing the type of missionaries sent to China,' the Rev. Monsma said." Yet the church has been providing financial support for her during a long stretch of years.

The Rev. Monsma assailed the policy of the Presbyterian Board of Foreign Missions for barring "fundamentalists" front its foreign service.

His attack apparently was prompted by a recent article of Mrs. Buck's written for *Harper's Magazine*, in which she gives her ideas of the proper function of missions and missionaries. In this article she vigorously criticizes the type of missionary who goes to China to "scrap" all of China's culture and substitute for it a narrow-minded, dogmatic doctrine. But she upholds missions when they are properly conducted. She thinks the missionary should first understand and sympathize the Chinese life, then live with the people and help them understand the great contribution that the example of Christ's life and teachings can make to their happiness. In short, she is anything but the kind of the missionary typified by the Rev. Davidson in the Maugham play "Rain."

Sex Treated Frankly in Prize Book

Her novel, *The Good Earth*, was hailed by critics as a beautifully written and wholesome book. The story of humble Chinese life, it treated sex matters very frankly, but without a trace of evil suggestiveness.

An interesting sidelight on Mrs. Buck's busy furlough in America recently was reported from Maryville. Mrs. Buck was known there as the sister of Grace Sydenstricker, who attended Maryville College, a Presbyterian Institution, while Mrs.

Buck was at Randolph-Macon. When it became known in Maryville that Grace Sydenstricker's sister had written a Pulitzer Prize-novel, there was a rush among some of the staid matrons of Maryville who knew Miss Grace to get copies of *The Good Earth*. But a number of them read only far enough to see that this was quite a different work from what they had expected of a young woman with such missionary and collegiate connections. In brief they were shocked and pained, probably in much the same way as the Rev. Monsma is.

Mrs. Buck Also Has Ideas About Women

Mrs. Buck has some ideas about women as well as missions. She has declared in an American interview that she thinks American women have gained greater financial freedom, but that they are still dependent on men.

"They are just as anxious to please men as ever and this reveals mental dependence," she said.

She believes every woman should cultivate outside interests. Hers is writing. She works in the attic of her old stone house in Nanking on her ideas and writing every morning from 8：30 until noon. Then she eats the luncheon her Chinese part-time maid has prepared. She cooks breakfast and dinner for her family, even if she is one of the world's outstanding women writers.

Speaking of China, Mrs. Buck said that the well educated Chinese woman, and few Americans know better than she, is well trained in practical affairs and less prone to impractical ideas than American women.

"Educated women in China do very much as they please," she concluded. "I think, too, that the Chinese man is liberal in his attitude toward women. They accept women—I'm speaking of the educated Chinese women, of course, as equals."

14. *East Wind*, *West Wind*, A Striking Novel, Set in China

The Sacramento Bee, Apr 26, 1930

East Wind, *West Wind*. By Pearl S. Buck.

The John Day Company, New York, $2.50

The clash of the older ideals in China with those imbibed by the younger generation under western influence has been the theme of many novels in recent years, but seldom, if ever, with the insight and understanding to be found in *East Wind*, *West Wind*, by Pearl S. Buck, herself said to have been long a resident of the Orient. The imprint of that residence is to be found on nearly every page of this unusually fine story.

Mrs. Buck understands perfectly the tenacity with which customs thousands of years old can be held and she is not unaware of the strength and sustaining social powers of such customs. Yet it is plain to be seen that she believes it is the leaven of the western idealism that is to be the salvation of the Orient.

The drama unfolded is presented through Kwei-Lan, daughter of a rich provincial official, who confides the events of the narrative to a white woman, her intimate friend. The crisis in her life comes when she is married to a Chinese physician with a background of twelve years in America. He wants a wife who is his companion and equal, not one thinks it heaven to worship her lord and master in all meekness and submissiveness.

On the other side is Kwei-Lan's brother, educated in the United States and wedded to an American girl, who is told when he comes home he must send her back and take the bride his father has chosen for him many years before. Otherwise he will suffer expulsion from his clan and disinheritance.

This is but a bare outline of the two chief themes of *East Wind*, *West Wind*. The writing itself is exceptional; and the novel a striking piece of work.

15. Sally Jessy Raphael to Host Buck Documentary
News Herald, Jun 2, 1993

Syndicated talk show host Sally Jessy Raphael, winner of the 1991 Pearl S. Buck Woman's Award, will host a preview viewing of "*East Wind*, *West Wind*: Pearl Buck, the Woman Who Embraced the World," Sunday, June 13 in the Cultural Center of the International Headquarters of the Pearl S. Buck Foundation in Hilltown Township.

Tickets for the fund-raising event must be purchased in advance and are $15 for general admission and $35 for Patrons who will enjoy a Patron Tea hosted by Ms. Raphael.

To order tickets, call the Foundation at 249-0100. Tickets are tax-deductible. The film will be shown at 1 : 30 p.m. and 4 : 30 p.m. with the Tea to take place in the Pearl S. Buck House from 3 to 4 p.m.

East Wind, *West Wind* is a 90-minute documentary film chronicling the rich and dynamic life of Pearl S. Buck. The film is a production of public television station WSWP-TV in Beckley, West Virginia and Refocus Films of Westport Connecticut. The film is narrated by actress Eva Marie Saint.

In 1938, the Nobel Prize for Literature was awarded to Pearl Sydenstricker Buck. To this day, she remains the only American woman to receive that distinguished honor. Pearl Buck is one of the most translated American authors of all time. Ultimately, however, she may be best remembered for promoting understanding between Asia and the West and for championing the cause of Amerasian children.

Highlighted by Pearl Buck's personal home movies as well as those of neighbors in Nanking, China, the film features a number of interviews with family members and friends who knew Buck best. Among those who candidly share their memories are her sister Grace Yaukey; fellow Nanking missionary, 103-year-old Cornelia Mills; and author James Michener. Historical perspective is provided by some of the world's great China scholars, including the late John K. Fairbank of Harvard, James C. Thomas of Boston University, and Nanjing (China) University Foreign Language Chair Liu Hai-Ping.

East Wind, *West Wind* follows the extraordinary path of a missionary child, born in West Virginia at the turn of the century and raised in rural China, who became one of the most popular writers of the 20th century. A blend of oral history and historical footage forms an intimate portrait of the multifaceted woman.

The film will have a national premiere at the Smithsonian Institute in Washington D.C. on June 10. The Pennsylvania premiere was appropriately picked to be at the site of her National Historic Landmark House, known as Green Hills Farm, where she lived for over 38 years until her death in 1973.

Though her best known novel is undoubtedly *The Good Earth*, Pearl Buck wrote over 100 books in her long career. She had a string of best sellers in the 1930's, 1940's and 1950's, but she was more than a popular novelist. In fact, she was an activist long before the term became familiar. Among the many causes she advocated in the 1930's and 1940's were woman's rights, civil rights, the repeal of the Chinese Exclusion Act, mixed race adoption and tolerance and understanding of retardation. The final segment of the film looks at what is perhaps her greatest legacy, the Pearl S. Buck Foundation, which strives to give life-long opportunity to Amerasian and other displaced children so they may rise above poverty, discrimination and other circumstances to be self sufficient and productive members of society.

East Wind, *West Wind* is the result of five years of rigorous effort and research by independent film producer-writer Craig Davidson and co-producer-writer Donn Rogosin.

16. Books Good and Not Good

The Honolulu Advertiser, Apr 13, 1930

East Wind: West Wind. By Pearl S. Buck, John Day. New York.

[By Charles Eugene Banks] Breaking up. Old China occupies a big stage. While the eyes of the world have been turned upon the ancient kingdom seeking to estimate the results of continual eruptions in civil and military life, the keenest observers have been able to no more than hint at China's probable future.

More difficult to fathom are the changes taking place in the structure of the ancient families. Few outsiders have been allowed entrance to the homes of the titled Chinese. What little has been learned of family life behind those walls and doors piqued curiosity but did very little to satisfy it. But here at last is a book, *East Wind*, *West Wind* that reveals not only the secrets of the age-old fashions, customs and habits among these people, but with originality, charm and pathos depicts the effect the adoption of many of the ideas of the West by the younger Chinese has had and is having on the intimate home life of the Celestial Kingdom.

Pearl S. Buck, the author, has lived in China all of her life. The story is told in a unique manner. A young Chinese wife confesses to the author the difficulties encountered by her in winning and holding the love of her husband. Kwei-Lan thus speaks with the charm of a language enriched by thousands of generations of students, poets who passed their lives in constant search for wisdom. She is married to the man chosen for her before she was born. She has been thoroughly instructed in the way of the bride to be. She goes to her husband with all those subtle arts which time and fashion have perfected to the minutest detail. But he is cold. He has become English in speech and feeling. A modern scientist, he believes in the equality of the sexes. The story of Kwei-Lan's conflict is as beautiful as she herself is beautiful.

Over against this main story is that of Kwei-Lan's brother, the only son, most precious in the eyes of his mother, for on him depends the continuation of the family. He goes to an American university and marries a professor's daughter. Returning home with his Western wife he finds the household turned against her.

Kwei-Lan's mother is wonderfully conceived. Through her we arrive at the wisdom of the ages. With the determination of a martyr, she stands firm against Western encroachment upon her family. Her nobility, wax-like beauty and exalted courtesy make of her a noble figure.

If one is interested at all in Chinese tradition and family life this book will prove fascinating. Kwei-Lan tells her own story to the author. Together with its delightful poetic prose and the charm of the reciter, we get a drama of power and force. The autobiographic manner of the book gives it an intimacy that would otherwise have escaped in the telling. It is said to be the first novel of this author, although she has written much for magazines. She is able to perceive and to conceive her readers that men and women, of whatever race or condition are compelled by like emotions to a like understanding, not only of general truths but of each other.

17. Where Yellow Takes Ways of White
The Pasadena Post, Apr 12, 1930

This story by Pearl Buck, who knows China, tells what is happening as the western culture crowds against the ancient customs of the most ancient nation, and awakens sympathy for souls caught in conflict.

East Wind: West Wind by Pearl S. Buck

New York: The John Day Co.

[By Zoe Johnson] This is the first novel by an author who has always lived in China, except for the time she passed in the United States going to college. She taught in the University of Nanking and the Government university under two national regimes. Her home is now in Nanking. Having always lived in the East, her understanding of the Chinese people, their age-old culture and beautiful traditions, has made for us a story which brings that far distant country very close to us. After all, men and women, both yellow and white, have too many emotions in common not to understand each other's experiences.

The story is told by Kwei-Lan, gentle and lovely daughter of old China, imbued with all her traditions and reared only to one end, marriage to the man to whom she was betrothed before she was born. Her childhood is passed in the secluded apartments of the women in the home of her father, where for 500 years her revered ancestors had lived in this ancient city of the Middle Kingdom.

Up to the age of 9 she plays with her brother, at which time he disappeared through the moon-gate into the men's apartments, and she seldom saw him again. She could not understand the reason for this cruel separation from her only playmate, and her grief and loneliness cause her much unhappiness.

She tells us of her august mother in whose presence she dares not raise her eyes, of her father's four concubines who live in the outer courts, the many children and servants and all the ancient customs of a Chinese household. We see her swinging her little bound feet over the edge of the bed to relieve the pain. We see her dreaming in the garden beside the lotus pool or walking beside her mother into the temple and reverently placing incense before the god.

As the years go by she hears strange whisperings about her brother, that he is taking up the western ways. She tells us of the horror and amazement of her mother when he dares to enter her presence in the hideous western clothes. He even goes to school in America, which causes her mother the greatest grief and suffering. Kwei-Lan also hears rumors that her own betrothed favors the western ways, but aside from these whisperings in the women's court, she leads a secluded life and patiently strives to become proficient in every art that will please her husband and her mother-in-law.

At seventeen she is married. Knowing nothing of the outside world, she comes to her westernized, modern husband, who, while courteous and gentle, scarcely recognizes her existence. In vain she practices every art taught her by her mother to capture his fancy. They do not live in the ancestral halls of his father, but move into a modern, westernized house. Her husband is a physician and a student, devoting most of his time to his books. In her loneliness she longs for the stately rooms of her old home, the black teak couches and chairs, the scarlet satin curtains in the doorways, the painting of the first Ming emperor above the table, the soft moonstone light coming through the rice-paper on the carved window frames—all this she thinks of as she sits stiffly on the edge of her chair in the hideous western house.

At the wish of her husband, she overcomes centuries of tradition and unbinds her feet. Her suffering then is far greater than in her childhood, but through it she and her husband at last find each other. From then on her life is swung between the passing old and the developing new, her devotions torn between her august ancient family and her modern husband.

Her supreme happiness comes when she presents her husband with a son. To a Chinese woman this is the fulfillment of her life.

Kwei-Lan's love for her husband, his love and devotion to her, bring about a gradual understanding of his change and the world's change, strengthening them to an unhesitating confidence in the future.

Interwoven with the story of her own life, she tells that of her brother's. He, too, as the years go by, becomes more and more westernized and even goes to America to attend college. Against the bitter opposition of his family and the traditions of his race, he marries an American girl and brings her home to China. The love between this Chinese boy and American girl is beautifully told.

They come first to the home of Kwei-Lan and her husband and wait patiently for an audience with their mother. She has been notified of their presence, but absolutely refuses to see the wife of her son. We hear of their long waiting and final reception of his mother, who refuses even to acknowledge the presence of the foreigner.

At the suggestion of his father they are allowed to reside in the outer court with the understanding that the American girl must live in the strict seclusion of the Chinese woman. He thinks that his son will soon tire of his new toy, give her up, and marry the woman to whom he was betrothed as a child.

The American girl, Mary, suffers from the close confinement and the curiosity of the other women, who are always peering and pointing at her, whispering and laughing with each other.

After many months, realizing that their waiting is useless, they move into a house near Kwei-Lan. The two women become good friends and help each other in the adjustment of their lives. Mary's open devotion to her husband shocks the little Chinese girl, who has been trained to suppress every evidence of emotion except in the privacy of her own home.

It seems most strange to Kwei-Lan that her brother and his wife should associate with each other as equals. Had she not been taught to enter her husband's presence quietly and wait until she had been spoken to? How embarrassing it had been when her husband had insisted that she precede him into the room when visiting his foreign friends. However, noticing his pleasure in their company, she strives to understand and like them, too.

Mary has been very happy since they have moved into their new home. She, also, presents her husband with a son, and in mutual joy and happiness the two women lose all thought of race or creed and together plan for the future of their children. When sewing for her baby, Mary had made a strange set of garments, all in white, and, upon being questioned by Kwei-Lan explains to her that six days a week her boy shall be dressed as a son of China, but on the seventh day he shall wear these white clothes and be an American.

Underneath the quiet charm of this story, we feel the throbbing heart of old China. The culture which has been so carefully built up through the centuries is being ruthlessly cast aside. The younger generation, eager for western civilization, is gradually breaking down the old tradition. Out of the change have come tragic confusion and conflict.

The old Chinese mother dies broken-hearted, firm in the conviction that her son has irrevocably offended his god and his ancestors.

What will this newer civilization do to China? This will be the problem of her children. There is so much that is beautiful and good in their own culture that we can only hope they will be successful in combining the best traditions of their ancient race with the modern thought and sciences of the newer peoples.

18. *The Good Earth*—Story of Chinese by Pearl S. Buck
Brooklyn Times Union, Mar 15, 1931

> *The Good Earth*. By Pearl S. Buck
> New York: The John-Day Co.
> Book of the Month Club Selection for March

Many stories and novels have been written about China, for the most part by authors remaining only for short periods in the big seacoast centers. These deal with life in the big cities and hardly scratch the surface.

Mrs. Buck, on the other hand, was born in China[①], the daughter of American missionaries; China has been her home except for the few years during which she was being educated in the United States; Chinese is as much her language as is English;

---

① Note: There is a mistake here. Pearl S. Buck was born in West Virginia, U.S. actually.

her home is in Nanking, where her husband is in the faculty of the College of Agriculture; she knows the Chinese of the soil.

And it is of these folk she writes in *The Good Earth*, her second published novel, a novel of the real Chinese, as was her first, *East Wind: West Wind*, a novel of the great mass who live within themselves and hardly know there are in the world persons in any way different from them.

Perhaps it is true—perhaps not—that it is only three generations from shirtsleeves and shirtsleeves. Many novels, likely only subconsciously, have been built on that theme. It is the theme of *The Good Earth*.

But the lives of these simple folk are treated with utmost sympathy by Mrs. Buck. Her characters are only a few of the millions and millions who are the backbone of China, living in poor mud huts, little holes in the wall for ventilation which are stopped by paper in cold weather; living near a stream in utmost poverty, a stream necessary if they would exist, for water must be found to keep the crops from dying, and yet a stream which is their great menace in times of flood.

Their homes are washed away, along with their crops, and again life becomes a struggle.

The Good Earth opens on the day of the wedding of Wang Lung, son of a sick father, whose wife is dead these many years. You see him leaving his bed that morning and deciding that as one will look that day upon his body he will use all the water available for a bath. You follow Wang that day about his tasks, always in his mind the thought that there is a woman coming into the home and no longer will he be called upon to do the household tasks, the cooking, caring for his sick father and all the other things he has been forced to do since the death of his mother.

Wang is poor; so is O-lan, the girl he weds, who has neither beauty nor hope of any existence other than one of poverty, slavery and child bearing. She had been a maid in the home of the Hwang, the only rich family in the province; a slave, virtually, sometimes beaten, never getting enough to eat, and never seeing any hope. Here was escape.

The sons in the house of Hwang are idle. Wang, on the other hand, is a worker and his wife is a slave in their humble home. By ceaseless toil and thrift, Wang Lung gets together sufficient money with which to buy a little plot from the estate of the house of Hwang—a rice field. He continues to toil.

This is his first step up the ladder of wealth, and by selling the plot, it is the first step down toward poverty for the house of Hwang. Then comes famine. Driven, with others, to other sections in search of food. Wang, O-lan and their first man-child reach the city walls.

The revolution comes. Wang does not know what it is all about, and he cares less.

The city is taken and he joins with others in the looting. With enough gold with which to restock his farm, he and O-lan and the child start back. They buy new fields from the house of Hwang; finally it all is held by Wang Lung. He is rich.

It is here that Mrs. Buck shows she knows her Chinese. The Chinese does not change. Wang changes his mode of life, but O-lan still is his property. He buys a tearoom girl, and O-lan remains in the kitchen until she dies, worn out by labor and child-bearing.

And the cycle is still there. Wang now is lazy, for he does not need to work. His sons, never having had to work, know nothing about it. Will their sons' sons be back where we found Wang Lung on his wedding day?

The Good Earth is a moving story, finely told and rich with humanity and the things which make up life.

19. About the Author of *The Good Earth*
Honolulu Star Bulletin, Jul 4, 1931

The John Day Co. has put forth a brochure containing an autobiographical sketch of Pearl S. Buck, whose novel *The Good Earth* reviewed in *The Star-Bulletin* March 21, still stands first on our private list of the best novels of the year.

Mrs. Buck, a daughter of American missionaries, spent her childhood in the interior of China. She was educated there by her mother, and later went to school in Shanghai, but learned a great deal also from her Chinese nurse, who told her stories of her own childhood and of the Taiping rebellion, and her father, who traveled widely in the course of his work and had many adventures.

At the age of 17 she was taken to Europe and America and completed her education in Virginia, returning thence to China. Two years later she married John Buck, an American, and they lived for five years in a town in north China, part of the time the only white people in the neighborhood.

"Outwardly our life was exciting enough," she writes. "We had a famine, with all that means; we had battles between bandits attacking the city, and bullets flew thick as flocks of birds over our little Chinese house, which clung to the inside of the city wall.

Sometimes we went into the country, walking sometimes, and sometimes, if it were far, I in a sedan chair and my husband on his bicycle. We went into places where white women had never been and I furnished topic for conversation for weeks, I am sure.

Mr. Buck for the last ten years has been head of the department of rural economics and sociology in the University of Nanking, and his book on Chinese agriculture will appear soon.

Mrs. Buck's own account of her life indicates clearly how she has been able to present Chinese life so naturally and convincingly and to make her characters so human and real.

"My chief pleasure and interest has always been people, and since I live among Chinese, the Chinese people," she writes. "When I am asked what they are like, I do not know. They are not this and that, but people. I cannot describe them any more than I can my own blood kin. I am too near them and have shared too closely their lives."

"For this reason I dislike all those writings about the Chinese which make them strange and outlandish, and my greatest ambition is to make the people in my books as real as they are to me."

Mrs. Buck has taught English literature in Chinese universities, but says she finds the work interesting chiefly because it brings her new knowledge through her students.

They have two daughters, one away at school and one, 5 years old, at home, who is studying Chinese reading and writing every day with the Chinese tutor who has also been Mrs. Buck's teacher in Chinese literature for many years.

20. Book Review: *The Good Earth*
The Ithaca Journal, Mar 26, 1931

The Good Earth, Pearl S. Buck
The John Day Company, 375pp, $2.50

Cornell's name continues to gather importance in contemporary literature, and is magnified materially by this new novel that comes out of the Orient. The authoress, while not an original Cornellian, took a Master of Arts degree here in 1925, and is wed to a Cornell man.

Mrs. Buck's literary touch is deft and skillful. With the sharp clarity of an etching she tells the simple, gripping story of Wang Lung, a poor farmer who worships his land and becomes wealthy.

The Good Earth is the current Book-of-the-Month, and with good reason. The story is told with a direct forcible style that remains uniform cover to cover, building up no conventional climax, but creating an impression that will be lasting upon the reader. Mrs. Buck employs an Oriental semi-poetic style which gives the flavor of something translated from the Chinese.

Though dealing almost solely with Chinese family life on the farm, the story is universal in its appeal. With a few changes, it might be applied to almost any locality. Wang Lung marries, he procreates, his crops are attacked by flood, drought and locusts. He takes his starving family into a southern city and pulls a jinriksha to keep them alive. Then comes revolution, and in a moment of good fortune he is given much money to spare a life. With it his goes back and buys more land, and still more, until he becomes a power in the town. Then he takes a concubine into his home, having tired of his slave-wife.

Always the reader feels the pull of the earth, like the undertow in a sea swell. A suggestion of Whitman's love of living—of feeling at one with the earth—is in these pages. Mrs. Buck is a stark realist, and the total effect of her book is not a little depressing.

The heart of the book may be summed up in these words of Wang Lung: "It is the end of the family—when they begin to sell the land. Out of the land we came and into it we must go—and if you will hold your land you can live—no one can rob you of land."

Despite the fact Mrs. Buck was the child of missionaries, she preaches no sermons. Her characters are quite pagan, and she is no prude. She has lived 39 years, and she knows the realities of life. She lived most of those years in China, and the insight she gives into Chinese rural life is deeply interesting.

Pearl Sydenstricker was graduated from Randolph-Macon College at Lynchburg. Va., in 1914, the same year her future husband, J. Lossing Buck, took his B.S. at Cornell. After years in China, they returned as man and wife to Cornell to take Master's degrees, which both achieved in 1925. They live in Nanking, and Mrs. Buck has taught at the University of Nanking and at the Government University there. Her first novel was *East Wind*, *West Wind*. Mr. Buck is an agricultural missionary.

(C. R. R.)

21. China's Charm Captured
The Pasadena Post, Apr 11, 1931

East Wind, *West Wind* by Pearl S. Buck. John Day Co., 1930

The Good Earth by Pearl S. Buck. John Day Co., 1931

[By Helen Stevenson] Last year a book entitled *East Wind*, *West Wind* appeared which may have escaped your notice and which is unlike anything of its kind that has been written. The author has lived practically all of her life in China and this novel reveals in a poignant manner the occidental influence in modern China. A charming little Chinese girl, reared in the traditional customs of her country, marries a Chinese who has been educated abroad. She retains the Chinese viewpoint while her husband has adopted western ideas. Her attempts to adjust herself to what seem to her shocking and revolutionary ways makes a touching and charming picture. Her brother, heir to the headship of the family, goes to America to study and brings home as his bride, an American girl. Modern changes and influence in China are thus portrayed in two dramatic situations which give the book its title. The author's genuine knowledge of China, and her penetrating sympathy for both the old and the new there, gives the story a tone of authenticity and unusual interest. Here is no touch of false sentimentalizing that occurs in most novels of life in China. *East Wind, West Wind* is a beautiful book written with simplicity, delicacy and charm.

It is referred to here especially not only because of its own merits and because it may not have come to your attention but also because Mrs. Buck has a new book this year, *The Good Earth*, which also depicts China.

This time it is a peasant Chinese and his passion for the soil. Both books contain that happy interweaving of Chinese customs and excellent characterization which make her writing notable.

22. Kappa Delta Writes "Book of the Month"
Clarion Ledger, Mar 18, 1932

[Letitia Allen] The "book of the month" selected for March is *The Good Earth* by Pearl S. Buck. Kappa Deltas who read the announcement realized with a thrill that Pearl S. Buck, author of a book which was listed by the American News company for many weeks as one of the six "best sellers," is a Kappa Delta from Theta Chapter.

The South is very proud in claiming Pearl S. Buck, as she was born in Hillsboro, West Virginia. Mrs. Buck was bred in a mission, has been herself a missionary, the daughter of one and the wife of another. Mrs. Buck has lived in China all her life and knows this country only from her experience in attending school at Lynchburg in Virginia. One may be permitted to wonder how many of the girls in the class of 1914 at Randolph-Macon have identified her with that strange Pearl Sydenstricker. After studying at Randolph-Macon and Cornell, Mrs. Buck went to China to teach in a Chinese university.

Her stories and articles appeared from time to time in *The Atlantic Monthly* and *The Nation and Asia*. Her first novel *East Wind, West Wind* is also about China. The *New York Times* Book Review comments as follows: In *East Wind, West Wind*, Pearl S. Buck wrote a novel of China which was generally hailed, in terms meant to be complimentary as a very promising first novel. In her second book *The Good Earth*, she has fulfilled that promise with a brilliance which passes one's most optimistic expectations. Laying aside the question of the locale *The Good Earth*, is an excellent novel. It has style, power, coherence and a pervasive sense of dramatic reality. In its deeper implications it is less a comment upon life in China than upon the meaning and tragedy of life as it is lived in any age in any quarter of the globe. Notwithstanding the essential difference in manners and traditions, one tends to forget, after the first few pages that the persons of the story are Chinese and hence foreign.

One cannot doubt that Mrs. Buck knows her China. Except for her college years in the United States, she has spent the greater part of her life there. But she portrays a China unfamiliar to the average reader, a China in which, happily, there is no limit of mystery or exoticism. There is very little in her book of the quality which we are accustomed to label "Oriental." Her interpretation of life in the Far East is as far removed from Lafcadio Hearn, on the one hand, as it is from Hollywood on the other.

23. Who's News Today
The Rock Island Argus, May 4, 1932

[By Lemuel F. Parton]
(Copyright, 1932, by The Argus)
[New York] At Randolph-Macon college, Pearl S. Buck, then Pearl Sydenstricker, got high marks in everything but English. The professor didn't like her stuff. It just wasn't up his alley. Of Teutonic descent, she was patient and persistent. Hence, *The Good Earth*—incidentally an epic of patience—the Pulitzer Prize, and renown which cannot divert her from her quiet, purposeful life. Like her own Wang Lung and O-Lan, she is unswerving.

When she was a child in the ancient city of Yochow, natives ascribed drought and misfortune to the foreign family. A mob approached their house. Her mother prepared tea and cakes and invited them in. It was a nice party and the visitors bowed and departed with profound appreciation of the hospitality shown them. In such contacts, the little girl learned the Chinese character. Back from college, she spent years reading the Chinese classics, but, she said later, it was not therein that she found her most salient material. There are no middlemen between her and the heart of old China— which, she says, is unconquerable.

Soon after her graduation from college, she was married to John Lossing Buck, graduate of Cornell. *The Good Earth* absorbed them both, for he wrote a book on *Farm Economy*, and is now head of the farm management department of the University of Peking①.

In her charming home at Nanking, Mrs. Buck still patiently carries on her work. In 1927, in the civil war, the Bucks lost their home and all their possessions, but this scarcely halted her work on *The Good Earth*. She plays the Chinese harp, entertains graciously and finds contentment in the ancient culture which she has so deeply penetrated. She is of medium height and stature, in her early thirties, black-haired,

---

① 此处原文可能有笔误,应当是 University of Nanking。

and always calm and reserved.

24. *The Good Earth* Wins Pulitzer Prize

Times Colonist, May 21, 1932

Pearl S. Buck, author of *The Good Earth*, was awarded the Pulitzer prize for the best American novel of the year, $1,000. The rules of the award were changed to enable the judges to honor this writer.

According to Pulitzer will terms, the judges are empowered to alter conditions of the award, which they have done.

The prize was supposed, originally, to go to the novelist whose book "shall best present the wholesome atmosphere of American life and the highest standard of American manners and manhood."

The Good Earth, which tells of the hardships of a Chinese farmer and his brother, was so outstanding that it caused the judge to alter the award conditions.

25. Young China Flames with Loves—Hates

1931 Pulitzer Prize Winner Writes a Novelet

The Des Moines Register, May 22, 1932

The Young Revolutionist, by Pearl Buck (John Day $1.50)

[By Zella Wallaces, Des Moines] Friends and admirers of Pearl Sydenstricker Buck who followed the adventures of Wang Lung through the fascinating pages of *The Good Earth*, Pulitzer prize winner for 1931, will find an unforgettable evening in the reading of this new and slender volume *The Young Revolutionist*. This time Mrs. Buck has chosen for her medium that neglected form of American art—the novelette that Willa Cather and Edith Wharton have found so satisfactory. It is a form of expression that permits extreme concentration and illumination of a smaller segment of life than the novel permits. It is the ideal medium for one-character portraiture.

Spirit and Power

The same qualities that distinguished and established Mrs. Buck in *The Good Earth* are here again. She writes with spirit, with power, and authenticity. Few occidental writers know the orient as Pearl Buck knows her China. She went there before she was old enough to walk and has spent her life there except when completing her education in America.

She writes a simple, careful rhythmic, often one-syllable prose that has something Biblical in its quality. But she knows not only China; she has that complete and sympathetic understanding of the human heart everywhere and once again she makes us feel the closeness of the soil, the warm sunshine and the fragrance of the upturned loam. (Her husband teaches agriculture at the University of Nanking.)

This is the story of a peasant Ko-sen whose parents during a severe illness dedicated him to the temple service of Buddha. This active youth rebelled against the darkened halls and deadness of the priesthood. So with his friend Fah-li they joined the army with the Revolutionists and dedicated themselves to the memory and the unfinished work of Sun-Yat-sen. They destroyed relentlessly the temples of Buddha, of Confucius and of the Christians.

Four Inch Feet

There is the impact of western ideas in the mind of this lad who from his boyhood can remember his little sister suffering and crying with her bound feet because her family had promised at her betrothal that her feet would not exceed four inches in length on her wedding day. We have here the love of a lad for his home and family, the flame of his patriotism, his devotion to blind ideals, the love of a soldier for his buddy—and there is the boom of guns and the spilling of human blood.

These are not thin themes. Mrs. Buck makes us not only see but feel the confusion, the chaos and disorder of emergent China but she closes with a hopeful note for the new order. There is something restorative in the work of this unassuming Pearl Buck. Again, and again she makes me feel—"I will lift mine eyes unto the hills from whence cometh help."

26. Pearl Buck to Live in Ithaca, Novelist Wrote "Best Seller"

The Ithaca Journal, Apr 7, 1932

Ithacans will be calling a best-selling novelist "neighbor" for the next year, now that Pearl Buck, author of *The Good Earth*, has decided to come to town. Mrs. Buck's husband, J. Lossing Buck, is to take graduate work at Cornell, and they will arrive from China in July.

Both are former students of Cornell. Mrs. Buck, formerly Pearl Sydenstricker, took a Master of Arts degree here in 1925. Her husband graduated from Cornell in 1914, and became a Master of Science here in 1925.

The family has since resided at the University of Nanking, where Mr. Buck is a member of the faculty.

The background from which Mrs. Buck wrote her famous novel, *The Good Earth*, was gathered from a childhood in China where she lived with missionary parents. A later novel of hers is now running in Cosmopolitan magazine, and her *The Young*

Revolutionist will be on sale the latter part of this month.

The Good Earth was the bestselling novel of 1931 in America and set a fashion for English novels against a Chinese scene. She has written her brother, Dr. Edgar Sydenstricker, director of the division of research of the Milbank Memorial Fund in New York, that she is being besieged by eight motion picture concerns for the rights to that novel.

The Bucks are at Present residing in Peiping.

27. Popularity of *The Good Earth* Was a Surprise to Pearl S. Buck
The Kansas City Star, Jul 22, 1932

The American-born woman who wrote a story of life in China that for more than a year has been a best-seller, and won for her a Pulitzer Prize, is today almost as obscure as when she sent her manuscript to her publishers with a note saying she feared it would not be liked.

Of all the figures on the literary horizon, Pear S. Buck is the cloudiest. Although it has been more than a year since fame knocked at the gate of her compound in Nanking, China, and critics leaped on the bandwagon to trumpet blasts of praise, she still is a mystery. Even so great a windfall as the Pulitzer Prize for the best novel of the year has not blown away the clouds that obscure her.

Editors clamor for stories about her. And all they get is that she is the daughter of American missionaries; that she was born in America and that she now lives in China.

So it has gone since an American publisher in 1930 saw fit to change the title of a manuscript from *Wang Lung* to *The Good Earth*.

As the number of her readers grew to hundreds of thousands, the mists surrounding her grew thicker, and when no silver lining showed itself, a few exasperated writers hit upon the idea that there was no such person as Pearl S. Buck. Would anyone, they asked, venture upon a literary career with such a name? Armed with this "clue," they jumped to the conclusion that the whole thing was a hoax behind which lurked someone of the stature of George Bernard Shaw or of Theodore Dreiser.

But It Is Her Real Name

Her real name is Pearl Sydenstricker Buck. Those who doubt her existence will, if her efforts to escape the searchlight of publicity fail, get a glimpse of her late in August. She is coming to America with her husband, J. Lossing Buck, who will spend a year at Cornell doing graduate work in agriculture in which he is regarded an authority.

It is doubtful whether anyone seeking copy will get Mrs. Buck to talk about herself. Modesty is not the word to describe her, rather one should call it humility which sets no value upon those things that concern self. If she is called abrupt, diffident, aloof or even "high hat" by interviewers on her arrival, it will not be because she objects to prying into her private affairs, but because she is convinced that she herself does not matter, the important thing being her work.

When her publisher asked for a biographical sketch, a request made of every new author, she wrote:

"I do not seem to find much in my life that sounds interesting to put on paper. I would like to be known not for myself, but for my books. The Chinese are very sensible about this. They take the artist as important only because of his art and are not interested in his personality and consider him unimportant except as a medium."

Mrs. Buck is more Chinese in her outlook upon life than she is American. Her attitude toward those things we take for granted and even consider of great importance is one of curiosity and surprise. When she received a cablegram informing her that the Book-of-the-Month Club had accepted *The Good Earth*, she wrote:

"I do not know exactly what it means since I do not belong to this club, but I looked up an advertisement of theirs and saw a very imposing list of names of widely known authors, and so I appreciate the fact that it must mean something for them to like my book well enough to put it on their list."

Saw Only the Honor Attached

She did not look upon the club's choice of her book in terms of an assured sale of 40,000 copies, but that it was an honor to be selected by it. In expressing her thanks, she wrote:

"It is very comforting and especially so because yesterday I happened to read a very astonishing article entitled 'Authors Are Awful.' It made me quite wretched to think there were persons such as this publisher described, and I wondered if perhaps all authors seem thus to all publishers!"

She nearly met a famous author when Will Rogers was in China. He planned to fly from Shanghai to Nanking to see her, but a storm prevented him making the trip. Mrs. Buck learned of his proposed visit from the American consul.

"I am afraid I did not know much about him," she wrote to a friend in America, "until the consul informed me very fully, and impressed upon me that I should feel it a great honor! I will wait until I see Mr. Rogers."

Whether her forthcoming trip to this country will acquaint her with it is doubtful. On her previous trips she was unhappy and went home just as soon as she was able.

Although brought up to call America home, Mrs. Buck's heart has never been in this country. She was born in Hillsboro, W. Va., and was taken to the far East as a child. Her missionary parents lived in many places far in the interior of China, but moved to Chinkiang when Pearl was a child. She spent her girlhood there studying English under her mother, who also prepared her for college.

Mother a Fearless Critic

"From my earliest childhood," Mrs. Buck says, "she taught me to write down what I saw and felt and she helped me to see beauty everywhere. Not a week passed without my giving her something to read that I had written and she was fearless, though kind, in her criticism."

When her lessons were over the girl roamed the hills and valleys of the country nearby, listening endlessly to conversations and absorbing the beauty and life of the people around her. At the age of 15 she was sent to a boarding school in Shanghai.

She was 17 when she arrived in America to complete her education. She majored in sociology and in at least one of her English classes her marks were not high. The professor, according to a classmate, did not like her style of writing because it was so unconventional.

"I did not enjoy my life in college," Mrs. Buck wrote in the autobiography submitted to her publisher. "It was too confining. I did not know of the life of which the girls talked so much and my life was as remote from them as though it had been on another planet."

Two years after she returned to China, she married an American student of rural economics and sociology. For nearly five years Mr. and Mrs. Buck lived in a town in North China where they were the only white persons during most of their stay.

"As a married woman," says Mrs. Buck. "I had more freedom than I had ever had to come and go and Chinese women would talk to me as woman to woman and friend to friend. Outwardly our life was exciting enough. We had a famine, with all that means: we had battles between bandits attacking the city, and bullets flew thick as flocks of birds over our little Chinese house which clung to the inside of the city wall."

These, Mrs. Buck adds, were the hardest and happiest days of her life and when Mr. Buck became head of a department in the University of Nanking. She left North China with regret. While he taught rural economics and sociology, she instructed in English literature.

From that time on they have lived in a brick house near the university. It has a garden of trees, flowers and vegetables and is surrounded by mansions and houses of thatch. There her two little girls play with other children and study Chinese reading and writing every day with their mother's old Chinese tutor.

The story of *The Good Earth* existed complete in her mind in the Chinese language before it was written. It took her only three months to put it down and she scarcely changed a word of the first draft.

Most of her readers, knowing of her missionary associations, have commented upon what they call her Biblical style, but Mrs. Buck says it is more Chinese than that of the Bible. She is firmly of the opinion, however, that the real Chinese does not exist in the writings of Confucius or other Celestial sages.

Much to Mrs. Buck's surprise the Americans liked her book. She glances at reviews her publisher sends and then throws them away. She keeps only those in which she has been criticized, the outstanding one having come from the pen of Younghill Kang, the Korean author who condemned her without mercy.

"I expected many more like his," she wrote. "I was sure young China would resent the book. They don't like to have the western world know about old China. They are ashamed of it."

(A. A. F.)

28. Pearl Buck Wins Nobel Prize
Award for Literature Based Principally on *The Good Earth*, Pulitzer Novel
The Decatur Daily Review, Nov 10, 1938

[By Associated Press, Stockholm] The 1938 Nobel prize for literature was awarded today to Pearl Buck, American author of *The Good Earth* and other novels dealing with China.

Mrs. Buck, formerly Pearl Sydenstricker and now Mrs. Richard J. Walsh of Great Neck, N. Y., was born in Hillsboro, W. Va., in 1892 and has spent much of her life in China. (Mrs. Buck's parents were missionaries in China and her first husband, J. Lossing Buck, was a member of the faculty of Nanking university. They were divorced in 1935.)

The Nobel award was understood to have been based particularly on *The Good Earth*, which also won the 1932 Pulitzer Prize for an American novel.

The Nobel literature prize amounts to 155,000 kroner, about $37,975.

Pearl Buck was the third American to win the Nobel award in literature, an honor she share in this country only with Sinclair Lewis, who was awarded it in 1930, and Eugene O'Neil, who received it in 1936.

She joined the company of such literary greats as Maurice Maeterlinck, Rudyard Kipling, Anatole France, William Butler Yeats and George Bernard Shaw.

She was the second woman of the decade to win Nobel recognition for her literature. The first, in 1928, was Sigrid Undset.

The Good Earth, probably best known of Mrs. Buck's works, won the Pulitzer award for the best novel of 1932. She also was awarded second prize in 1933 O. Henry

Memorial awards for her story, *The Frill*.

29. Pearl Buck Led Dual Existence
The Interests of Nobel Prize Winner Were Always American, but Her Life Was Chinese
St Louis Post Dispatch, Dec 11, 1938

[By Virginia Irwin, New York]

Talking with Pearl Buck is like taking a sedative. Not that the lady puts you to sleep, but her calmness is contagious. She has an amazingly placid personality, an air of detachment, that lends composure to anyone privileged to spend more than 10 minutes in conversation with her, and yet her voice, soothing as the strains of your favorite serenade, is compelling.

Recently, in the offices of her husband and publisher, Pearl Buck talked to me of the honor that has come to her in the form of the Nobel Prize for literature, of her plans for the future and of the war that has so long been going on in China. And as she talked the noises outside on Madison Avenue, one of Manhattan's busiest thoroughfares, seemed to recede and the room in which we sat seemed strangely quiet, as if Pearl Buck's ability to detach herself from her surroundings might be a physical rather than a mental power.

"Frankly," Mrs. Buck smiled, not with her face, but with her eyes, as we talked of the prize awarded her just a month ago, "it all happened as a complete and tremendous surprise to me. I had no idea even that the committee convened at this time of the year and I had never given a thought to being considered. But now that I have been singled out for this honor, I feel a great responsibility. The thought came to me at the time that it would perhaps have been better had the committee waited another decade before they so honored me for my work. But now that I have won the prize—not only for my *Good Earth*, but for all my work—I am determined to do better work. There are so many plots, so many books begging in my mind to be written."

As the third American to win the Nobel award, this rather shy, solemn woman shares that honor in this country with only Sinclair Lewis and Eugene O'Neill, and now joins the company of Maurice Maeterlinck, Rudyard Kipling, Anatole France, William Butler Yeats and George Bernard Shaw. This international recognition in literature is understood to have been based particularly on *The Good Earth*, which won the 1932 Pulitzer prize, and made China a living reality to American novel readers.

"So many people think when they see my name signed to anything that it must be another story about China and the Chinese," Mrs. Buck continued as we talked of her writing. "And people have the idea that it was my years in Chinese that made me a writer. Actually I have written because I have always wanted to write and that my first writings were about China is explained by the fact that China was in the foreground. I would much rather have had the subconscious out of which writer writes American rather than Chinese, but I would not want to wipe out my Chinese experiences."

For many years, Mrs. Buck says, she has planned not to limit herself to books about China, and *The Patriot*, her latest volume, is American in theme. Her next story will be called "The American Legend" and will concern itself with the strange love which America gives to her heroes.

"It is an American phenomenon, the idolatry that is lavished upon a man who happens to fly the Atlantic alone or who hits more baseballs than anyone else," Mrs. Buck said. "The idolatry lasts for a short time and then the hero is forgotten. In no other land in the world is this so and in all other lands a national hero is one who has made some definite contribution to the life or culture of his country and because of that contribution is held in honor and respect by his countrymen, not for just a short time, but for life and even afterwards."

Born in America, but with 38 years' experience in China, Pearl Buck regards herself as having lived a dual existence. Her interests, she says, have always been American, and behind her were American traditions, but her life was Chinese. She hopes to visit China again, but never again makes it her home.

"I had never lived in peace until I came to America," she told me quietly. "Always in China there were civil wars and one never knew what might happen from one day to the next. And conditions there are even worse now."

China, Mrs. Buck believes, may eventually yield to Japan, but she says that the real war will be fought after all big battles are over—the war to control the spirit as well as the area of China.

"Two years before this war broke out, the Chinese were anticipating just such a war," Mrs. Buck explained. "And China knew that she could never hope to meet Japan with equal arms. She knew then and she knows now that she may be compelled to yield, but she also knows that she can never be vanquished in real defeat. To the world she may be the conquered nation, but her civilization will be unchanged. Japan may bomb one great city after another, control the sea coast, but that is as nothing, for the real civilization of China is in the interior. You know 80 percent of China is rural and China is not dependent on foreign trade or on trade centers. Her communities are self-sufficient, and if Japan were to occupy all the large Chinese cities, she would not have control of China. It is a physical impossibility to control China and her spirit, too."

"China was never controlled even by her own officials, because, while a Chinese accepts family control as right and just, he has never, and will never, be amenable to government dictation. Chinese families will go on living as they have lived for centuries, regulated only within themselves, and refusing regulation from outside the family circle. And it is just such refusal to accept other than family control that keeps Chinese life strong. When human life is too regulated, it becomes weak and wastes away."

On the subject of Hitler's persecution of the Jews, Catholics and political opponents of the Third Reich, Mrs. Buck predicts that history will look upon the Fuehrer's campaign as "the most awful blot" ever placed upon civilization. "Whatever excuses anyone may find for his principles, certainly no one could find any justification for Hitler's methods," Mrs. Buck frowned. "After all, one simply doesn't pick a person's pocket and then send him out into the world to starve."

Until six years ago, Pearl Buck had no permanent home in this country. She was born in West Virginia and taken to China at an early age by her father, who was a missionary. She had no formal schooling until she went to a boarding school in Shanghai at the age of 15 and by that time, she says, she had ceased to think of herself as different from the Chinese. For 10 years, from 1921 to 1931, she taught at Nanking University, Southeastern University and at the Government institution in Chental①. For five years, she and her first husband, John Buck, lived in an out-of-the-way town in northern China, where for months at a time they saw no white people, and learned there the beauty and the feel of the real China of the interior.

Now Pearl Buck is the proud possessor of a permanent home in Bucks County, Pa., and there with her present husband, Richard J. Walsh, New York publisher, she lives with her children and does most of her work.

"But I can work any place," she explained. "I am not like some writers who must have some one room, some one place in that room, and must use the same pen. I work wherever I happen to be, because I have the ability to be able to concentrate on what I want to do. If I am in a room full of people, all talking at once, I can go right on thinking out a plot, or doing whatever happens to be foremost in my mind, because I just don't listen if I don't want to."

Perhaps it is this ability to detach herself from her surroundings that gives Pearl Buck the suggestion of remoteness that is about her and adds to the impression of solemnity that not even a perky hat and the latest in costume suits could erase from your correspondent's mind during this interview. This solemnity is most apparent in her soft, large, blue eyes and gives her a look of sadness which vanishes only when she smiles. And Pearl Buck smiles often, but like the Chinese, she seldom laughs.

---

① Editor's Notes: Couldn't verify the word "Chental". It might be Central, referring to the Central University.

30. Pearl Buck's Years of Training for Writing

The Province (Canada) , Jan 7 , 1939

[By Professor W. T. Allison] The award of the Nobel Prize to Pearl S. Buck, recently, was probably based upon her novels of Chinese life. When *The Good Earth* appeared in 1931 it was received with applause in the United States, Canada, and Great Britain, and proved to be the world's best seller since Sinclair Lewis was lifted into fame by *Main Street*.

It brought to Mrs. Buck not only a fortune in royalties but the Pulitzer Prize in 1932, a Yale M.A. honorary degree in 1933, and two years later from the American Academy of Arts and Letters thc William Dean Howells medal for fiction. And now has come the crowning honor, the Nobel Prize, all the more acceptable because Mrs. Buck (now Mrs. J. Walsh) is the first American woman to be chosen by a committee of foreigners as worthy of this distinction.

Like so many successful authors, Pearl S. Buck rose to greatness because she was fortunate in her subject, her education, and her experience of life. When she was only two months old her father and mother went as missionaries of the Presbyterian church from Virginia to the interior of China. This was forty-five years ago when the people of the celestial kingdom looked upon white men and women as foreign devils.

Mrs. Buck's home was once mobbed in a city where the members of her family were the only foreigners; her father, who with the greatest courage went on lonely journeys throughout the district brought back stories of his narrow escapes from death and colorful descriptions of his mission work in villages along the banks of the Yangste (should be Yangtze) River. These stories and those related to the growing child by her old Chinese nurse who served the Buck family for eighteen years, laid a basis for her knowledge of native life.

Her Mother Her Only Teacher for Years

Her mother was her only teacher for many years. She taught Pearl to study the customs and institutions of her adopted country sympathetically and to see beauty everywhere; she also encouraged her to write, and gave her wise criticism. When she grew up, Pearl married a young American professor and taught English literature on the staff of the University of Nanking. By this time, she had become a deep student of Chinese literature. Over a period of ten years, she read all the classic novels of China. This required infinite application, for she had first to learn between 10,000 and 20,000 Chinese characters.

Her formal study, added to her keen observation of the full tide of daily life at a time when China was being swept by the struggles of bandits and war-lords and by social and educational change, formed the abundant resources of a novelist who had learned to paint the thing as she saw it for people thousands of miles distant from the Nanking garden where she wrote *The Good Earth*.

This novel which has won for its author such renown is a sincere and skillful interpretation of Chinese character. It discourses to us of "the still, sad music of humanity"; humanity, it is true, with a yellow skin and oblique eyes, and with ways and modes of thoughts far different from ours, but in its trials and temptations, essentially the same as those of the western world. The western reader is, perhaps, most impressed by Mrs. Buck's characters, for they seem so understandable; there is nothing mysterious about them, nothing exotic as in so many stories of the Orient. If it were not for the local color and the extreme poverty, the floods, droughts, pestilences and revolution, we might imagine we were reading about Canadian or English people.

"These people," as an authoritative critic has written, "are born, play, toil, suffer and dream as all humans have done, under whatever sun, or whatever patch of common earth."

31. Divorce "Without" Passion

Daily News, Jun 16, 1935

[By Ruth Reynolds] A new high in modern divorce methods has been reached by a woman, who, after twenty-seven years of marriage, agreed not only to give up her husband to a prettier rival, but lived on friendly terms with her successor during the six weeks both were establishing divorce residences in Nevada.

But there were tears in her eyes when the gray-haired little woman, Ruby Abbott Walsh, moved with determined steps into Washoe County Courthouse at Reno to charge her 49-year-old spouse, Richard J. Walsh, New York publisher with "cruelty I can neither forgive nor condone."

And she fled by the rear entrance five minutes later—after the District Court had granted her petition for divorce, not waiting to see Pearl Sydenstricker Buck, also newly freed, meet Walsh at the courthouse door and hurry away, radiant and flustered, to a second marriage.

Her Husband, Friend Had Fallen in Love

For six months and more, Mrs. Walsh faced the inevitable and acquiesced quietly. She knew her husband and her friend had fallen in love—a love deeper and more demanding than the passions of youth. There was nothing she could do about it. So when the time arrived to set the wheels of divorce in motion, Mrs. Walsh agreed that she and Mrs. Buck might as well go through the divorce mill together.

Mrs. Walsh, her friends say, has seen with amazing clarity this true life plot so similar to the pieces of fiction Pearl Buck has written.

No one knows better than Ruby Abbott Walsh that the meeting of her husband and the author was no more significant than his meeting with numerous other women writers.

Ruby Hopkins Abbott married Dick Walsh a year after he finished Harvard. He was a reporter and special writer for the Boston Herald.

He advanced rapidly and she watched with pride while he worked as assistant secretary of the Boston Chamber of Commerce, promotion manager of the Curtis Publishing Company, advertising writer, editor of *Colliers' Weekly*, associate editor of *Judge*, and finally in 1926 president of the John Day Publishing Company.

The Lyons, Kan., son of Joseph and Elizabeth Walsh made a place for himself in the world—was a member of the United States Food administration staff during the war, first president and honorary member of the Art Directors' Club, member of the Council of Foreign Relations, wrote several books and a number of articles. And Ruby Abbott Walsh was proud of him, as she bore and reared his three children, Natalie, Richard and Elizabeth.

She was particularly pleased when he told her that his publishing company had a new find—Pearl Sydenstricker Buck, daughter of missionaries and wife of a professor at Nanking University in China.

And when Mrs. Buck came to New York in 1929 to see about publication of her first book, *East Wind: West Wind*, Mrs. Walsh was extremely interested in the author's unusual life.

Her parents, Absalom and Caroline Sydenstricker, Mrs. Buck said, were Presbyterian missionaries and just happened to be in this country when Pearl was born at Hillsboro, W. Va., on June 26, 1892.

They returned to China immediately with their baby. Pearl and a younger sister, grew up among the Chinese and absorbed their culture. Because her parents wanted her to be educated in the United States, she studied four years and received her A. B. degree at Randolph Macon College at Lynchburg, Va.

She was most unhappy from her matriculation until her graduation in 1914 because she felt more Chinese than American. She had little in common with her fellow students.

She hurried back to China and plunged into teaching at a mission school and at Nanking University. There she met the man who was to become her first husband, John Lossing Buck, professor of agriculture, who had come out from his home in Dutchess County, N. Y., to teach there.

He was a slim, sensitive little fellow with brown hair, smoked glasses and a small, reddish-blonde mustache—and she fell in love with him. They were married in

1917.

For years their life was placid and ideal. Several years after their marriage Carol, now 15, arrived. Then Janice, now 10, came along.

When she had time, Pearl Buck wrote about the only things she really understood—China and the Chinese people. Much of her manuscript was returned to her with rejection slips. Finally the John Day people saw *East Wind: West Wind*, and thought it was good.

That first novel had little sale. Her second, *The Good Earth*, won the Pulitzer prize of 1932. It was then Mrs. Buck became a celebrity and a real friend of Ruby and Dick Walsh.

She made enough money from her books, *The Good Earth*, *Sons* and *A House Divided*, to do as she chose. She suggested that her husband spend his sabbatical year in work and study at Cornell University, as he had done back in 1926, when she received her master's degree there. He agreed, and the Bucks came to New York State to live.

Said She Couldn't Stand Bustle of City Life

She was a domestic looking person—buxom, blue-eyed, wavy brown-haired.

She said, in a voice low and subdued, that the bustle and feverish tempo of New York life seemed so futile, so useless, so puzzling. She couldn't, she said, stand living in New York City. Her husband had a farm up the Hudson—but she was going to spend her time with him at Ithaca, writing and studying at Cornell.

Ithaca is a long way from New York City but Mrs. Buck had numerous reasons to be in the city of her publisher during the next twelve months. When she spoke her mind about missionaries and finally, after a row, resigned as one of them, her publisher stood squarely behind her, issuing statements and advising her.

Pearl planned to return to China with her husband at the end of the college term, June, 1933—but she didn't. She stayed on for one thing and another and stopped in Hollywood to see how the movie of *The Good Earth* was coming along.

And when she did finally get to China she found, in her own words, that she was "thoroughly dissatisfied."

Instead of raising her two daughters in Chinese ways as she had intended to, she brought them back to America in 1934, sent them to camp, arranged for their American schooling, and settled down in New York City to write.

She had changed greatly. She was slimmer, more vital, more self-contained, and certainly prettier. She no longer talked of preferring the Chinese and disliking the bustle of New York City. She was, she said, intensely interested in all things American—intended to write a novel about Americans.

Anyone with half an eye could see she was falling in love with some one—and Ruby Abbott Walsh knew his name.

But Mrs. Walsh, intellectual as she is, couldn't blame Mrs. Buck, either for the drastic psychological and physical change which had come over her, or for her mature unprofessional interest in the publisher. She could only fear, and wait, and hope for the best.

Buck, on the other hand, was too deeply interested in Government work he was doing for Henry Morgenthau in Northwestern China to think too much about his traveling wife. And when he finally heard she wanted a divorce, he acquiesced—agreeing everyone must live his own life. As for the children—a far-sighted agreement of property and custody made between the Bucks in 1925—had given them to their mother.

In the same spirit—that she could do more harm than good by standing in her husband's way—Mrs. Walsh, too, agreed to a divorce. Their property and custody agreement was signed last May 6.

What was more natural to both these friends than that they live together during their six weeks' Reno residence? Or that they should employ the same attorney, George A. Whiteley? They shunned the limelight. Mrs. Buck constantly refused to talk before the Reno women's clubs. Mrs. Walsh's identity was not revealed.

Last Tuesday, Mrs. Buck took 20 minutes to get her divorce, charging cruelty. She smoked nervously. Two hours later, in the home of the Rev. Brewster Adams, Baptist minister, the words pronounced by the Rev. R. C. Thompson, Dean of Men at the University of Nevada, made her the second Mrs. Richard Walsh, bright and blooming at 43.

And in another part of town her good friend, Ruby Abbott Walsh, was trying not to cry.

32. American Woman in China's War Knew Heroes, Gangsters, Martyrs

The Commercial Appeal, Oct 10, 1943

Battle Hymn of China, By Agnes Smedley. A. Knopf. $3.50

[Reviewed by Mrs. Mark Clutter] "Their country has offered them nothing but sorrow and hunger, cold and suffering. Still, they offer their lives for it. They died by the thousands on deserted battlefields. Other thousands stagger to the rear, look ruefully at their uncared-for wounds, their eyes searching the mountain paths and the highways, yearning for help that never comes." Thus does Miss Smedley characterize the heroic army of China.

While Miss Smedley is not a Communist by personal conviction, she has a great interest in the ideological pressure that the Soviet Union has exerted upon the Chinese. She finds the soldiers of the Red Armies of China are more united in purpose, more eager for education, and more willing to sacrifice themselves than those of the Kuomintang Party.

Aside from the fact that this is a well-documented book of recent history, written with the impartiality of a good reporter, it is also worthwhile reading for its interesting sidelights on personalities that we have seen from one viewpoint only. She does not hesitate to criticize Chiang Kai-shek and she dares to suggest that Lu Hsun is a greater author than Lin Yutang. She came in contact with Hu Shih, Claire Chennault, Pearl Buck, George Sokolsky, General Stilwell, T V. Soong, Edgar Snow and a number of other colorful and famous persons.

She impresses the reader time and again with the stupidity and indifference displayed by America in allowing war materials to be sold to the Japanese. "The Japanese murderers were without a sword," she quotes a Chinese general as saying. "America gave them a sword."

This book, however, is not primarily concerned with the intricacies of international politics. It is a book about people. She knows about war lords and gangsters and at one time was forced to flee from the dreaded "Blue Shirt" gang. She also knows the courage and loyalty of the great mass of China's common people for whom she has labored hard to organize medical care.

33. Comments on Pearl S. Buck in Agnes Smedley's *Battle Hymn of China*

The attitude of Chinese and foreign Christians toward Pearl Buck was an interesting one. Among them she was noted not only for her books on China but because she had left her church, divorced a husband, and married a second time. As many political parties often attack former members, so the missionaries looked askance on Pearl Buck. They hinted that she would deteriorate, and when she obviously did not, they were much put out.

Many Chinese disliked Pearl Buck's books because she did not always show her characters dressed in their Sunday best. A Chinese colonel once announced to a friend of mine that Pearl Buck was "finished" because she wrote an article about the Eighth Route Army, calling it "Guns for China's Democracy." She was henceforth isolated from China, he declared, washed up. What nonsense! Such were the rumors that hateful people spread about Pearl Buck.

34. Pearl Buck Tells Audience That China-Japanese War Is Being Won Through Non-Resistance

The Daily Journal, Oct 23, 1939

After explaining the vast difference between the Chinese and Japanese peoples, Pearl S. Buck, noted writer, told a large audience at the Vineland High School auditorium, Saturday night, that the Chinese have adopted a new method of resisting the invasion of the Japanese, which is, by not resisting at all.

This astonishing information brought smiles to the audience until the lecturer explained that the Chinese philosophy believes that "war is won by the person who stays alive when it is over," and said in her opinion, that she does not believe Japan can ever conquer China.

She advised her audience that the United States "might do well to consider this Chinese philosophy in these threatening times," adding that the Chinese are just wearing their enemy out, using guerrilla warfare as their only offense, and merely to harass the Japs.

The Chinese people have withdrawn into their vast interior, Miss Buck said, as the Japanese have bombed most of the seacoast cities in China, and captured many of the important ones. These victories have not bothered the Chinese at all, she declared, as they have calmly moved elsewhere when their homes were destroyed, and are establishing new centers of their age-old culture and civilization in the hinterland.

She quoted a Chinese proverb: "'There are 36 ways of escape and the best is to run away,'" to show how the Chinese people feel toward the Japanese invasion. She pointed out that the Chinese were not cowards but were not interested in war.

She criticized by implication this country for its aid to Japan through exports, declaring that Soviet Russia is the only nation which has befriended China, and that Russia has not done enough.

Miss Buck predicted that Japan could not continue its present war if this nation stopped exporting products to the islands. She declared, in answer to questions, that she believes China is further from being conquered today than ever, and that warplane bombings in China have aroused the inhabitants to hatred of the Japanese but have not broken their spirit. "The bombings have strengthened the temper of the Chinese," she said.

She asserted that Soviet Russia does not want to fight any nation, but merely wishes to add to the existing confusion in her aim for a world revolution. She explained that China is carrying on trade, despite capture of her seaports, by re-opening her old trade routes, and declared she believes the Japanese want "certain powers" in China more than territory—and that Japan will "go beyond China" in her quest, if given the chance.

Referring to the exports of American goods to Japan. Miss Buck pointed out that China can't buy United States' products, as they have no way of getting them. Pointing out that this country's trade agreement with Japan expires soon, the speaker asked, "are we going to continue our trade with that country? Leave it to you to determine the justice of the problem, Japan couldn't carry on her war with China if it were not for the United States."

Introduced by Dr. Ada Walker, president of the Vineland Woman's Club, the speaker was accompanied by Prof. Edward R. Johnstone, director of the Vineland Training School.

She told of the differences between the Chinese and Japanese races by describing their different temperaments, their modes of living, their physical points, as well as their psychological attitudes, and geographical set-up, all of which, she indicated, are as different as day and night.

Japan is a world power, she said, imbued with a tremendous and fierce energy which she has poured into the war. She believes nothing is impossible to Japan in its present position, except to have faith in the Chinese ability to withstand being conquered.

China, she pointed out, is one-half again as large as the United States, and has cold barren areas in the north, and lush, tropical sections in the south, as well as deserts. China is in reality a continent, while Japan is a number of small islands, which are the most beautiful in the world. Japan is sea-girt and storm ridden, and tortured almost continually by Nature, in the way of earthquakes and other disasters. The people there have become so accustomed to such catastrophes that they are not even mentioned in the Japanese newspapers. "That sort of environment breeds a certain sort of person," she said, while big China makes for friendly, good fellows, the people having a sense of humor and easy-going ways. Japanese, on the other hand, have tremendous physical courage, but are dour and suspicious, as well as more serious than the Chinese.

"The Chinese enjoy life," she said, "while the Japanese enjoy beauty. The Japanese have little food while the Chinese are happy-go-lucky about everything. We in America do not know the Chinese. Those whom we see are Cantonese." She said the true Chinese of Central China is a physically handsome creature and the women are beautiful.

Dr. Walker mentioned in her welcoming address that the attractive programs were printed by pupils of the Training School, for whose Research Department the lecture will benefit. The Woman's Club sponsored the lecture. It marks the second time Miss Buck has appeared in Vineland under the auspices of the club.

Vocal selections were rendered at the opening of the program by Leonard Tremper, tenor, of Philadelphia, with Mrs. Dorothy Boersig as pianist.

35. How China Can Win

The Index Journal, Mar 16, 1939

Mrs. Pearl Buck, author of *The Good Earth*, and a recognized authority on Chinese affairs, doesn't agree with many of the war experts that Japan never will be able to whip China. She expresses the opinion that China has started a "tremendous trek" westward to revive her small industries as a means not only of relief, but of occupation for youth.

"China cannot win the war by arms and she knows it," Mrs. Buck says, "so she has decided she will have to live the war and in spite of the war. Her policy has been to withdraw—not run away, but withdraw. There is a tremendous trek to the West, the hinterland of China, their real strong hold."

Mrs. Buck estimates that Japan had captured about 70 percent of the large industries in the Chinese cities, as a result of which the Chinese had turned to the West and its "way of working for centuries in small industries," such as weaving, and manual arts. The aim she said, was to establish thousands of cooperative local industries.

"It is relief, but also it putting to work the brains of young people." she observes. "If China can hold to her raw materials, encourage her people in small industries and keep her spirit, she will win even though the end is far off."

36. In a New Novel About the Far East, Pearl Buck Writes of China and Japan Today

Chattanooga Daily Times, Mar 5, 1939

The Patriot. By Pearl S. Buck. 372 pp.

New York: John Day Company. $2.50.

Mrs. Buck has interrupted her series of not altogether successful books about western life "to sing us again of Mandalay"; to tell us more about those circumstances of life with which she is most familiar, about China and Chinese, and this time their relations with their neighbors, the Japanese. In *The Patriot*, Mrs. Buck regains immediately her old mastery, her old achievement of so thoroughly immersing her reader in these strange, exotic circumstances—less strange now, though, than once they were, in no small measure due to Mrs. Buck, but largely attributable to the war, which has brought books and journalistic accounts of value for their interpretation of both the old and new attitudes of the Far East—that he reads it with the same ease and familiarity that he does a story about New York or New Orleans or Los Angeles. Nor is that all: Mrs. Buck returns to the simple, almost primitive, manner which so distinguished those early books—*The Good Earth*, *The Mother* and the others—a manner somewhat strange to western ears, but attractive and appealing: one which leaves the reader with the impression that he might have heard the story told by an old Chinese, rather than read it in a book by an American. And it is a vitally interesting story.

In the series of books about the Wang-family, Mrs. Buck wrote about the rise of a peasant family from poverty and ignorance to wealth and some degree of education. In doing this, she also informed her readers about the Chinese history of the last fifty years; about the change from the primitive China, which existed down to this century, to the modern China, an awakened youthful China, interested no less in western political and economic ideas than in western machinery.

The Patriot is not about the Wangs, but otherwise it picks up where *The House Divided* left off. This time we follow the fortunes of the Wus, a family of aristocratic and wealthy background. I-wan, the younger son of a Shanghai banker, is our hero. I-wan was a revolutionary idealist. He, like many other of his generation, both east and west, felt "this was a time when a deeper unity than blood united." His interest in the poor and oppressed overcame the strong and traditional feeling of family ties which most Chinese have. I-wan and his friend, En-lan, who was the leader of the movement in Shanghai, looked for the accomplishment of the revolution by Chiang Kai-shek. To their dismay, though, they barely escaped the fury with which he exterminated the revolutionaries when he took Shanghai. I-wan was sent by his father to a friend in Japan. There he saw something new in life—order. "China was used to the lawlessnesses and unruliness of people who loved freedom." In Japan he found a people who were "devoured with a sense of duty." There, also, he found Tama, whom he married. They established a home; two sons were born to them; I-wan had begun to forget the differences between himself and the Japanese, and they had begun to think of him as one of them, and then, one day, there were reports of difficulties in China. The soldiers began to leave in transports. New levies were called up. I-wan began to wonder about them. Finally, the urge became too strong. He was Chinese, and so he went back to discover that at last China was united; communist and supporter of Chiang Kai-shek fought, each in his own way, against the invader. And there we leave I-wan, wondering how it is all coming out, but determined to fight.

In this story, whose quality as entertainment is in no sense submerged in an attempt merely to inform—Mrs. Buck is far too wise and great an artist for that, there is not only the usual contrast of west and east, but there is in addition the presentation of the differences between Japanese and Chinese, differences no less great than those between Chinese and westerners. Mrs. Buck has attempted in all this to be impartial. Her sympathies are unquestionably Chinese, but that doesn't cause her to distort or propagandize solely. Her material in both instances is human beings, essentially the same despite obvious differences. Japan gave I-wan much. "Tama had somehow changed him. She had taught him to love order and right behavior and grace in everyday acts." So when he sat down to wonder over the outcome, he knew that Japan's militarism was wrong, but so was China's chaos. The Chinese were honest and simple, but "their simplicities were not enough. Enlightenment and knowledge, order and grace, these were things life must have, too." That was what China must strive for. Must not all peoples?

37. Chinese Family in War: Pearl Buck's Vivid Novel

The Philadelphia Inquirer, Jan 21, 1942

A Stirring Story of Invasion and Heroic Peasants
Dragon Seed by Peal S. Buck. The John Day Co., $2.50.

Pearl Buck's *Good Earth* has now become the scorched earth.

Her new novel is once more of China, but this time it is a China which has been invaded and laid waste by the ferocious "dwarf men" from the "East Ocean". There have been several novels to come out of this war which is now in its fifth year, but none has depicted Japanese cruelty and barbarism and Chinese stoical resistance so vividly, so powerfully, and so feelingly as this one.

Family Fortunes

As was *The Good Earth*, this is the novel of a family, and what happens to it is what has happened to uncounted thousands of Chinese families. It came to know death, despoliation and disease, but through the vicissitudes of war it remained adhered, and we are left in no doubt that heroic families like this one of Ling Tan will in the end conquer the conqueror.

Ling Tan lived in a village outside the gates of a city that is apparently Nanking. He was a simple, untutored farmer, but he and the others of the village were the inheritors of a rich and ancient culture. They could not read or write, but they were civilized human beings.

A Tiny Universe

Ling Tan knows nothing of an enemy and nothing of foreigners; his universe is bounded by his rice fields.

He owns his earth and as he tells it, he reflects that deep down below, on its other side, the foreigners must walk with their heads downward. He laughs at the thought. One day, over the rice fields, came the flying ships of the dwarf men.

They dropped silver eggs, which caused the earth to fly about. One of them dug a large hole, and the lucky farmer who owned the land exulted because he had always wanted a pond. He and his friends thought this must be a new machine for making ponds.

Eggs of Death

They were soon undeceived. The silver eggs dropped also on the city and laid it in ruins. Refugees filled the roads. Enemy soldiers pillaged the countryside. The war caused the dissolution of Ling Tan's family, and created a traitor in the person of his son-in-law, a city man.

Mrs. Buck traces the fortunes of the family through the months of war, shows us how it grows stronger through the infusion of new blood, and finally, how it is transformed into a centre of patriotism and guerrilla resistance. The Biblical simplicity of her style enhances and adds impart to a fine and compelling narrative.　（A. K.）

38. "Mental Laziness" of Women in America Appalls Pearl Buck; Research, Writing, Editing and Children Keep Writer Busy
The Akron Beacon Journal, Feb 18, 1940

[By Naomi Bender]
Pearl S. Buck, sitting on the arm of a chair in her modernistic New York apartment. She doesn't like to have photographs taken but, characteristically, made no fuss when asked to pose.

[New York] The women of America worry Pearl S. Buck, writer, lecturer and Nobel prize winner, known in private life as Mrs. Richard J. Walsh, wife of the president of John Day Publishing Co.

"Their lack of knowledge about their own history, that in itself is shocking," she said, decisively.

We were sitting in her New York apartment, a large, light, beautiful place, filled with Chinese paintings, screens and objects d'art, that made a singular but interesting combination with the modernistic furniture in blue and gold.

Reads Manuscript

Pearl Buck comes to New York but one day a week. The rest of her time she spends at her home in Buck (should be Bucks) County, Pennsylvania, where she writes, reads manuscripts for the John Day Company, and takes care of her children, five of whom are adopted.

"If only American women would study their own historical background," she continued, a little woefully, "it might help them. But look, right now congress is considering the passage of a bill to prohibit married women working. Why it will push women back years and years, and what are they doing about it? Nothing," she said in her rather high-pitched, clearly enunciated voice, as she sat on the comfortable divan, her capable, blunt-tipped hands resting quietly on her lap.

Takes History Straight

Pearl Buck is an enthusiast about history of all kinds. She prefers it to fiction.

"But I like my history straight," she said, quickly. "I can't abide historical novels."

She reads a lot, she says, aside from her manuscript reading for John Day— biographies and better fiction, as well as history. Stein-beck she admires tremendously.

"And I don't consider his *Grapes of Wrath* a social document; it is a very good novel, belonging, I would say, to the Dickens tradition."

Everything in life must be related to our past, she believes. And again and again she returns to the problem of American women who are in danger of losing the freedom they now hold so precariously. First, she would have them learn about great women in American history. Elizabeth Cady Stanton, for instance.

Mental Laziness

"She was the great American in the history of women," she said, "and we should do our utmost to see that women of this kind receive the recognition that is their due."

Typical of American women's mental laziness, Pearl Buck says, is their habit of listening to interminable lectures.

"But then they do absolutely nothing about what they hear," she pointed out. "Of course," she continued, smiling, "this habit of listening to people is an easy way to get information without working. But yet, what have women done about such necessary legislation as child labor laws? As I see it, this going to lectures is just a simple way to pass the time."

There's no insincerity or pretense about Pearl Buck. She knows what her beliefs are and has no hesitancy in expounding them.

Teaching for Men

She thinks, for instance, that women should have less to do with the education of children.

"Men in this country are dominated by women from infancy," she explained. This is unhealthy, she believes, and she would like to see more men become teachers.

In her own home, in Bucks County, Pearl Buck follows a fairly rigid schedule of work. In the morning, she writes four hours at a stretch while her children are at school.

She has a cook and a nurse, "for the four little ones," but she has no housekeeper. She does her own marketing. Occasionally, she likes to go into the kitchen and cook a meal.

"But I don't like washing dishes," she said, with a soft laugh, "or making beds." She doesn't play bridge or knit but "occasionally," she said, "I do like to make a pretty little dress for my two-year-old girl."

Her latest novel, *Other Gods*, has just been released by John Day Co. Already this energetic woman is working on another novel, with three others in mind.

She never works from an outline. "I get the whole book in shape in my mind before I set down a line," she explained. "If I spent too much time over an outline, I would be stale before I began to write."

"The worst period in writing a novel, she finds, is the middle. "That's where almost every writer bogs down," she said. "In the beginning I start with a rush and do practically no rewriting. My enthusiasm carries me along through the first third. In the last section, one is busy tying up all the loose ends and that is fun. But the middle," she sighed, with amusement. "That's the tough part to get through."

Stops for Children

But even when she is writing at fever pitch, she's always willing to stop if her children need her.

"I try to gear my day to my children," she said. "And I never want them to feel that they're interrupting me."

What working wives should do about their children and their home, she couldn't say. "But that of course depends on the wife, don't you think? Of course, I feel that I'm very fortunate to be able to do my work at home, so that that need not be a problem for me."

She has very little social life. "I don't care for crowds," she asserts, "I don't feel that I get anything from them. Once or twice a month, my husband and I go to the theater in New York."

With her writing, her editorial work, her children and her outside interests—last week, for instance, she was one of the forum speakers for a Chinese relief meeting—Pearl Buck's life is very full, indeed.

Simplifies Life

"But I simplify life," she said, "by doing only what interests me. Fortunately," she added with a laugh, "I find many things interesting and amusing."

Naturally, she has a keen interest in China's future since this country, its people and philosophical viewpoints have gained her love and respect.

"The war between China and Japan will drag along until there is a stalemate," she believes, "There will be no victory."

Will of Iron

Born in 1892, Pearl Buck look much younger than her years. Her hair drawn softly back in a small knot at the nape of her neck, free of make-up, her soft-skinned face and blue eyes are alive and expressive as she speaks.

But underneath her softness, one senses an iron will and strong determination to act on her beliefs. That is why she is so disappointed in American women. Here, she points out, they have such wonderful opportunities which they shamefully neglect. She would like to see women free, individuals all of them, who with marriage refuse to lapse into a vegetable state. If they want children, fine. If they don't, that should be their privilege. If they want careers, all to the good. But, if they don't, she feels they should still make some active contribution to the American way of life.

Above all, she hates any sort of distinction between men and women.

"Fundamentally, they're alike," she believes. "And there's no excuse for women being unprogressive."

39. Open Chinese Relief Drive
Fund of 1 Million Sought by Emergency Committee
The Kansas City Times, Nov 15, 1940

[By the Associated Press, New York] A nationwide drive to raise 1 million dollars for the relief of the war-stricken people of China was opened tonight by the newly formed China Emergency Relief Committee. Inc., headed by Pearl S. Buck, author.

Miss Buck announced that Mrs. Franklin D. Roosevelt was honorary chairman.

As part of the opening ceremonies, the committee had planned to have Madam Chiang Kai-shek, wife of the Chinese generalissimo, speak by short wave radio from Hong Kong, but the National Broadcasting Company was unable to make radio connect with that city at the scheduled time.

Miss Buck said that all money raised would be spent in the United States for medical and surgical supplies.

40. Richmond Paper Yesterday Carried a Picture, with the Caption "First Lady Aids Chinese Relief—Mrs. Franklin D. Roosevelt Presented a Check for $100.00 to Mrs. Buck"

The Daily News Leader, Dec 19, 1940

Pearl S. Buck, author and chairman of the newly-created China Emergency Relief Committee, at the White House Sunday to launch a national drive to raise $1,000,000 for medical supplies for war victims in China.

This is of special interest here, due to the fact that Mrs. Buck is the niece of Mrs. N. J. Doyle and Mr. C. S. Stulting, and a first cousin of Miss Mabel and Ruth Doyle, well known and prominent citizens of Montcrcy.

Mrs. Buck is the daughter of the late Absalom A. Sydenstricker and Mrs. Caroline Stulting Sydenstricker, well known citizens and former residents of Highland and Pocahontas county, W. Va., and who for many years, were missionaries to China, and where the daughter spent many years, and has published a number of books, dealing with life and conditions in China, and only a few years ago, was the winner of the Nobel prize in literature, and on the book *The Good Earth*.

Mrs. Buck is also the author of a number of other books, all dealing on her observation and knowledge of the Chinese people, after spending a number of years in this country. Mrs. Buck attended and graduated from the Randolph-Macon Woman's college in Lynchburg. She has visited her relatives here on a number of occasions.

She is now busily engaged in her new task of raising funds for the relief of those with whom she came in contact during the time her parents were serving as missionaries in this now-oppressed country.

41. Any Day May Be Too Late

Wisconsin State Journal, Apr 5, 1941

Calling the United States the "Rip Van Winkle of the Nations," Pearl S. Buck, Nobel prize novelist, urges American to "wake up to reality" and help the people of China, in an article in the April Issue of *Coronet*.

If Japan should conquer China, "it maybe she will become overnight our most dangerous enemy," Miss Buck asserts. "Yet still we do not wake from our sleep. Our help to China is far below what it should be; from government loans to Red Cross relief, our help has been too slowly given, and too scanty where given."

Miss Buck condemns the continued sale of war materials to Japan.

"Our obsolete ideas have not let us see how absurd it is to oppose Fascism in Europe and encourage it in the Far East. That is what we have been doing. Japan is only a couple of days farther away than Hitler—nearer than Hitler, if Hawaii is America. But our backward comprehension did not grasp this fact. We went on blandly selling materials of munitions to feed that war. It was exactly as though now we should send Hitler most of the scrap iron and gasoline and oil that he needs, and then protest to England how sorry we are for her and how much we always did like the English. Exactly that is what we have done for China, for exactly same war has been and is being fought in China that is being fought between Britain and Germany today."

Buck declares, "She will never yield, but she is growing desperate. She knows very well the war she is waging. It is the war of democracy against fascism. Where are her friends? Where is America?... "Any day may be a day too late. China needs help. She needs airplanes and would be grateful even for a few..." (Note: Several months later, Pearl Harbor Attack happened on Sunday morning, December 7, 1941.)

42. Questions China Aid Policy
Messenger Inquirer, May 28, 1941

American aid has not only helped bolster Chinese morale, it has cured the sick and fed the hungry. Here a group of formerly famished and broken down refugees line up for their daily clinic visit at an American supported hospital run by the American Bureau for Medical Aid to China, one of the member agencies of the United China Relief drive to raise $5,000,000 to extend and maintain such projects of civilian relief such as this.

A city wide "China Day" will be observed by city churches on Sunday, June 8, sponsored through the Owensboro Ministerial association by the Nation-wide United China Relief committee. The United China Relief is a combination of the seven different organizations and movements providing work, rehabilitation, relief and medical supplies for the Chinese in their resistance of Japanese aggression.

To eliminate overlapping or duplication among the various agencies, they have united under the chairmanship of James G. Blaine, of New York. The campaign for funds is headed by Eugene Barnett, international Secretary of the Y. M. C. A. Other members of the board of directors include Pearl S. Buck, William C. Bullitt, Thomas W. Lamont, John D. Rockefeller, III, Theodore Roosevelt, Jr., David O. Selznick, Mrs. Franklin D. Roosevelt and Wendell Winkle. Agencies participating include the American Bureau for Medical aid to China; American committee for Chinese War orphans; Associated Boards for Christian Colleges in China; China Aid Council; China Emergency Relief Committee; Church Committee for China Relief; and Indusco, a committee sponsoring industrial cooperatives in China, sometimes called "vest pocket industries." The Rev. Walter W. Harvey is chairman of the local church committee for

"China Day."

43. A Letter from Pearl S. Buck

Dear Miss Martin:

I am writing to you with the hope that you will help in the making of a list of motion pictures which could be recommended to audiences across the Pacific as being really representative of life in America. Motion picture theatres have greatly increased in number in those countries in recent years and have become enormously popular. American films are shown more often than any others, and among them have been many, of course, which have not been a good sample of everyday American life. Gangster pictures, pictures full of Hollywood ideas of luxury, slapstick comedies, and Westerns have done their share to puzzle the East. It would interest these peoples, few of whom will ever see America except in pictures, to know what Americans consider their good films.

Will you therefore help us by making a list of ten or more films which you would like to have shown to people who do not know America? These films ought to be of the 35 mm commercial variety, but they need not be chosen entirely from the most recent films, since films made within the past five years or so are still circulated abroad. I do not wish to influence your choice, but merely as an example I suggest that *Mr. Deeds Goes to Town* might be a suitable one, but *The Great Dictator* would not, since the latter does not deal with American life.

I should greatly appreciate your cooperation and would especially value your opinion.

Yours Sincerely,
Pearl S. Buck

44. Broadcast to Chinese Children
The Daily Journal, Oct 28, 1942

Authoress Pearl S. Buck directs two Mandarin-speaking youngsters, Eddie Hsia and Mei Mei Lin, during the recording of a broadcast, to Chinese children of one of a series of programs that she wrote for the East and West Association. T, C. Hsjung, of the China Institute of New York, stands behind the youngsters. Mei Mei Lin is the youngest daughter of Lin Yutang, famous Chinese author.

45. Pearl Buck Explains Why Allies Must Take Asia Initiative Now

Star Tribune, Jan 3, 1943

To the Editor: I read with approval the editorial in the *Minneapolis Sunday Tribune* of Dec, 13. You put the truth very succinctly when you said:

"Our greatest danger in the Pacific is not that we cannot win; it is that, in winning, we shall do unwittingly the very thing we want most to keep Japan from doing: unite the people of Asia against us."

The word "UNWITTINGLY" is well chosen. I believe that ignorance of the peoples of Asia and of the situation in Asia has been at the bottom of our mistakes there.

The first mistake was Pearl Harbor. Ignorance was certainly the real cause for unpreparedness.

The second mistake was failure to reassure China at once that we intended to make the Pacific a front equal with Europe. This reassurance could have been given by treating China as an equal, in war councils and war strategy, at least to the extent of giving to Generalissimo Chiang Kai-shek's personal representatives in Washington the same treatment that has been given to England's representatives, and by sending war supplies to China, at least to the extent of their extraordinarily modest requests.

There has been no such equality. The Chinese representatives in Washington have been so ignored that the military mission there, sent directly from the generalissimo, has, after months of fruitlessness, been ordered to return home. The war supplies sent have been practically nothing.

Our third mistake was the loss of Burma. The consensus of opinion among Chinese and others who took part in the Burma campaign (and I have this first-hand) is that Burma need never have been lost had the importance of the Pacific front been understood.

Two things account for that loss: the refusal to allow Chinese troops to come into Burma until Rangoon, the capital, had already fallen; and the continued retreat of the British forces, which resulted in the destruction of the three divisions of the finest Chinese veterans, who fought valiantly.

This retreat cannot be laid to cowardice, for the British are not cowards. The truth seems to be that the British forces, both soldiers and officers, were not sufficiently informed to understand the importance of Burma in the whole Allied strategy. British soldiers, and even officers, said, "What's the use of us wasting our lives here? If we win the war Burma will be given back to us, anyway. If we lose, we lose it, anyway." In other words, they did not dream of having to take back Burma again, foot by foot, because Burma is of prime importance in our war against Japan.

Burma is the bridge between India, the channel of war supplies, and China, the only base for air attack upon Japan.

It is tragic now to know that immediately after Pearl Harbor, Chinese set to work to make many airfields on their soil for us to use against Japan. They thought that of course we would want to attack Japan directly and at once, and they threw thousands of people into the work of making the necessary airfields. These people were the ordinary folk, and they had only their hands and their farming tools, but they made airfields with incredible speed—airfields never used.

Only now, and let us hope it is not too late, are we beginning to talk of the necessity of retaking Burma. It will now cost lives that might have been saved, had we understood the importance of our Pacific front earlier Air and land forces alone can do it. There must be strong sea support in the Bay of Bengal. The British navy must help us there.

But embittered Chinese are saying that Britain does not want to put up a real fight for Burma now because she wants to finish with Europe first in order that she can be in at the "kill" in Asia and then get her empire back intact, including Hongkong, which the Chinese feel must never again be a part of the British empire.

Granting by all means that Hitler must be defeated, our failure to recognize the full meaning of our losses in Asia—not only military losses but even more serious losses in prestige and good will—cannot but cost us heavily.

It Is Impossible for Anyone Who Knows the Facts to Be Optimistic

The moment has passed for any easy optimism. I will not say the moment has passed for hope, for I put my faith in the good sense of the freedom-loving American people.

But the danger is that the American people do not even know what is happening.

It is time they did know, and I commend the part you are taking in telling the truth about our situation in Asia.

R.F.D. No. 3, Perkasie, Pa.—Pearl S. Buck.

46. Belittling Gallant China's War Effort

The Montreal Daily Star, Aug 21, 1943

[By Rodney Gilbert] Formidable amphibious operations will, of course, be needed to re-establish open and adequate communications with China; and while these may have to wait upon the collapse of German resistance, or an investment of German land and sea power within the Reich and the Baltic, they may not. Japan cannot now greatly alter the present distribution of her army to strengthen any one position.

The Mediterranean will presumably be wide open to the shipment of supplies before Germany folds up.

So far as man-power goes, the new Indian Army should be more than adequate for the reoccupation of Burma, Siam, Indo-China and Malaya.

With air and naval superiority in the Indian Ocean and the Bay of Bengal, which certainly will not be hard to establish if Japanese showings elsewhere mean anything, the Indian Army may be qualitatively adequate and stage a walkover—or it may not.

At any rate it can and must be done by Indian or Occidental forces, until reconquest has been pushed far enough toward South China for air power based on recovered territory to support the Chinese in offensives against Japanese forces on their own soil.

That is when the spirit which Ch'en Cheng's men in the upper Yangtse Valley recently displayed will begin to count and when Japan's calamities will begin to grow by geometrical progression, until actual contact has been made and overwhelming air power is actually behind the Chinese front lines as just a little air-power was behind Ch'en Cheng at Ichang—unless Mr. Baldwin's observers are right and Japan has not wanted to knock China out of the war at any time, nor to gain all the favorable positions she might have taken during these last six years, but has just been conducting profitable exercises there.

The sources of this line of twaddle are very well known to the Chinese and, if the latter were a less tolerant and understanding people, they would be making the position of those Occidentals in China who are doing their best for Chia, because they believe that they are with the winning team, extremely difficult.

But, as I have said, there is no reason to believe that it is malicious or even purposeful. It is just wrong-headed.

There is now another movement, however, to discredit China's leadership, the administration under which republican China is united as she has never been united before, the only administration that we can possibly rely upon to keep China in the war until the United Nations can get in behind China's hungry legions. Its publicity is not accidental and hap-hazard, like that which is given the gossip of the military sceptics in Washington.

It is concerted and purposeful. It is not consciously malicious or destructive, for it is knowingly or innocently spread by persons who are as passionately pro-Chinese as they are anti-Japanese. None of these persons is ignorant of conditions in China. All of them have worked and traveled there; and some are as familiar with the language and traditions as they are with the country. Their purpose is not the immediate overthrow of China's leadership or of China's united front.

Their immediate purpose is to undermine the moral credit of China's leadership in this country and to build up the credit of the Chinese Communists, so that when the time comes for the latter to seize the fruits of victory over Japan, after the war, such an achievement, whether by coup or by revolution, will not alienate American sympathy from China, vis-a-vis Japan, or elicit a revulsion of feeling against the Red "Democrats" and with it armed support for their suppression.

This is the major purpose and hope behind the whole volume of sad, sympathetic laments about the clouding over of China's "democratic" future, which the reader of Far Eastern chit-chat has found in a variety of publications for several months past. A corollary purpose and hope is, of course, to win enough "liberal" American sympathy for the currently circumscribed political activities of the Chinese Communists to influence policy in Washington, and thence to win from the Chiang Kai-shek administration more freedom and scope for the Communists to prepare for the exploitation of victory.

Now I am quite ready to believe that many persons who have done highly appreciated spade work for this movement are unaware of these purposes and would not knowingly forward them, but have been enlisted as publicists through appeals to their "liberalism." I am persuaded that there was nothing more than this, for example, behind Mrs. Pearl Buck's contribution to *Life*, May 10 of this year, of an article entitled "A Warning About China." Yet that article was no sooner on the news-stands than two Chinese who hold no position under the Chinese Government, who are not members of the Kuomintang (the party behind the generalissimo's one-party dictatorship) and who owe no fealty whatever to the Soong family, advised me to read it with the gratuitous comment that Mrs. Buck had evidently come under the influence of the "leftists." I must say that, being then unaware that there was any "leftist" promotion of plaints against the governing regime, I should have suspected nothing of the sort, for most of what Mrs. Buck wrote about the state of gloom and foreboding in isolated China was then strictly true.

Looking back later upon her implication that Madam Chiang did not speak for the Chinese people in this country, her suggestion that the bureaucracy around Chiang was something to do away with in a democracy, her allegations that the war was ceasing to be a people's war, that freedom of speech and of the press were suppressed by "an organization far more severe than the secret service of a democracy ought to be," and that the students and intellectuals, silent now, were losing faith in the future of Chinese democracy—looking back now, it is impossible to avoid the conclusion that she was either doing spade work for the "leftists" by sheer coincidence or had indirectly absorbed some "leftist" propaganda.

I am by no means so ready to be persuaded that the inspiration of T. A. Bisson's article entitled "China's Part in a Coalition War," which appeared in Far Eastern

Survey of July 14, published under the auspices of the American Council, Institute of Pacific Relations, was so indirectly or innocently absorbed. He is for the Chinese Communists and says so. There is no space here for full analysis; so these quotations must suffice: "A year or more before Pearl Harbor... two Chinas had definitely emerged... One is now generally called Kuomintang China; the other is called Communist China. However, these are only party labels. To be more descriptive, the one might be called feudal China; the other, democratic China."

These terms express the actualities as they exist today, the real institutional distinctions between the two Chinas. The argument is that "feudal" Kuomintang China is slipping in efficiency and is militarily passive. To get the maximum out of China as an ally, the United Nations should exert their influence to unify the two Chinas "on the high plane of social advance and democratic reform." Since Chinese democracy and Chinese Communism are one and the same thing in Mr. Bisson's vocabulary, the argument is clearly one for United Nations action to force more Communist "reform" upon Kuomintang China—to give the Reds all the scope they want, in short, to get ready for the post-war showdown.

47. Unrest in China[1]
San Bernardino County Sun, California, Aug 19, 1943

There is enough smoke, however, to indicate that all is not well within China. Pearl Buck, in her article "A Warning About China" in the May 10 *Life* magazine, said:

The great liberal forces of the recent past in China are growing silent. There is now no real freedom of the press in China, no real freedom of speech. The official implement of repression is an organization far more severe than the secret service of a democracy ought to be. The division between the Eighth Route army and the National army still continues, in spite of the fact that all accept the generalissimo as their leader. There are forces around the generalissimo which keep apart these two great bodies of the people who ought not now to be kept apart.

There is other testimony. Creighton Lacy, member of a missionary family, declared in his volume *Is China a Democracy?* that "some of the factions within the Kuomintang" are of much "concern to true democrats in China." There are at least two groups which have warranted the epithet "semi-fascist" because they are "more antagonistic to Chinese communism, and possibly to constitutional democracy, than

---

① This article cites a paragraph of Pearl Buck's article "A Warning About China—A Great Friend of the Chinese People Points to Dangers That May Lose USA Valuable Ally".

they are to the Japanese. The tragedy is that their memberships include some of the most prominent cabinet ministers, generals, and diplomats."

48. Pearl Buck Here, Says Japs Can Never Appease Chinese
Daily News, Oct 19, 1943

Japan's change in policy from terrorization to conciliation will never succeed permanently in China.

Pearl S. Buck, the author who "thinks in Chinese," gave this opinion yesterday at a press conference at the Chapman Park hotel shortly after her arrival here to speak in behalf of the War Chest. With her is Richard Walsh, her husband and president of the John Day Publishing Co., which publishes her books.

"For years Japan tried a campaign of terrorization in China but it didn't work," said the writer, whose books have won her both Nobel and Pulitzer prizes. "Now they are trying to win over the people in the territories they have occupied. In some places this policy apparently has begun to work, but it will never succeed permanently.

"I can't imagine my Chinese"—her tone softened as she said these words—"permanently being won over. China has bided her time before and she is doing the same with Japan now."

Chinese armies are hungry and exhausted but they will not collapse, Miss Buck said. However, this country need not send food to China, for the rich agricultural regions of that country can supply ample amounts—it is a question of money and transportation.

Asked in what way the United States can best aid her ally, Miss Buck answered immediately: "She should be treated on an equal basis with the other United Nations. We should do as much for her as we do for Britain."

At present we are not doing proportionately the same for China as we are for Britain, in Miss Buck's opinion.

She parried the question as to whether she thought it true that certain elements in Britain were avoiding a battle in Burma because they hoped for a weak China. "I am certain the Labor party would have no such policy," she said, smiling.

The quiet-spoken Miss Buck said she did not presume to question military strategy, but she believed that the war with Japan can certainly not be considered a secondary war; though it may be secondary in time it is not secondary in importance.

"No European country can appreciate our position," she stated. "It is one peculiar to us in the United States."

Americans have not been "humanly aware" of the sufferings and trials of other peoples and races, the writer believes.

"It isn't our fault—we've been too comfortable. This war might never have happened if we'd kept informed of what was going on outside of our own comfortable country. No one now should think that because he's given $50 to the War Chest he has done enough," she said vehemently. "That's only the beginning, relief such as that. We must go on and learn about people and their cultures."

Such books as *The Good Earth*, *Dragon Seed* and *All Men Are Brothers* have given new concepts of the Chinese to millions of Americans who formerly thought of China as a country of laundrymen and cooks. Miss Buck has just completed another book *The Promise*.

"When is it going to be published?" She inquired of her publisher husband.

"Next month," he said, adding to the reporters, "It's about the campaign in Burma."

Walsh also said that in addition to her writing, Miss Buck finds time to manage the 200 acre farm in Quakertown, Pa., where they live.

She finds that the Pennsylvania Dutch farmers are much like the Chinese farmers in their methods and love of the "good earth."

She raises cattle, too, as another contribution toward the war effort, but would rather "carry a gun than knit."

Miss Buck modestly disclaimed any credit for forwarding relations between China and this country through her writing, but warmly commended Chinese writer Lin Yutang for what he has done in this regard.

Chinese was Miss Buck's "first language" and she speaks Mandarin fluently.

Following the press conference, Miss Buck and her husband were honored at a reception in the Gold room of the Ambassador hotel, given under auspices of United China Relief, one of the agencies included in the War Chest.

Tomorrow morning Miss Buck will address a rally of War Chest leaders at a breakfast in the Embassy room of the Ambassador.

49. Pearl Buck's Democracy Plea Derails Solons' Jap Inquiry

Daily News, Oct 22, 1943

A state senate fact finding committee yesterday returned to the well worn rails traveled by trains of thought of previous committees gathering evidence opposing the return of Japanese to the west coast.

But it did so after suffering a surprising derailment by Pearl S. Buck.

The Nobel Prize novelist had the committee members gasping for breath, or lunch, or air, or whatever, before she finished her 40 minute surprise appearance in the State building just before noon yesterday.

But, refreshed with lunch and things, the committee returned to its hearing room in the afternoon to get back on its single track. It heard more of the same evidence collected by the Dies committee and the Tenney committee, opposing return of the Japanese whether citizens or aliens.

Miss Buck livened the hearing room with her testimony, however. Before she concluded her appearance she had made such statements as:

If you plan to exclude the Japanese, then you must exclude the Germans; if you desire to take the property of Japanese nationals or citizens of Japanese descent, then you must take the property of German nationals and citizens of German descent.

The visit of Admiral Dewey in a battleship to Japan, and the Japanese exclusion act of 1924, contributed to the attack on Pearl Harbor.

The United States should treat all enemies as enemies and all allies as allies, and not discriminate against one or another.

Unable to parry her statements and finding that each question they asked brought an undesired answer, the committee members fidgeted in their plush chairs.

State Sen. Jesse Dorsey of Bakersfield tried to interrupt her: "Why, ah, we all have reservations and things, Miss Buck, and thank you very much."

He rose from his chair, but Miss Buck kept talking.

The committee's sergeant at arms whispered in Senator Dorsey's ear, but this move failed to distract the novelist.

Finally, one of the senators shot: "Say, isn't it time for lunch? I'm hungry." And the hearing adjourned. But it didn't end until Miss Buck had said what she thought "every intelligent American should know."

"Our attitude toward the Japanese here today is being carefully watched throughout the world as a portent of the future," she said.

"All the great colored races of the world—the yellow, the brown, the black—are watching you, gentlemen. The decisions reached right here in California will form the pattern for the future—a pattern for peace; or a pattern for fresh wars."

On the question at hand—the resettlement of evacuated Japanese and American citizens, Miss Buck said: "When we put aside even for war the rights of American citizens, we jeopardize the whole country and all the democracies abroad."

The committee members tried to trap her on a question regarding the intelligence of Gen. John DeWitt's eviction order.

"I refuse to discuss the military aspect with you, gentleman," she said. "I do not feel, myself competent to discuss this any more than I feel you are."

Besides, she said, the important question is not what should be done now, but what should be done after the war.

"I do not believe in the discrimination against any group, nation, race or color," she said.

"I believe that we shall have war as long as, or until we learn to deal with human beings as human beings, and justly."

Miss Buck said the exclusion laws of 1924 killed the liberal movement in Japan.

"Japan might have been a democracy today had it not been for those laws discriminating against Japanese."

One of the senators asked her what she thought about immigration from the orient.

"Isn't it the function of this committee to consider the question of returning the Japanese already in this country?" She whipped hard.

Again, a senator asked her what she thought of the job being done in relocation centers now housing Japanese.

"Considering the emergency," she said, "I would say the government has done a rather excellent job!"

One senator interrupted with: "We hear stories that these Japanese in camps are receiving too good treatment, receiving luxuries and so on that are denied to us here."

"Well," Miss Buck parried, "I would rather err on the side of goodness than on the side of evil." To every question about Japanese espionage here, Japanese atrocities abroad, Japanese loyalty to the emperor, and Japanese treatment of prisoners, she said: "So have the Germans." Or, "Don't forget, gentlemen, that Germany is our enemy, too. Don't forget the bunds in the east. Don't forget that on the east coast we feared a German invasion as much as you feared one from Japan."

In fact, this was the theme of her entire testimony. If Japanese and citizens of Japanese extraction should be interned, then so should the Germans, she said: "We have arbitrarily placed the Japanese in a class of their own, and by so doing we are breeding another war," she said.

Just before the morning session adjourned, one of the senators tried to impeach Miss Buck's testimony with this question:

"You say you have spent considerable time in the orient. Just how long were you there, Miss Buck?"

"From the time I was 3 months old until I was 42," she answered, clipping each word out like bullets.

Earlier, Carey McWilliams, also an author and former state immigration and housing commissioner, testified that few Japanese newly relocated in other states planned to return to California.

However, he added, the Japanese still interned, and owning property here, hope to regain their homes.

In the afternoon session, the committee assembled some more testimony opposing return of Japanese, evicted from the west coast after Pearl Harbor.

Sheriff Carl Rayburn and Dist. Atty. John Neblett, of Riverside county, said the residents of that county opposed return of the Japanese.

Rayburn said about 90 percent of the people opposed return of the Japanese during the war, and about 80 percent opposed return of them "at any time."

R. E. Combs, chief investigator for the Tenneyun-American activities committee of the legislature, presented testimony similar to that he had given before. He told of the riots at Mcnzanar between loyal and subversive Japanese, how two were killed by deputies seeking to quell the riot.

Interesting contrast during the afternoon was the testimony of three women, all of whom have sons now prisoners of the Japs.

Mrs. E. H. Snipes, of the "Women of Wake," warned against discrimination toward American Japanese. She said such discrimination would result in reprisals to Americans now prisoners of Japan. At the present time, she said, she believed these prisoners were not suffering.

"Women of Wake" is a group of 200 Southern California housewives whose husbands or sons are prisoners of the Japanese.

But Mrs. Verona K. Trowbridge, president of the Bataan auxiliary, United Philippine War veterans, said members of her organization were "very bitter, very bitter," toward all Japanese. She warned that return of the evicted Japanese would bring trouble.

Mrs. Florence H. Allen, with a son and a son in law imprisoned in Manila, said she agreed with Mrs. Snipes that hardships to Japanese in this country would bring reprisals in Jap prison camps where Americans are interned.

50. Japan, China, the United States and the Road to Pearl Harbor, 1937—1941

Between 1937 and 1941, escalating conflict between China and Japan influenced U.S. relations with both nations, and ultimately contributed to pushing the United States toward full-scale war with Japan and Germany.

At the outset, U.S. officials viewed developments in China with ambivalence. On the one hand, they opposed Japanese incursions into northeast China and the rise of Japanese militarism in the area, in part because of their sense of a longstanding friendship with China. On the other hand, most U.S. officials believed that it had no vital interests in China worth going to war over with Japan. Moreover, the domestic conflict between Chinese Nationalists and Communists left U.S. policymakers uncertain of success in aiding such an internally divided nation. As a result, few U.S. officials recommended taking a strong stance prior to 1937, and so the United States did little to help China for fear of provoking Japan. U.S. likelihood of providing aid to China increased after July 7, 1937, when Chinese and Japanese forces clashed on the Marco Polo Bridge near Beijing, throwing the two nations into a full-scale war. As the United States watched Japanese forces sweep down the coast and then into the capital of Nanjing, popular opinion swung firmly in favor of the Chinese. Tensions with Japan rose when the Japanese Army bombed the U.S.S. Panay as it evacuated American citizens from Nanjing, killing three. The U.S. Government, however, continued to avoid conflict and accepted an apology and indemnity from the Japanese. An uneasy truce held between the two nations into 1940.

In 1940 and 1941, President Franklin D. Roosevelt formalized U.S. aid to China. The U.S. Government extended credits to the Chinese Government for the purchase of war supplies, as it slowly began to tighten restrictions on Japan. The United States was the main supplier of the oil, steel, iron, and other commodities needed by the Japanese military as it became bogged down by Chinese resistance but, in January, 1940, Japan abrogated the existing treaty of commerce with the United States. Although this did not lead to an immediate embargo, it meant that the Roosevelt Administration could now restrict the flow of military supplies into Japan and use this as leverage to force Japan to halt its aggression in China.

After January 1940, the United States combined a strategy of increasing aid to China through larger credits and the Lend-Lease program with a gradual move towards an embargo on the trade of all militarily useful items with Japan. The Japanese Government made several decisions during these two years that exacerbated the situation. Unable or unwilling to control the military, Japan's political leaders sought greater security by establishing the "Greater East Asia Co-Prosperity Sphere" in August, 1940. In so doing they announced Japan's intention to drive the Western imperialist nations from Asia. However, this Japanese-led project aimed to enhance Japan's economic and material wealth so that it would not be dependent upon supplies from the West, and not to "liberate" the long-subject peoples of Asia. In fact, Japan would have to launch a campaign of military conquest and rule, and did not intend to pull out of China. At the same time, several pacts with Western nations only made Japan appear more of a threat to the United States. First, Japan signed the Tripartite Pact with Germany and Italy on September 27, 1940 and thereby linked the conflicts in Europe and Asia. This made China a potential ally in the global fight against fascism. Then in mid-1941, Japan signed a Neutrality Pact with the Soviet Union, making it clear that Japan's military would be moving into Southeast Asia, where the United

States had greater interests. A third agreement with Vichy France enabled Japanese forces to move into Indochina and begin their Southern Advance. The United States responded to this growing threat by temporarily halting negotiations with Japanese diplomats, instituting a full embargo on exports to Japan, freezing Japanese assets in U.S. banks, and sending supplies into China along the Burma Road. Although negotiations restarted after the United States increasingly enforced an embargo against Japan, they made little headway. Diplomats in Washington came close to agreements on a couple of occasions, but pro-Chinese sentiments in the United States made it difficult to reach any resolution that would not involve a Japanese withdrawal from China, and such a condition was unacceptable to Japan's military leaders.

Faced with serious shortages as a result of the embargo, unable to retreat, and convinced that the U.S. officials opposed further negotiations, Japan's leaders came to the conclusion that they had to act swiftly. For their part, U.S. leaders had not given up on a negotiated settlement, and also doubted that Japan had the military strength to attack the U.S. territory. Therefore they were stunned when the unthinkable happened and Japanese planes bombed the U.S. fleet at Pearl Harbor on December 7, 1941. The following day, the United States declared war on Japan, and it soon entered into a military alliance with China. When Germany stood by its ally and declared war on the United States, the Roosevelt Administration faced war in both Europe and Asia.

51. Proving Our Friendship
The Miami Herald, Apr 10, 1943

Congressional action to eliminate a direct insult to China and other Oriental allies which has been included in U. S. immigration laws for 60 years will rob Japan of a most effective propaganda weapon. Influential groups are now sponsoring a measure to admit to the country and eventual U. S. citizenship Orientals from nations now allied with us against the Axis. It will not, however, permit the entry of Japanese.

Present U. S. immigration laws, excluding all Orientals, have provided Japanese with verbal ammunition in their penetration and conquest of the Far East. "You are good enough to fight for America and die for America." the Japs tell conquered Chinese, Malays and Burmese, "but you are not good enough to live in America." The worst part of this propaganda is that our restrictions back it up.

If the exclusion clauses are repealed, our Oriental allies would be admitted on the quota basis governing immigration from European countries. At most the quota would allow 105 Chinese to enter each year. Under the same regulation, 100 from India, 100 from the Philippines and 100 from each of the autonomous or semi-autonomous areas of the Pacific would be allowed entry. The total admitted legally probably would be less than that smuggled in before the war.

The Chinese exclusion act, dating from 1882, was the result of mass importation of Chinese coolies to work on Western railroads. American labor could not compete against Chinese, willing to work for a bowl of rice a day.

American labor does not oppose repeal. Today CIO unions approve lifting the exclusion ban and AFL may take a similar stand. Both unions have admitted Orientals to membership in West Coast unions. The United Auto Workers last June called for repeal of the exclusion act and cited its value as propaganda to the Japanese.

Although Mme. Chiang Kai-shek did not publicly discuss the proposal during her visit to Washington, it is known she hopes America will make this gesture of friendship. Pearl S. Buck has actively supported this movement.

President Roosevelt does not oppose revision of the law, although he prefers to leave action up to Congress.

A bill has been introduced in Congress by Rep. Martin J. Kennedy to permit Chinese to enter U. S. and Rep. Walter Judd is preparing another on a wider all-Oriental, except Japanese, basis. Congress and the nation should urge immediate passage.

China and our other Oriental allies are fighting our battle. It is little enough to welcome them into our homeland.

52. Pearl S. Buck Urges Repeal of Exclusion Act
Redding Record Searchlight and the Courier Free Press, May 21, 1943

[Washington (AP)] Pearl Buck, author of Chinese novels, told the house immigration committee that the Chinese exclusion act should be repealed as a war measure, for the good of both the United States and China.

"All Chinese know about the exclusion act which as barred them from entering into this country for more than 50 years," she testified.

"I've spent four-fifths of my life in China and have been asked that question (why the act has not been repealed) many times, much to my embarrassment. The Japanese are using it in their propaganda program in China. They are taunting the Chinese by telling them ' Look—Is America really your ally? —You are being discriminated against.' "

The measure under consideration would allow China an annual immigration quota of 107.

James L. Wilmeth, of the Junior Order of United American Mechanics, opposed the bill, arguing that the influx of Chinese workers, who would accept low wages, would be "ruinous for our people."

53. Favor Bill to Repeal Chinese Exclusion Acts

Will Allow Chinese Immigration to the U.S. on a Quota Basis

The Daily Advertiser, Oct 7, 1943

[By the Associated Press, Washington]

In a surprise move today the House Committee on Immigration voted 8 to 4 in executive session to report favorably a bill to repeal Chinese exclusion acts and allow Chinese immigration to this country on a quota basis.

The swift action was understood to have been the result of an effort to get a bill out of committee this week to honor the anniversary next Sunday of the founding of the Chinese Republic. The leader of the opposition to placing the Chinese on a quota basis—Rep. Allen (D-La)—was not present at today's executive session and his proxy, along with several others, was reported not to have been voted. The measure, on which the House may act next week, would repeal the Chinese exclusion acts dating back to 1882, place the Chinese on a quota basis under the immigration act of 1924, allowing approximately 105 to enter the United States annually, and amend naturalization laws to allow the Chinese citizenship.

54. A Warning About China

—A Great Friend of the Chinese People Points to Dangers That May Lose Us a Valuable Ally

Life, Oct 05, 1943

Pearl Sydenstricker Buck, whose novels about the Chinese people won her the Nobel Prize in 1938, knows China as well as she knows America. She was brought up by her missionary parents in Chinkiang on the Yangtze, came back to Virginia to college (Randolph-Macon), and then returned to China to spend the next two decades. Her first husband, Dr. John Lossing Buck, taught rural economics at the University of Nanking; she herself taught English. In 1934, after the success of *The Good Earth*, she returned to the U. S. for good. She lives on a Pennsylvania farm with nine children and her second husband, Richard J. Walsh, who is editor of the magazine *Asia*.

Although Pearl Buck has not been in China since 1934, she still has a "Chinese self," and is one of the most understanding spokesmen the Chinese people have. Because she knows and loves them well, she has their confidence and can say things to and about the Chinese that would come from most Americans with bad grace. For the frightening situations described here, however, she does not blame China, but puts the blame where it belongs: on America's failure to understand in time the necessity of helping China, so that

China can help us.

(Pearl S. Buck) Madame Chiang Kai-shek's tour of the United States has been an extraordinary personal triumph. Everywhere she went the American people gave ample proof of their appreciation of her appearance and of their friendliness, through her, toward China. She came as a representative of China, and she conquered by her individual beauty and charm.

Now that the tour is over, how can we assess its value? That it had great value is undeniable. To many Americans, Madame Chiang brought the knowledge of a new type of Chinese. They saw someone whom they were able to understand—not a remote and esoteric creature who might have stepped from a Chinese fan, but a woman, however fragile in body, yet of considerable will and determination. She spoke in a language which, if it was above the heads of some, was nevertheless our language. In brief, America saw in the person of Madame Chiang a modem woman, a woman who is at home in any country; and through her China has for millions of Americans suddenly become a modern nation. Perhaps nothing else could have taught so many people this much-needed lesson so quickly.

If Madame Chiang's visit has done this for the people of America, what has it done for the people of China? To suggest that it has done something less than it might have done is not to put the blame on anyone, except perhaps on ourselves. It must have been difficult for Madame Chiang to discover how little we know about China, and even about the war that has been fought there for nearly six years. In her speeches she did not mend our ignorance until she reached Los Angeles. There, in her last address, she told something of her own experience in the early period of the war and its progress up the Yangtze River. She shrank, she said, from seeming to want to exploit in a foreign country the sufferings of her people. For this we respect her. But the fact remains that it would be well for us to know the exact position where the Chinese people now stand, especially if we are to be able to put into practical form the results of this visit. It is not enough for China that we acknowledge Madame Chiang's personal charm, nor that we give our personal gifts. China needs far more than that from us, and this for our own sake as well as China's.

For we cannot win the war against Japan if China is not held. The soil of China must be the base for our final attack on Japan. We may lose that base before it can ever be used if we do not sustain the spirits and bodies of China's people. A China disarmed and totally subjected in body would be helpless in spirit. Occupied China today is not quite helpless, because hope still remains that before it is too late the Allies can reconquer Burma, the access to China. But were that hope taken away, all free China, as well as occupied China, would settle back into long deep darkness, out of which she could struggle only after centuries, and far too late to save America. It is time we

Americans were thoroughly frightened.

American friendship for China has at this moment reached a popular height which brings it to the verge of sentimentality. The Chinese are being exalted into persons such as cannot exist in our fallible human race. A dose of common sense is needed. If the dose is not taken in time those who have rushed to give gifts, those who have sold valued possessions, as some have, to make a gift, are going to wake up one morning condemning China and all Chinese, and then they will regret their possessions and feel ashamed of their emotionalism, and isolationists will make the most of this disillusionment. But the Chinese people deserve neither adoration nor condemnation. They do deserve understanding and help, and that we may give what they deserve, it is necessary for a friendly diagnosis to be made now of China's present condition.

To put the condition briefly, China is ill. Her lifeline was choked off with the loss of Burma. Transport service has not been sufficient to supply what China needs for healthy maintenance of war activity. As in any starving body, latent ills spring up. The danger now in China is that the war against Japan may dwindle because of the increasing weakness inevitable under present circumstances, and that in this subsidence those who would make peace with Japan may come to power.

The Chinese people realize their danger with fear and dismay. They are bewildered, stalemated and silent. Their resolute resurgent voice, which used to be so clear, is silent now. In 1937, when the Chinese people led that government into what they supposed was a war for national democracy, they called the warning to the world. But today one of the major paradoxes of this war is that although Madame Chiang is our most eloquent wartime evangelist, the Chinese people themselves are voiceless.

Already, undemocratic forces, which could not do their evil work so long as China was hopeful of her place as an equal ally of the United States and England, have been strengthened by our policy which has relegated Japan to the place of a secondary enemy, allowing Burma to be lost and the line to China cut. In the isolation and helplessness of China those in the government there who were voices for the Norte and for democracy cannot speak loudly and clearly as once they did, as they did when they were promising their people effective aid from us. Division within China is deepening in spite of the fact that the leadership and the genius of Generalissimo Chiang Kai-shek are not yet being challenged. He has become a legend among the Chinese people, and though they may reject others around him, they do not reject him. Chiang Kai-shek is still the rallying point and the center of unity for China's war. So long as this remains true, it can still be said that the war is a people's war.

It started altogether as a people's war. The government was reluctant to begin it, knowing that China was ill-prepared to face Japan's war machine. The people knew that, too, and yet they saw that the war had come upon them, whether they were ready or not, and that there were only the two alternatives—either they had to fight with whatever they had, or they had to surrender to Japan without fighting. They chose as Americans would have chosen, as any independent self-respecting people would have chosen, they chose to fight. Chiang Kai-shek chose with them, and Left and Right alike, the people united under him. They understood very well that there were forces connected with him and playing upon him that were not good forces from the point of view of the people or of the common fight against Japan, but in their need they had to accept the evil with the good. Moreover, they were convinced that Chiang Kai-shek was still stronger than these forces. They knew him to be an unsentimental man at heart, and a man who would not, therefore, allow personal emotions to sway him too deeply. They believed that he had passed the stage of personal greed. He had wealth and power sufficient for him and the need for these things was not a disease with him as it is with some.

Around the figure of Chiang Kai-shek, then, the people centered. He became the symbol of their unity, and so he has continued to this day. The people still hope and believe that when the clouds are cleared away from the point where they now stand, at least his figure will still be there, ready for the future. Even the Leftists, now once again bitterly repressed and ignored by the bureaucrats, believe that it is still possible to find national unity in Chiang Kai-shek.

It is the people of China, then whom we must thank today for the years of resistance to Japan. Those intrepid, reckless, plain people did for us in Asia what English people did in the West—they proved the enemy was not invincible. All over China the plain people were roused—they were fighting for Chinese soil, as the Russian people are fighting for theirs today.

But it is only common sense to realize that even a great and brave people rallying around a beloved leader cannot win a war without weapons. Their only hope for these was from America. The weapons are not being sent and there are three reasons for this: we are allowing ourselves to be persuaded that Japan is only our secondary enemy; we are allowing ourselves to be shaken by the reports that all China is being demoralized; we are allowing ourselves to be too easily persuaded that the problem of transportation cannot be solved.

We cannot alter the decision to fight and beat Hitler first. Even if we could perhaps we should not. But neither can we dare neglect the war against Japan or risk the loss of China. To America at least, and I believe to all democracies, Japan is an enemy of equal danger to us with Hitler. It may take Japan several years to consolidate her gains to equal the resources of Germany, but she is not allowing the strengthening of her military forces to wait for this. She is increasing and building up her fighting power. Nothing which is now being done, either by Chinese forces or our own, is impeding that growth. No American can afford to forget this. It is dangerous to be deceived by the small military actions now taking place. We have not yet met Japan's main forces. The efforts bring put forth by ourselves in the Pacific and by the Chinese in China do not engage any great proportion of the Japanese Army. The British efforts in Burma are feeble indeed, because the British feel that the time has not come to invade on a big scale.

55. Still a Change

The Lincoln Star, Aug 14, 1945

Lincoln, Neb.

To the editor of *The Lincoln Star*:

In the last number of *Asia*, Pearl S. Buck writes about "American Imperialism in the Making," deploring the fact that those who were supposed to represent Americanism at San Francisco and Potsdam were silent while Stalin insisted that all colonies must ultimately have independence. For some time she has also given word pictures of the achievements of the Russians under Stalin, making it plain that Russians accomplished more under Stalin than Americans did under Jefferson. Then, Russia, like Saul, now stands a head higher than all other Imperialisms in the experience of man. Bismarck built German Imperialism on Luther's foundation. "Ein Fester Burg 1st Unser Gott," with Prussian militarism as the corner stone, while Disraeli built British Imperialism on forts and battleships. May we hope that our victory now will result in an Imperialism, with Woodrow Wilson's "Self-determination" as the cornerstone. Hitler tried to wag Russia as a part of his big dog tail and the Japs tried to wag China as a part of their big dog tail and get digested and assimilated as a proper part of their anticipated Imperialisms.

56. China's Best Friend

The Wichita Eagle, Aug 1, 1948

Her Novels Have Won Understanding and a Wide Sympathy for China

In 1931, Pearl S. Buck was a little-known instructor of English literature at a small college in Nanking. A year later, as the author of *The Good Earth*, she was one of the most widely read writers in the United States, the winner of a Pulitzer Prize and the owner of an international reputation. It was a Cinderella story, but actually Pearl Buck's ascent to fame from obscurity was not accomplished with the ease that these contrasts imply. It was an arduous climb full of pitfalls and rockslides.

Miss Buck, whose 15th adult novel, *Peony* (John Day and Company, New York)

has been one of the strongest best-sellers on the summer fiction lists, wrote her first book in Nanking during the 1920s. She completed the manuscript in 1926 and planned to send it to New York for publication the following spring.

Novel Went Up in Smoke

In March 1927 Civil War broke out, and Nationalist troops stormed Nanking, looting and killing foreigners. With her husband and their three small children, Miss Buck hid in a cave until rescued by an American warship, but their home was burned and her novel—representing five years of conscientious work—disappeared in a thin, white column of smoke. "I console myself now," she said recently, "by thinking that my first novel probably was not any good."

Pearl Sydenstricker Buck was born in 1892 in Hillsboro, W. Va., but her parents, who were missionaries, took her to China when she was five months old[1]. She spoke Chinese before she spoke English, attended Chinese schools and after graduating from Randolph-Macon College in Lynchburg, Va., in 1914 returned to China to teach.

During these years she wrote stories, novels, articles, all of which received an apathetic reception from New York publishers. In 1923 she had an article published in the *Atlantic Monthly* and the following year one appeared in *The Forum*. Then, after her first novel had been destroyed by fire, she wrote another—*East Wind*, *West Wind*, published in 1930. *The Good Earth*, in 1931, made her famous.

Of her subsequent novels, all but one have had China as a background, and it is this concern on which her reputation has been built. In 1938 she became the first American woman to win the Nobel Prize in literature. In accepting she paid a tribute to China, "which is like my own to me."

Through the years Mrs. Buck has carried a double-edged sword. She has written novels as readable as any produced in her time, and in them she has carried the banner for China and its people. To millions of Americans, Pearl Buck's Chinese have become good neighbors and friends.

57. Fight Shames Pearl S. Buck

Tucson Daily Citizen, Jun 30, 1950

[Cape May, N J., AP]—Pearl, S. Buck said yesterday that "I think what we did in Korea is necessary." but "as an American I feel a deep sense of shame, rather than national pride."

Miss Buck, a winner of the Nobel prize for literature, is the author of many novels

---

① 应该是 3 个月大的时候。

about China. "If you use force," she told the Friends general conference here, "you admit your failure and if that is all we can do, we have failed."

She said American military backing of invaded South Korea was necessary since "we are in a sense responsible for Korea because of our occupation government and our postwar division of the country."

But, she added, "we have nothing to do for Taiwan and our defense of it means that we now face the protection of the whole of Asia."

She told an audience of 3,000 Quakers that she had changed her mind about the possibility of friendship with Communist China.

"I do not think today that we can be friends with the Chinese people, which is a far different view than I held six months ago," she said.

She asserted that mistakes in American foreign policy toward China have "created an abyss between us".

58. Pearl Buck Tells Haddonfield Group
U.S. Could Lose All Fighting China

Courier Post, Oct 18, 1950

[By Edmund N. Watkins] If America should engage in a war in China proper, "we could lose everything we have and be taxed out of existence," Pearl S. Buck, world-famed author, said Tuesday night.

Speaking in the Haddonfield Memorial High school under the sponsorship of the Haddon Fortnightly, Mrs. Buck said: "I cannot imagine anyone fighting a war in China and winning."

The Nobel prize-winning novelist and authority on the Far East said she used to talk about China easily and with freedom, but because of events that have taken place, she has lost that freedom. Now, she said, "my very presence there would put my friends into danger merely because I am an American."

Taught to Hate U. S.

"Americans once were the most favored by the Chinese of all the western peoples," she said. "But now the Communists are teaching them to hate us above all other peoples." Recalling that 40 years of her life were spent in China, Mrs. Buck declared that Synghman Rhee, president of the Republic of Korea, never had the support of most South Koreans.

"I have never heard any remarks about Synghman Rhee except from South Koreans," she said. "And I know many, many South Koreans who do not like Synghman Rhee. They accepted him because they hoped they could get more benefits from us in that way."

Taught to Avoid Truth

Mrs. Buck said that Rhee is supported only by a "little circle of personal friends."

Asserting that "we are taught not to speak the truth" because in doing so we might help the Communists, Mrs. Buck recommended speaking the truth and acting on facts even if the Communists have said the same things.

Criticizing Chiang Kai-shek, Mrs. Buck said that if he had been able to do so he would have become emperor of China rather than president.

Terms Chiang Warlord

"When Chiang came in, he was not elected," she said. "He took over because he was the most victorious warlord, and that followed the usual Chinese pattern." The author added that Chiang Kai-shek "never knew what democracy was." "He grew up with other ideas," she declared, adding that "we made a mistake when we expected him to be something that he is not. We dealt with him as though he were a modern American, and he is not, and never could be."

1,000 Hear Speech

More than 1,000 persons attended the lecture, which was sponsored for the benefit of the research funds of the Vineland Training school. Mrs. Buck was introduced by Dr. Walter Jacob, director of the school, who said it is hoped that before long it will be possible for anyone to bring a child to the school for diagnosis.

"There is no such place in the country at the moment," said Dr. Jacob, introduced by Mrs. Warren Danzenbaker, president of the evening section of the Haddon Fortnightly. Dr. Bryant T. Kirkland, pastor of the Presbyterian Church of Haddonfield and member of the board of directors of the training school, also spoke.

59. Prestige Low in Asia, Says Writer
The Bristol Herald Courier, Mar 2, 1951

"The United States has lost a considerable amount of prestige in Asia during the past five years, but Americans can still regain their former position of great influence if they will only try to understand the deep desire Asiatic peoples have for independence," Pear S. Buck, noted American author, told Bristol Forum Association audience here last evening.

Speaking before a capacity group of listeners at the Sullin College auditorium, she said that the United States stood in position of unparalleled world influence and strength at the close of World War II, "but we made a fatal mistake in not declaring ourselves as being in favor of national independence for the peoples of Asia." And she added:

"What makes this so tragic is that the countries of Asia, who were sick to the death of colonial rule by the Dutch, British and French, felt so sure that America, since we had won our own independence by breaking away from colonial rule in 1776, would certainly be the champion of the peoples of Asia in their desire for independence."

Ran Out on Obligation

"But what did we do, pray tell?" she continued. "We stated that we would have nothing to say or do about national independence in Asia. We did this for political reasons, fearing that we might turn the French and Dutch against us. And the news reached Asia that we were deserting them, and they had counted so much our help."

Mrs. Buck stated that the mistake in Korea came when we divided the country in half and the Russia rule one half while we ruled the other, for like all the countries of Asia, little Korea desired national independence most greatly. South Korea failed stop the North Korean invasion, because the South Koreans had lost faith in the men we sent to occupy their country. The American men in South Korea knew nothing of Korean history and customs, and the result was that we did a pretty shabby job occupation. When the invasion came, the morale of South Korean was very low.

Mrs. Buck believes that the United States should change its attitude towards participation in such United Nations organizations as the World Food Organization, the World Health Organization and the World Education Organization. "Our refusal to cooperate whole-heartedly with these groups has already cost us much prestige in the world, especially in Asia, and we should be pouring billions into these movements rather than to continue building bomb after bomb which will not settle any problem in the long run," she stated.

Too Much Power

She also believed that American military men are acquiring too much power, and that extreme bad public relations is apparent in the use of such phrases as "Operation Killer" in connection with a military effort in Korea. She also deplored such statements by American military authorities as "our main objective in Korea is to kill as many Chinese as possible."

Mrs. Buck says that the teaching of Buddhism, one of the religions of Asia, is that it is very wrong to take away human life. "Consequently," she says, "such statements by our authorities are bound to make Americans appear repulsive in the eyes of the Asiatic. If we have a military job to do in Korea, we should do it without such bad public relations."

Turning to legislation under consideration in Washington, Mrs. Buck said that the *Universal Military Training Law* about to be enacted does not have the "review every two years" clause which has always been the custom with regard to military legislation in this country. "Unless this clause is put in the new law," she stated, "the United States will be faced with a permanent military conscription program which is certainly foreign to the ideals of America."

"We are in a nice nasty mess," Mrs. Buck says, "but there is still a chance to redeem the situation if we take the lead in a positive program to better the world's standard of living and stop depending so heavily upon bombs and machines of war as a means of setting Asia's problems."

60. Pearl S. Buck and Her Husband, Richard J. Walsh

The Tennessean, Jun 10, 1951

Most husbands of authors are naturally proud and excited whenever their wives write a new book.

Richard J. Walsh, however, becomes doubly so since he's a publisher and she's Pearl S. Buck.

Here's a literary and marital partnership that is really ideal since their interests are so similar and their co-operation so congenial.

Any publisher would give his eye teeth to have such a popular and distinguished author as Pearl Buck on his list (her latest, *God's Men* is among current best-sellers). Walsh is president of John Day, which issues most of her work.

Besides being perhaps the firm's most popular writer, Mrs. Buck also reads many John Day manuscripts and performs other editorial duties. These services are especially valuable since the firm specializes in books about the Far East.

Friendly, Sincere People

Two more friendly, sincere people would be hard to find than genial, pipe-smoking Richard Walsh and his Nobel prize-winning wife. He has done a bit of writing himself, so he really understands the besetting problems of authors. He has written several books and has contributed innumerable articles to magazines. He was once editor of Colliers, and has headed *Asia* magazine since 1933.

Few famous people wear their honors so lightly as Pearl Buck. Though she deeply appreciates them she has refused to let them change her essential being, steadfastly retaining "a humble, contrite heart" for life and her fellow men.

In talking to her one is immediately struck by her sincerity, her belief in people. One quickly realizes that here is a person who fully understands the deep responsibility and seriousness honest writing entails. She regards authorship as a high calling indeed, not a mere economic profession. She "feels" every one of her books, though she has written many—perhaps 30, she says.

"I believe books must come out of travail and the fullness of personal experience, that's why I've never written any historical novels."

Parents Missionaries

How long have you been writing, Mrs. Buck?

"Ever since I can remember. As you know I have spent most of my life in the Orient, having been taken to China when I was two years old. My parents were missionaries and extremely bookish. My father was very proud of his library which contained most of the standard authors. I fairly grew up there and read Dickens and other old favorites through and through at an early age. I was writing little stories even then and my folks encouraged me. Mother liked to write, too. Father was a tremendous reader and quite the scholar." she said.

Would she ever write a book with an American setting?

"I hardly think so. You see I have spent most of my life in China and the East. I really know little about the United States. I did go to college here, graduating from Randolph-Macon in 1914, but soon I was back in China again. It was only in 1934 that I came here to live. One lifetime is all too short in which to know any one country thoroughly. I'm still somewhat of a stranger here, though I'm trying hard to understand my own people and the meaning of our institutions."

Well, then, how about an autobiographical or semi-autobiographical book? Surely her many readers would be interested in an account of such a colorful life as hers.

Not Subjective Writer

"I don't think I'll ever write about myself," she paused and thought a bit, "primarily because I'm fundamentally a 'story teller.' I'm not a subjective author. I'm more interested in action than description."

Do you enjoy writing. Mrs. Buck? Does it come easy to you now?

"That's a hard question to answer. Let me say that I do feel a sense of fulfillment and pride of accomplishment when I have produced a book which I think goes home. Writing has become almost a necessity to me, a sort of compulsion. I don't think of it in terms of enjoyment exactly. Then, too, it has compensated for many things in life, has helped me solve many problems which at times have been vital," she explained, "it's relaxing, too."

"It is never exactly easy, especially the gestation. I have developed a certain proficiency and speed in the actual composition, which come with practice and the observance of regular writing habits through the years. I write best in the morning and usually work straight through from 8 until 1 o'clock, I once wrote a children's book in one day. I compose both in longhand and on the typewriter. Fortunately, I have never needed much sleep. I do quite a bit of my reading late at night, thanks to my insomnia."

What about work in progress?

Started New One

"I've just started a new one which will deal with the relations of Japanese and Americans. This will be a bit more difficult for me perhaps than some of the others about China. I have never learned to read Japanese."

Out of the many books she had written did she have any particular favorite, one which she felt stood out from the others?

"I think I feel like many other authors do in this respect," Mrs. Buck smiled. "The last one is always the best, until you start another one."

Did she consider a writing career all-encompassing, a full enough life within itself to make up for the lack of divergent activities which make up the average person's existence?

Mrs. Buck didn't think so. "Books must come out of a writer's full life," she considered. "His life, however, must be an entity. There must not be too many extraneous things. In my case everything hinges together, my family, we have four adopted children, my home and my writing. I have little time for any alien activities. My one hobby is cooking. This may be understood, perhaps, since we live in Bucks County, Pennsylvania, with Quakers on one side of us and the Dutch on the other. Chinese food is fascinating, too."

What about the present tendency of young American writers to accent futility and violence? Mrs. Buck explained that the young always wrote of frustration, that there was nothing new or alarming about it. She admitted that she hadn't read many of America's sad young men, but that she did like Hemingway, whose naturalism she found closely akin to that of many Chinese writers. She admired, too, the early Steinbeck.

Advice to Writers

Many budding authors must have brought her their problems, particularly youngsters thrilled with romantic ideas of literary fame. What advice would she give them?

The author of *Dragon Seed*, *The Good Earth*, *Pavilion of Women*, *The Mother* and *House of Earth* carefully considered and replied:

Writing is a terribly exacting profession with the chances of success extremely thin. Don't expect to earn your living by it for many years. If you approach it as at trade you are lost as a real artist. The hours of apprenticeship are long and arduous and the pains of creation agonizing. I don't believe starving in a garret really aided in the production of works of genius. You can't worry and write; fear dries up the creative well."

"But if you truly believe in yourself and really have something to say nothing should stop you from writing."

61. Pearl Buck Eloquently Disproves Saw of the East and West Never Meeting

Daily Press, Feb 20, 1955

[By William D. Patterson]

The tragic truth in the jingling couplet "East is East, West is West, and never the twain shall meet" may still be true of most of the world today, but it could never apply to Pearl S. Buck. Two civilizations have fused as completely and gracefully in the distinguished author as seems humanly possible.

In her autobiography, *My Several Worlds*, the Nobel Prize winner writes with maturity and eloquence of her varied life and of the two worlds of China and the United States, in which she has lived her years almost equally.

This book may be her finest achievement. Certainly, it is humanity and craftsmanship have combined to make it stand out on *The Saturday Review*'s list this week of books being most widely read and enjoyed around the country. Other best-readers were:

The Tumult and the Shouting, by Grantland Rice (Barnes). A lifetime spent covering sports all over the world is summed up in this informal but constantly interesting book.

The View from Pompey's Head, by Hamilton Basso (Doubleday). Youthful dreams in a small Southern town are memorably contrasted with mature success in New York City in this splendid novel.

The Fall of a Titan, by Igor Couzenko (Norton). A former Russian official writes a powerful, fascinating novel of life and death in Soviet Russia.

Soldier of Fortune, by Ernest K. Gann (Sloane). This is a fast-paced tale of derring-do in Hong Kong and Communist China by a skilled storyteller.

Song of the Sky, by Guy Murchie (Houghton Mifflin). A flier turned author writes beautifully of the phenomena of sky and air and space in which airmen live.

Almanac of liberty, by William O. Douglas (Doubleday). A magnificent series of daily essays on the landmarks of American freedom by the Supreme Court Justice.

Remarkable Book

Out of her remarkable life Mrs. Buck has distilled a remarkable book. Warmth and wisdom are on every page. These attributes come not only from her own gracious personality and literary skill, but from the years of growing up, living, working, observing that she passed in China and the Far East as well as in the United States. Of these two worlds she has made a superb synthesis. "We have no enemies, we for whom the globe is home," she writes. "for we hate no none, and where there is no hate it is not possible to escape love."

This autobiography is written with love, although she has not forgiven the colonial powers or native rulers who exploited the good people and the good earth of the Orient for their own selfish ends.

Growing up in China, as a small child she lived easily in the white world of her missionary parents and in the yellow world of her Chinese playmates and friends. Slipping effortlessly from one to the other and hack without any awareness that there were two worlds, she still remembers the shock when the Boxer Rebellion of 1909 forced her family to flee from their small hill town to Shanghai. In Shanghai she saw, and never forgot, the signs in the parks reading: "No Chinese, No Dogs."

At a time when we must understand China and the other peoples of the Far East this book is a rich and rewarding reading experience with its minute details of life, history, cooking, philosophy, love and family in the Orient.

Revealing Story

Of our parochial ignorance of Asiatic culture, Mrs. Buck reports revealing story of a conversation with an associate at the revered Academy of Arts and Letters, of which she is a member. She asked why there was not a single Eastern book included in the hundred books, those classics selected by scholars to embody civilization. Her friend replied, "Because nobody knows anything about them." Mrs. Buck comments, "Nobody? Only millions of people! Ah well..."

But the United States under the stress of the world situation is learning. The author writes: "In spite of embarrassing mistakes and alarming missteps in the process of learning our world lessons, I see the American spirit reaching new levels of common sense and enlightenment. We are already beginning to give up our destructive prejudices in color, creed and nationality, and we are no longer so boastfully sure that we can lead the world. Indeed, the idea of world leadership is becoming distasteful to us, and we are considering co-operation instead of leadership."

"We are not empire builders. How important this fact is no American who has not lived in Asia can appreciate. We do not want an empire because we do not enjoy the task of ruling. It goes against our conscience, which is a very tender part of the American spirit."

"I am therefore hopeful. In spite of dismaying contradictions in individuals in our national scene, I feel the controlling spirit of our people, generous, decent and sane."

This is a beautiful book, one to read with care and pleasure, and to ponder with profit long after it is closed.

Born in West Virginia in 1892, Pearl Sydenstricker Buck grew up in the interior of China, where her parents were missionaries. She learned to speak Chinese before English.

Although she left China at the age of 17 to enter college in the United States, she returned to China on graduation. There she lived, married, taught and wrote until the turbulent march of history so transformed that friendly nation that she felt compelled finally to move permanently to the United States in 1932.

After the dissolution of her first marriage to a young America agriculturist in China, she married Richard J. Walsh, head of the John Day publishing firm. With their adopted children, she now lives on a farm in Pennsylvania.

For her novels, essays, children's books, translations of foreign classics Mrs. Buck has received many awards, including the Nobel Prize, the Pulitzer Prize, honorary degrees and membership in the American Academy of Arts and Letters. Her passionate hobbies are racial equality and writing. (W. D. P.)

62. Pearl Buck Sees Red China As Reality U.S. Must Face

The Herald News, Nov 15, 1961

[By Philip Chen] Communist China today is a reality that the United States must face and learn to live with, Pearl S. Buck, 69-year-old Nobel Prize winner, said yesterday.

Speaking before a capacity audience of 2,000 at the gymnasium of Paterson State College, yesterday afternoon, Miss Buck said the reluctance of the United States to adopt a more liberal policy toward China was an "outdated" mode of diplomacy.

"The unchangeable law of the universe is the law of change," she said. "If we maintain our unwillingness to change, we will soon find ourselves in an even worse predicament than the present."

The predicament she apparently was referring to is the situation the United States faces on the question of recognizing Communist China.

The United States adopted the passive strategy of asking the United Nations General Assembly to postpone consideration of the Chinese representation issue for the past decade. But it has met with increasing difficulty in recent years due to the waning popularity of Nationalist China.

Expounding on her topic, "Understanding of China Today," Miss Buck, who won international fame with her penetrating novels about the Chinese, further urged that it is "imperative" for the United States to precipitate communication with the Chinese people.

"We should try to get communication going as soon as possible, so that neither side will judge the other by what is told to them," she said.

Meanwhile, Miss Buck said, she saw several contending schools of thought that sought to solve the so-called China impasse. One advocates seating Communist China in the General Assembly while permitting Nationalist China to remain in the Security Council.

"Absurdity!" she said.

She contended that Communist China would certainly be voted into the United Nations, and satisfactory solution might be worked out for Taiwan.

....

Miss Buck, who had come earlier from her home in Perkasie, Pa., appeared punctually at 1 : 30 yesterday afternoon at the gymnasium where an overflow crowd of students, parents, and school officials gathered.

Introduced by James Lepore of Wayne, a junior student, after opening remarks by Pat Carson, an art sophomore, Miss Buck immediately launched into a detailed account of Chinese history and culture that prepared the background for her talk on today's China.

Miss Buck said China, being a monarchal state throughout her thousands of years of history, has never known democracy advocated by the Western-educated revolutionary elements led by Dr. Sun Yat-sen who overthrew the last imperial dynasty in the early 1900s.

She noted that as the old form of government was destroyed, leaders of the new order failed to enlist the understanding and support of the peasants who were alien to the thought of being democratic.

"In this respect," Miss Buck continued "Mao Tse-tung shows himself a true Chinese. He combines intellectuals with peasants who form the backbone of Chinese society, and it is that that makes him so successful."

....

"The outlook is not dark, only if we have courage," she said. "As I mentioned earlier, one thing we must learn is that if you don't change, you die."

The speaker, who won the Nobel Prize in 1931 and the Pulitzer Prize for her novel *The Good Earth*, has written more than 40 novels on China.

A recent one, *Letter From Peking*, published last year, brought a barrage of denunciation from the Chinese Communist organs and Radio Peiping, charging her as the chief reactionary of the United States professing the "division of the two countries."

The revelation of the ruling finally led to the rejection of her visa to visit mainland China, and the trip was later taken by an American correspondent, Edgar J. Snow, who wrote for *Look* magazine early this year.

63. Pleads for Justice for Negroes
The Central News, Oct 23, 1941

With a real passion for justice for the colored Americans, Mrs. Pearl S. Buck, distinguished novelist who makes her home in Bucks county, asked that more than 200 professional women, representing Soroptimist Clubs from six Eastern States, make it a point to obtain real knowledge of the racial issue in connection with the colored Americans and then take strong, swift and courageous steps to have these oppressed peoples get their rights as American citizens.

Mrs. Buck, who spoke at the Fall conference of the North Atlantic region of the American Federation of Soroptimist Clubs at a luncheon meeting on Saturday at the Doylestown Inn, asserted it takes intellect and will to break down the instinct of race prejudice.

Mrs. Buck explained that she has written 12 outstanding American men and women, asking them to give of their time and talent to do something about the condition of the colored Americans. She related how she wrote letters to President Roosevelt regarding the situation here and that in his answer he said: "I can go no faster than the people want me to go."

She also told how she presented Dorothy Thompson, columnist to two groups of colored Americans, one a simple, almost naive, workers' type and the other well-educated, cultured and sophisticated in order to interest the woman columnist in also fighting for the "oppressed colored Americans at home" and not only the oppressed peoples abroad.

"Miss Thompson", continued Mrs. Buck, "really is somebody and I want to tell you that after the educated, sophisticated colored American group got through with her she begged off and said she had another engagement which had to be kept. I have noticed that in her writings she now mentions the oppressed colored Americans."

Saying that just before she came to the luncheon meeting, she had received one answer to the 12 letters she has written to men and women, Mrs. Buck explained that Raymond Gram Swing, radio news commentator, said he "didn't have time." "I am not sure that I like Raymond Gram Swing any longer," said Mrs. Buck, who deplored that he didn't want to or wish to give only two hours of his time. "I wrote also to Winston Churchill about the oppressed peoples in India, where I lived for some time and know both points of view—the English and Indian and his answer was quite different from that of our own President," said Mrs. Buck, who added the Prime Minister gave only the English point of view. Declaring the race prejudice and oppression is the greatest contradiction to the democracies of the world, the author of *The Good Earth* said: We know now the totalitarian nations have handled it, but how are the democracies going to do it?"

64. Education Is Not Meeting Needs, Says Pearl Buck
Covington Virginian, Nov 4, 1950

[Richmond, AP] Virginia Negro educators have been told that American education does not fit its youth for the needs of the world. Mrs. Pearl S. Buck, Nobel prize winning novelist, called for "complete revision" of the present school curriculum yesterday in an address before the Virginia Teachers Association here.

"What must we teach, and how can we teach it, when we don't have the materials?" Mrs. Buck asked some 3,000 Negro teachers and educators attending a general session of the convention yesterday. Modern textbooks, she said, "are obsolete." "What you need to teach, you won't find in textbooks," the authoress declared. "You must tell your children that they are going to have to return good for evil, to speak to save peace and let peoples of other nations know that they can be our friends. This they can do if they can remember high dignity and the necessity of being human."

65. U. S. Race Bias End Seen by Pearl Buck
Courier Post, Nov 14, 1963

[By Charles Q. Finley] Pearl S. Buck, world-famed novelist and Nobel prize winner, said last night and American Democracy will overcome the race problem peacefully.

The author spoke at the 15th Annual Executives' Night Dinner of the Camden Chapter of the National Secretaries Association at which Dr. Reuben L. Sharp of Mount Laurel, Camden physician, received the Boss of the Year trophy. Dr. Sharp, former president of the Camden County Medical Society, has practiced since 1929.

Miss Buck told the nearly 100 persons attending the meeting at Cherry Hill Inn.

Prejudices Skin Deep

"Despite all the eruptions about color when personal experiences are involved we see that prejudices are strongest among people who are not well educated."

After the session she told the Courier-Post:

"We are having growing pains now but I feel optimistic that our Democratic way of life has ample room for a solution without violence in time. All races should be judged not as races but as individuals and we are beginning to see this."

Miss Buck discussed the history and operation of "Welcome House," an adoption agency she founded in Bucks County, Pa., 15 years ago. She told the group she hopes to expand the agency so that it may help children in other countries who are not in a position to be brought to this country for adoption.

Scholarship to Camden Girl T

The $500 Ruth D. Kimsey Memorial Scholarship was awarded to Anna A. Martin, Camden High School graduate now studying business administration in Philadelphia.

Peggy Crossan, chapter president, extended a welcome. Veronica M. Kidder, dinner chairman, also addressed the secretaries and their bosses.

Miss Buck is chairman of the board of "Welcome House."

66. Pearl Buck Finds a Miracle
The Record, Apr 13, 1964

[By Miriam Taylor Petrie]

Harry Holt, who runs an orphanage for children of Asian-American parentage, is a 1-man miracle, according to author Pearl S. Buck, who drove from her home in suburban Philadelphia to White Beeches Country Club, Haworth, Saturday night to attend a charity ball for the Holt Orphanage.

Speaking to 250 members and guests of the Junior Woman's Club of Tenafly, Miss Buck said it was the first time she had attended a benefit for this orphanage.

"Such institutionalized children are fortunate," said Miss Buck. "Other thousands roam Korea and other Asian countries, devoid of food and the other necessities of life."

"These unwanted, unloved children are called Americans by their countrymen and, paradoxically, Korean when the fortunate few reach American homes in the U.S.," she said.

Miss Buck pointed out that the children of American and Asian parenthood are unusually beautiful and of generally superior intelligence.

"At least this is true of those who manage to survive abandonment and camp-following," she said.

It is for these children who will never reach American shores or know any home that the author has founded the Pearl S. Buck Foundation, which is working with the South Korean Government seeking a solution to the continuing problem.

Miss Buck was escorted to the ball by Theodore Harris, executive director of the Foundation. She said there will be a benefit next Saturday for her foundation at Convention Hall, Philadelphia.

Arrangements for Miss Buck's appearance were made by Mrs. Donald V. Joyce of Cresskill, publicity and public relations chairman.

Mrs. Frank B. Hennessy, president of the juniors, introduced Miss Buck. Mrs. John Auld of Dumont was chairman, assisted by Mrs. Mathias O'Gorman, Mrs. George Deubel, and Mrs. Dominic Telesco.

67. The Babies

Daily News, Jul 12, 1964

Outcasts in their homelands, thousands of Asian children fathered by indifferent GIs face almost hopeless future.

[By Christina Kirk] The squalor of Korea's teeming, mud-crusted streets came as no shock to American author Pearl S. Buck when she made her first postwar trip to the Orient four years ago. A daughter of missionary parents, she had lived half her life in China and knew well the sight and smell of poverty. Even the barefoot children who pulled at her skirts and begged for a bowl of rice were sadly familiar—until one day she chanced to look into the almond-shipped blue eyes of the red-haired urchin.

"It makes one feel very strange," sad Miss Buck, "to have a beggar child put out his hand for a penny and look down into the eyes of the child unmistakably American."

68. Pearl Buck Has No Time on Hands

The Sacramento Bee, Apr 8, 1965

[By Gay Pauley, New York—UPI] "Me tire? From what?", asked Pearl Buck.

At 72, the woman who has written close to 60 books and holds the Nobel and Pulitzer prizes for literature, is still writing.

She is also involved in enough other activities to exhaust most women half her years.

She is studying dancing, and as she said, "I can do a cha cha if I have to." She is making movies. And she is busy with a new project to aid children of American servicemen and Asian mothers.

It is for this last she has established the Pearl S. Buck Foundation, of which she is board chairman and treasurer. The foundation carries several steps further the work she has been doing with children of mixed Asian-American blood, through Welcome House, Inc., an adoption agency which since its founding in 1949 has located permanent homes for many hundreds, she said.

"But adoption can't meet all the needs," she said in an interview. "I've visited Asia recently. There are thousands to be cared for."

These, Miss Buck said, are the pathetic cases because "they're not treated the same by either side. They're outcasts without opportunity."

"We'd like to see that they get a chance in their own country."

Miss Buck estimated there are at least 50,000 children of mixed blood in Korea, that at the end of the United States occupation in Japan there were 200,000. She said the United States army put the figure at 5,000, and there are "unknown numbers in Okinawa and now Viet Nam."

The foundation will work through established institutions in the Asian countries, but a representative from the foundation will also be on the scene. "In Korea for instance, we'll be working right through the government's child placement service," she said.

Miss Buck's interest in dancing is helping to raise money for the foundation. A student at a dance studio for the last two years, she has gotten the 350 some studios affiliated with the chain to stage balls with proceeds going to the foundation.

Harry Evans, president of the firm, explained the studios had pledged at least $ 1 million to the foundation to be raised in the next five years. And Miss Buck puts in guest appearances at the functions.

She is scheduled to be in Sacramento next week during a full spring trip cross country which will find her in Honolulu by May 8th.

Meanwhile, two more of her books, *Death in the Castle* and *The Big Fight* will join A Joy of Children and Welcome Child currently in the bookstores.

"How do I find time for everything?" she replied. "Well, I never think of time. And children's books write easily."

Then she talked of her interest in Stratton Productions, Inc., whose latest film is *The Guide*, made in India. Miss Buck is coowner of the film company (and) coauthor of the screen play.

The author was born Pearl Comfort Sydenstricker, in Hillsboro, WVa., June 26th, 1892. As an infant she went with her parents to China where they served as Presbyterian missionaries. The China in which she grew up provided the background for her *The Good Earth*, which won her a Pulitzer in 1931. In 1938, she received the

Nobel prize, the first American woman so honored. Miss Buck was married in 1935 to Richard J. Walsh, the president of the John Day Company, her publisher, and the editor of *Asia* Magazine. Walsh died in 1950.

69. China: New Perspectives on Oriental Mystery
The Jackson Sun, Jun 19, 1977

> *The Committee of One Million*; "*China Lobby*" *Politics* 1953—1971.
> By Stanley D. Bachrack. Columbia University Press: $14.95.
> *A Revolution Is Not a Dinner Party*;
> *A Feast of Images of the Maoist Transformation of China.*
> By Richard H. Solomon with the collaboration of Talbott W. Huey.
> Anchor-Doubleday: $9.95.

[By B. Franklin Cooling] For a long time, it was fashionable to be interested in pre-World War II China a la Pearl Buck, then Americans fretted about who lost China (when it wasn't ours to lose). Now, we are getting down to the post-Korean War saga—who lobbied about getting China in or keeping China out. Who supported Taiwan, and what mysterious forces conspire to link lobbyist—CIA agent—high government official in pursuit of the latest American goal on the Asian mainland. For a nation that regards its most potential enemy in Europe, we sure spend a lot of time worrying about the Chinese.

Stanley D. Backrack has performed some fascinating investigative reporting in tracing the influence of the so-called Committee of One Million, that right-wing, anticommunist, anti-People's Republic of China group who worked for years to keep the Red Chinese out of the UN and safely under wraps as far as normal American relations was concerned.

Finding CIA linkage, vast influence on Capitol Hill and an "eighteen-year" crusade under Congressman Walter Judd (former China missionary), Backrack has given us more than just a fascinating look at Sino-American relations. He suggests the tentacles which lie behind much of U.S. foreign policy in the wake of our first Asian debacle of modern times—Korea.

He shows how members of Congress, not just the executive branch of government have conspired, suppressed information, manipulated money and influence—in pursuit of foreign policy (their own foreign policy). Maybe we shouldn't be so amazed at Korean influence-peddling on the Hill—apparently they have simply copied the experience of other Asia tics—the Nationalist Chinese—who for years held the Congress and country captive to outmoded, meaningless policies in sad need of reform.

But, what of the "enemy" of the China lobby—the People's Republic of China?

Better to ask, as have the publishers of Solomon's book on the mainland country, "what is your conception of China?" They go on to suggest what we all know—it is generally mythically inaccurate, racist, prejudiced and patently untrue.

It is not just Fu Manchu, Kung Fu, Charlie Chan and the local neighborhood laundryman. Americans have seen China as a land of empire (the European as well as native variety), land of opportunity (especially for western capital and exportation of democracy) and as a threatening Communist state. Most of us will get to Vienna, London, Rome and Paris before we ever venture to Peking. We probably won't see the Great Wall or the wallboard "graffiti." TV repeats of Nixon's triumphal reopening of the closed society (with some other president instead of Nixon), will hardly quench anyone's thirst for the mysteries of Red China.

Solomon seeks to combine pictures and text in an exploration of our stereotype view of China. If read along with the China Lobby book, we shall come to know just what we are missing and what Americans for three decades have been missing. Perhaps elsewhere in the world—eastern Europe, Africa, South America—we won't be so prone to dismiss everyone now as just another misguided people to be saved. Understanding and education are necessary keystones to enlightened, modernized perspective on the world to come. China and Russia are as good a place to begin as any!

70. Critics of U.S. Foreign Policy
Honolulu Star Bulletin, Jun 12, 1965

A prominent social worker, Miss Addams was the co-winner of the Nobel Peace Prize in 1931.

Among the national and honorary sponsors of the Women's International League for Peace and Freedom are singer Marian Anderson, authors Erich Fromm and Pearl S. Buck, Socialist leader Norman Thomas, Vijaya L. Pandit, Bertrand Russell and Albert Schweitzer.

Mrs. Marion Kelly, president of the Hawaii branch of the league, said the "Open Letter to President Johnson" was not the first publication of protest by the local league.

She said funds to have the Vietnam letter published were obtained by sending letters to 450 persons thought to be in sympathy with the peace movement and opposed to President Johnson's actions.

The local league was only the sponsoring organization, but the 62 co-signers of the letter are not necessarily members, she said.

Almost all of the co-signers reached by the Star Bulletin said they had not known what other names would appear with theirs, until the published list appeared.

The signers did affirm, however, that they were in agreement with the content of the letter which in addition to rejecting the Vietnam policy, urged an immediate ceasefire and conference of all nations concerned to negotiate a peace settlement.

In a statement to the *Star-Bulletin*, Mrs. Kelly wrote: "The women's International League for Peace and Freedom believes that the continued escalation of the Vietnam war increases greatly the danger of a third world war. Since nuclear bombs will kill people of all political persuasions, all people, regardless of their political beliefs or personal histories, have an equal right and duty to speak up on behalf of reason to help pull the world away from disaster."

71. Timely Observations
St Joseph News Press Gazette, Jun 22, 1967

Pearl Buck observes her 75th birthday anniversary: Monday. Mention the name of Pearl Buck and the average American immediately thinks of *The Good Earth* and Paul Muni. The association is not entirely fortunate. A woman who has given away more than $7 million to square the America conscience deserves to be known for more than a movie that some sophisticates like to down grade.

In her autobiography, *My Several Worlds*, Pearl S. Buck wrote that as a result of her early education—with lessons from her American mother in the morning and from a Chinese tutor in the afternoon—she became "mentally bifocal." It's reported that she spoke Chinese before she spoke English and that she became suddenly aware that she was a foreigner in China only when, at the age of nine, her family was obliged to flee for safety in the Boxes Rebellion. They returned to their home in Chinkiang when peace was restored.

Pearl Comfort Sydenstricker was born in Hillsboro, West Va., on June 26, 1892. Her parents had been Presbyterian missionaries in China, and they went back to that country when she was only five months old.

The missionary heritage is perhaps the central explanation of Pearl Buck's life. She is best known for *The Good Earth* and the other volumes of the *House of Earth* trilogy—*Sons* and *A House Divided*. But she received the Nobel Prize for literature in 1938 primarily for the biographies she had written of her parents, *The Exile* and *The Fighting Angel*.

"The decisive factor in the Academy's judgment," wrote the critic Anders Osterling, "was, above all, the admirable biographies of her parents... two volumes which seemed to deserve classic rank and possess the required prospects for permanent interest." As for the novels, the Nobel committee observed in its citation that they were outstanding for "rich and genuine epic portrayals of Chinese peasant life."

Pearl Buck announced on May 21—as she prepared to leave on a tour of Asia—

that she was giving her estate and most of her earnings—more than $7 million—to her own special welfare project for half American children living in Asian countries. She has signed over her television and motion picture royalties worth some $6 million, her suburban Bucks County, Pa., farm, her Vermont property, and all future book royalties to the Pearl S. Buck Foundation.

The explanation is simple. "I was in Asia, making a movie," she said, "and I saw the children of American men and Asian mothers. And I was really quite ashamed." The story of the camp follower and the soldier is legend. Homer wrote: "The sex is ever to a soldier kind." The novelist's foundation in a way is an extension of her own life. She has 10 children, nine of them adopted Amerasians.

Mrs. Buck has been able to look at two cultures clearly and with understanding and love. She published in 1933 a translation of the classic Chinese novel *Shui Hu Chuan* under the title *All Men Are Brothers*. The title makes an appropriate text for observance of her birthday.

后记

　　一位诺贝尔奖获得者去世，一国总统为此发表声明，这是绝无仅有的。为什么尼克松总统赋予赛珍珠"人桥"的赞誉？要回答这个问题，需要更深入、更广泛、更全面地了解和研究赛珍珠，看到她为自己设立的使命是什么，她的动力又从何而来。

　　本书呈现给读者的这些报刊资料，印证了赛珍珠几十年来始终不渝作为东西方文明的"人桥"所做出的努力和贡献——为使她的中国家乡摆脱战争、摆脱贫困、摆脱帝国主义的压迫，为消除西方世界对中国的陌生、误解和对立，为促进中美交流和关系正常化，即使是在中美关系极其困难的时期和极其复杂的环境中，她也不曾放弃。更为不易和可贵的是，她所进行的广泛宣传和辩论，几乎是孤军奋战。

　　赛珍珠在中国的成长经历奠定了其对中华文化的强烈认同，正是在这种背景下，她写出了几十本关于中国的小说。赛珍珠不仅是一位著名的文学家，她还是一位哲人、一位社会活动家，更是一位公平正义的捍卫者。中国的文明、文化和智慧，赋予她无与伦比的洞察力和坚韧的毅力，使她具有卓越政治家的思想和远见。

　　站在中美两国各自的历史上观察，赛珍珠是中美交往绕不开的重要历史人物。1972 年，尼克松的访华被认为是中美交往的"破冰之旅"，而事实是，中美两国的秘密接触比这和 1971 年的"乒乓外交"要早得多。即便是在新中国成立后，赛珍珠的"人桥"作用也未曾停止发挥其积极影响。

早在 1950 年，赛珍珠就指出，朝鲜战争不是美国的自豪。"如果你使用武力，你就承认了你的失败，如果这是我们所能做的全部，我们就失败了。"

1955 年，赛珍珠说"东西方有共同点"。

1961 年，赛珍珠直言新中国是美国必须面对的现实，呼吁美国要了解今日中国。"两国领导人将找到共同利益与合作之道。""中国人民从历史上就认为台湾理所当然地属于大陆。"

1962 年，赛珍珠呼吁美国总统肯尼迪取消对中国出售谷物的禁令。她的呼吁遭到了当时美国舆论的批判，而她本人被指责是在援助"红色敌人"。

1964 年，赛珍珠指出，中国拥有核武器"对世界和平来说是个好兆头"。

沟通文明需要桥梁，捍卫文明需要斗争。这些记录了赛珍珠沟通中国与世界之努力的历史片段，将在中美交往和东西方人文交流的历史长河中永远闪烁发光。

本书完稿后，我开始了对赛珍珠社会关系的研究。例如，我发现赛珍珠和雅各布斯共同交往的朋友及相关重要人物，其中有报刊记载的有八十多位，涵盖了美国总统、政治家、外交人士、律师、作家、艺术家、大学教授、社会活动家和普通民众，具有一定的社会代表性。这也许为认识和研究赛珍珠提供了一个新的视角。人们对赛珍珠的研究，或侧重于她的小说和传记，或侧重于她的慈善事业。而要真正理解赛珍珠，需要更深入的思考。这是一个历史研究的系统工程。

也许，发现新的线索，继续认识和研究，是我们这一代人的责任和义务。

在本书的写作、翻译、校对和出版的过程中，镇江市赛珍珠研究会和江苏大学出版社给予了极大的、多方面的帮助，这进一步激发了我对于赛珍珠研究的热情，借此对他们一并表示深深的感谢！

匡　霖
2023 年 11 月 23 日
于美国弗吉尼亚州